The Wilson Gove

The Wilson Governments 1964–1970

Edited by
R. Coopey
S. Fielding
N. Tiratsoo

PINTER
London and New York

Distributed in the USA by St. Martin's Press Inc.

P I N T E R
A Cassell imprint
Wellington House, 125 Strand, London WC2R 0BB, England

First published 1993
Paperback edition first published 1995

Distributed exclusively in the USA by St. Martin's Press, Inc.,
Room 400, 175 Fifth Avenue, New York, NY10010, USA

British Library Cataloguing in Publication Data

A CIP catalogue record for this book is available from The British Library

ISBN 0 86187 188 X (hardback)
    0 85567 343 6 (paperback)

Library of Congress Cataloging-in-Publication Data

A CIP catalog record for this book is available from the Library of Congress

Typeset by Florencetype Ltd, Kewstoke, Avon
Printed in Great Britain by SRP Ltd, Exeter

Contents

List of figures

List of tables

List of contributors

Richard Coopey is currently a Research Fellow in the Business History Unit at the London School of Economics where he is working on the history of 3i. He has previously worked on the labour process and technology in the car industry. His book on *Supervision in the US Auto Industry* will be published by the University of Illinois Press.

Steven Fielding is a Lecturer in the Department of Politics and Contemporary History, University of Salford. He has previously taught History at the University College of Swansea, Lancaster University, East London Polytechnic and Teesside Polytechnic. He is the author of *Class and Ethnicity. Irish Catholics in England, 1880–1939* (Open University Press, 1993).

David Horner was a Research Fellow at the Technology Policy Unit, Aston University, and is currently a Lecturer in information policy at the University of Brighton.

Lewis Johnman is a Senior Lecturer in Economic History at the University of Greenwich and Visitor at the Business History Unit, the London School of Economics.

Dilwyn Porter is a Senior Lecturer in History at Worcester College. He is the co-author of *Modernization Frustrated: the Politics of Industrial Decline since 1900* and author of articles on the history of financial journalism.

Robin Ramsay is a graduate of Hull University and the editor/publisher of the magazine *Lobster*. With Stephen Dorril he wrote *Smear! Wilson and the Secret State* (Fourth Estate, 1991). Since 1978 he has written widely for what used to be called the 'radical press', for the last few years chiefly for *Tribune*. He is currently working on a political thriller.

Peter Thompson is completing a PhD at the Centre for the Study of Social History, University of Warwick, and working on a book about politics in the 1940s.

Nick Tiratsoo teaches at the Centre for the Study of Social History, University of Warwick. He edited *The Attlee Years* (Pinter, 1991), a companion volume.

Nicholas Woodward is a Lecturer in Economic History in the Department of History, University College of Swansea. He has published widely in the field of labour economics. Currently his main research interests are the area of Twentieth Century macroeconomic history, particularly for the period since 1945. His most recent publication is the *The British Economy Since 1945*, jointly edited with N.F.R. Crafts and published by Oxford University Press.

Chris Wrigley is Professor of Modern British History at the University of Nottingham. His numerous publications include *David Lloyd George and the British Labour Movement, Lloyd George and the Challenge of Labour, Arthur Henderson, A.J.P. Taylor: A Complete Bibliography* and three edited volumes, *Warfare, Diplomacy and Politics, A History of British Industrial Relations Vol. 1. 1875–1914* and *A History of British Industrial Relations Vol. 2. 1914–1939*.

Introduction: The Wilson Years

Richard Coopey, Steven Fielding and Nick Tiratsoo

When the Labour Party, led by Harold Wilson, won the 1964 General Election, many felt that Britain was headed in an entirely new direction. There was a widespread recognition that the country had languished under the gentlemanly Conservative amateurs Macmillan and Home, an unease highlighted by the economic progress of competing nations. Wilson, how-ever, brought hope of a new dawn, one in which Britain could emerge refashioned to take its place in the 'modern' world. The new prime minis-ter's very character and background – his grammar school education, economic expertise and scientific literacy – seemed to symbolize the change that had occurred. Wilson's own success appeared to indicate the existence of a rising meritocracy that would break through the old, strangling class antagonisms of Britain's social structure.

The general election of 1966 increased the anticipation of progress. Labour had achieved power in 1964 only by a narrow margin, but was returned to office with an overall majority of 97. At long last, the Party seemed to have achieved full power in a situation where it was not ham-strung by crippling handicaps or constraints. In this sense, the contrast with previous Labour administrations was striking. Wilson was politically inde-pendent unlike the minority MacDonald Governments of the inter-war years; he was also free of the problems confronted by Attlee in 1945, when Britain had stood on the verge of bankruptcy after six years of total war. To any contemporary surveying the scene in 1966, it seemed more than poss-ible that Labour would be able to implement its reforms unhindered by outside pressures.

When Labour's new dawn failed to materialize the optimism of 1964–66 was transformed into bitter cynicism. As a consequence Labour was attacked by critics drawn from both right and left. Wilson, the commentators averred, had promised too much and delivered too little. 'Moderniza-tion' was judged as essentially a sham. The economy was alleged to have stumbled from crisis to crisis under Labour's mismanagement, while key questions, like the future of the trade unions, had been simply avoided. Moreover, effective social reform remained as far away as ever. The whole shoddy episode seemed to be summed up by Labour's desultory perform-ance at the 1970 general election, when it lost to a Conservative Party which few, except the most partisan, saw as formidable.

Since that defeat a consensus has emerged which stipulates that the period 1964–70 was disastrous both for Britain and the Labour Party. Writing in 1990, K.O. Morgan noted that, over the previous two decades, the Wilson years had 'served as a paradigm of economic failure, social indirection and political paralysis'. He added:

The reputation of the 1964–70 Wilson government is the reverse of Bernard Shaw's. It has no friends and even its enemies don't like it. Like Ramsay MacDonald's government of 1929–31 it has become a major point of reference in charting the inadequacies of British democratic socialism as a programme for power.[1]

Indeed, it can be argued that the Wilson administrations are almost unique in the scale of disapprobation they have received. Critics are drawn from many different spheres – party activists, career politicians, newspaper col-umnists, academics – with diverse political allegiances and sympathies. This point can be established by briefly reviewing the copious literature which now exists on the subject.

The most compelling characteristic of those who have criticized the 1964–70 Governments was that many were either Labour members or sympathizers. This was because according to David Marquand, 'few modern British governments have disappointed their supporters more thoroughly' and because – more poetically – the Wilson era was one of 'lost innocence, of hopes betrayed'.[2] For those intellectuals who had invested much emotional fervour in Wilson's pre-election campaign of 1963–4 which launched his vision of the 'New Britain', the descent into disillusion was especially acute.[3]

However, other detractors have been drawn from those on the left who see Labour as an inherently flawed and fundamentally dishonest party. Typical, here, were those reviewers of Wilson's 1971 account recording his period as prime minister who gladly took the opportunity to attack Labour's supposed lack of principle and morality. As E.P. Thompson concluded, 'One rises from this book with an enhanced contempt for parliamentarians, and for the parliamentary Labour Party in particular.' The Government's lack of commitment to 'socialism' at home and its failure to condemn American involvement in Vietnam also aroused fury. The tenor of such criticism was essentially that, under Wilson, Labour had abandoned socialism in favour of administering capitalism, a view outlined in 1967 by the May Day Manifesto Committee.[4] This remained the dominant means of viewing the Government among left-wing activists and academics for the remainder of the 1970s and 1980s.

Of course, to such commentators this was merely the chronicle of a death foretold. In their eyes, the Wilson administrations formed a crucial part of the 'wasted years' which followed Labour's 1951 general election defeat. According to John Saville, during this period, 'the Labour movement in general has slowly but inexorably fragmented the diffuse radical consciousness which gave the Labour Party nearly 14 million votes in 1951'.[5] This argument is at its most forceful in the works of David Coates, James Hinton and Ralph Miliband. According to them, the Wilson Governments of necessity sought to 'curb and subdue' working-class militancy because they were committed not to building socialism but, instead, to constructing a more dynamic form of capitalism. This meant that they had ultimately to accede to the demands of the Treasury, International Monetary Fund and multinational corporations. The logic of the economic programme which was consequently pursued meant that Labour had to enforce a wage squeeze and, finally, mount an assault upon trade unionism. The promises of greater social justice, made to the administration's mainly working-class electorate, were therefore quickly withdrawn. As a result Labour alienated support in its natural constituency, leaving itself open to a successful Conservative challenge. Thus, although Wilson solved the severe balance of payments problem which confronted him on taking office, this was accomplished at the expense of working people. Yet, in Miliband's words, 'The government could have had all the support it required from trade unionists, had it been seen to be genuinely engaged in the creation of a society marked by greater social justice.' However, the very nature of the Party meant that it could not explore this radical option: it was too committed to making capitalism work. Thus, according to such left-wing critics, if the Wilson Governments have any merit at all, it was in finally proving the bankruptcy of Labour as a party of socialism.[6]

Even those not wholly convinced that Labour was an intrinsically flawed vehicle for progressive change remain convinced that the Wilson Governments were a failure. They at least grant that some of the social reforms were beneficial. However, the Labour leadership still stands condemned for allowing the inherited balance of payments crisis to undermine ambitions for economic modernization. This at least possesses the virtue of suggesting that an element of choice was involved. Wilson, for example, need not have resisted devaluation until 1967 thereby condemning the economy to a prolonged period of government-induced deflation. Thus, whilst not disagreeing with the overall assessment of anti-Labourist historians, such critics at least imply that failure was not inherent to the character of the Government. Failure was not the result of ideological inadequacies but more a question of mismanagement.[7]

Such a view logically leads to a search for the reasons why mistakes were made and, therefore, ultimately to the problem of leadership. Virtually every commentator accepts that Wilson proved unable to provide an adequate command. His reputation was certainly damaged by Paul Foot's brilliant, if partisan, assault.[8] More fair-minded critics have been drawn to follow Foot's lead. As Clive Ponting has it, 'The final judgement on Wilson must therefore be essentially negative and the blame for the government's overall failure has to rest largely with him.'[9] The question of leadership has been most vigorously underlined by those who defected from Labour in the early 1980s to form the Social Democratic Party. To them, the principal cause of the Labour Governments' difficulties was the absence of Hugh Gaitskell. According to Stephen Haseler all would have been well under a Gaitskell premiership, for he would have:

created that most elusive of British needs: a party of reform with mass support amongst the working people, but a party steeped in the political traditions of the country (patriotic, democratic) that was nevertheless not encumbered by the cultural and class problems presented to the British people by the Conservatives.[10]

Not only would Gaitskell have probably won a larger majority than Wilson in 1964, but he would also have been better able to deal with a whole range of problems once in power.[11] In contrast to the alleged 'sheer moral force' of Gaitskell Wilson was the 'guilty man', the unprincipled compromiser who 'placed his own political skin above his nation'. Wilson's 'strategic incompetence' caused him to allow the extreme left to embed itself within the Labour Movement thereby fatally changing Labour's character. Thus, his leadership was responsible for the decline of the right within the Party and their ultimate decision to form the Social Democrats.[12]

Many Cabinet members who have left a record of their time in office have echoed these attacks on the Wilson premiership. Of those who have laid blame at Wilson's door, Denis Healey, as is his way, has been especially forthright:

He had no sense of direction, and rarely looked more than a few months ahead. His short-term opportunism, allied to a capacity for self-delusion which made Walter Mitty appear unimaginative, often plunged the government into chaos. Worse still, when things went wrong he imagined everyone was conspiring against him. He believed in demons and saw most of his colleagues in this role at one time or another . . .[13]

Parallel with criticisms originating from the left or from within Labour's own ranks are those which have come from various parts of the right. From this perspective, the 1960s have been condemned as immoral and the Labour Government found guilty by association. As soon as it was over, the decade was seen as a shoddy, shameful time of personal excess, one defined by mass gullibility, irrationality and illusion.[14] The Wilson administration was condemned in similar terms. As Christopher Booker put it:

Rarely can any Government have lived and acted to such an extent in the make-believe world of public relations, of press leaks, of meaningless language, of ill-considered actions performed primarily for their immediate effect on people's minds rather than for any lasting effect on events.[15]

Alongside this moral critique, the right also focused on Labour's economic difficulties. Wilson, it was argued, proved once again that Labour could not be trusted in office. The Party would always put its own narrow electoral interests above those of the nation, and thus exacerbate the country's real economic difficulties. From this it has been deduced that any government based upon social democratic values is incapable of managing the British economy: therefore the market solution remains the only viable alternative to decline.[16]

One of the key elements in the triumphant Thatcherism of the 1980s was that the moral and economic arguments were conflated. Early on, Labour's alleged promotion of the permissive society was linked to economic decline as were high taxes and the demise of such 'traditional' values as hard work and honesty.[17] This is what Mrs Thatcher meant by her caustic reference to those politicians who possessed a 'Gannex conscience'.[18] Such an analysis gained popular purchase because of the electoral and economic success of the Conservatives in the 1980s. After 1979 the people were insistently informed by the media that a revolution had occurred in Britain. By embracing laissez-faire policies and emasculating the trade unions a resolute Conservative Government had caused a turn-around in the country's economic fortunes. Britain had been saved from the consequences of the 1960s and Wilson's Labour administrations.

Taken together, these various comments and claims clearly amount to a formidable case. Yet, close examination suggests that many of the allegations against Wilson are not as securely based as they initially appear. Bias and prejudice colour much of the criticism; moreover, the hard evidence produced in some of the broadsides is remarkably thin. Whole areas of study which might have contradicted the generally damning conclusions have been ignored. For example, very little has been written of the 'low' politics of the period, while important Wilson initiatives, such as the Ministry of Technology (Mintech) remain largely unexplored. In these circumstances, it may reasonably be concluded that a re-evaluation of the Wilson years is overdue, and this perception forms the starting point for this collection of essays. The remit given to the different authors was simply to explore again some of the leading questions of the period in order to establish how far received myths (of the type prevalent in the accounts outlined above) conformed to realities.

This meant, in effect, confronting three particular points which are repeated in most accounts of the 1964–70 Wilson administrations. The first concerns one of Labour's key initial aims on taking office – the 'modernization' of Britain. Wilson's image at the time was closely associated with various facets of this concept, and in folk memory he is still remembered for his famous 'white heat' speech. Yet most commentators have assumed that there was no real commitment to the issue and dismiss it as another example of Wilson's cynical political expediency. However, the extent to which 'modernization' was more than a rhetorical device designed to win votes needs to be seriously considered.

The second point relates to Labour's actual performance in government. The Wilson administrations are typically portrayed as being directionless, tossed between a series of self-inflicted crises which could not be fully resolved due to Wilson's cowardly and self-seeking pragmatism. This, in turn, is linked to the perception that under Wilson Labour lacked both strategy and principles. The Prime Minister, it is said, was only really concerned to hold on to power, and this has led to an enduring image of Wilson as a virtually psychotic plotter and intriguer. The veteran

Communist Jack Dash's verdict vividly reflects a more general feeling: 'in the field of politics', he wrote, 'Harold Wilson could do an about-turn smarter than any of the sentries at Buckingham Palace'.[19]

Clearly, these charges enjoy some grounding in reality: no one can seriously deny that Wilson was a consummate politician. Yet, in the rush to judgement, those who have sought to condemn Wilson have often wildly exaggerated their case. Moreover, few have entertained the notion that Wilson sought to achieve anything of substance or accept the possibility of the existence of any constraints on government action. It is certainly at least possible that the Prime Minister's endless manoeuvring was because he confronted exacting foes on difficult terrain.

The final issue to be addressed concerns the Labour leadership's effect on its own supporters, both in the party and in the wider electorate. One of the most ingrained truisms about the Wilson years is that they seriously damaged Labour as an electoral force, by demoralizing activists and driving a wedge between the Party and its traditional working-class base. In some accounts, Wilson is blamed for laying the seeds of Thatcherism. Typically, Ken Livingstone presents a familiar litany of 'betrayals' that are alleged to have marked the 1964–70 period and then adds a chilling admonition:

Politicians who raise the hopes and capture the imagination of ordinary women and men only to betray that trust do more to undermine faith in democracy than any fascist could ever do.[20]

If Wilson was culpable in this regard, which leader of a major political party cannot be similarly condemned?

Having surveyed the main themes to be explored in this collection, it remains only to indicate what the various authors have made of their particular subjects. The first three chapters deal with the period prior to Labour's triumph in 1964. Porter provides a general survey of the Conservative ascendancy of the 1950s and early 1960s. He argues that Britain was entering a 'crisis of modernization' but suggests that the Conservatives were unable to fully respond to it due to their historical and ideological inheritance. Fielding and Horner concentrate on what Labour was doing during these years, and in their different ways explore how it was that 'modernizing concerns' – for example, the relationship of science to socialism – came to dominate the Party's programme. They show that the new orientations were not adopted for reasons of expediency, but reflected a particular analysis of what Britain was like and where it was going. This, as the authors underline, had been worked out over a number of years with the aid of numerous outside experts.

The second section of the book deals with various aspects of Labour's record in government. Woodward presents an overview of the administration's macro-economic policy and in so doing punctures some common myths. He shows that Labour had to deal with significant external and internal economic difficulties during this period. Although mistakes were made Labour's record was not overwhelmingly bad; in any case, as Woodward shows, there were no easy solutions. Coopey adopts a tighter focus in his study of Mintech. He argues that this initiative was a significant and well thought-out departure from past governmental practice and as such illustrates Labour's serious approach to modernization. That Mintech largely failed, Coopey concludes, should be blamed less on the absence of political will and more on bureaucratic resistance and technological inertia.

The next two chapters deal with issues which stand as acid tests for the argument that Labour lacked principles. Wrigley looks at Wilson's foreign policy, long a major bone of contention amongst the Party's left-wing critics. Although unimpressed by the administrations record, he does not see failure in terms of 'betrayal'. This was mostly due to Labour's long-standing illusions about Britain's 'great power' status and the Party's strong commitment to the 'special relationship' with the United States. Moreover, Wilson cannot be accused of bad faith in foreign policy matters: he had proper motives on many occasions, but these were often overlaid by other, narrowly political considerations. Thompson surveys Labour's relationship with the alleged rise of permissiveness in Britain during the 1960s. He argues that the Party helped shape a good deal of the critical legislation in this area and demonstrates how some in Labour's ranks felt that reform was needed to make Britain a more civilized society. Yet, it is clear that not all the Party's sympathizers were happy with these developments and some resisted liberalization.

The chapter following returns to the theme of constraints. Robin Ramsay has built up a considerable reputation for his expertise on Britain's 'secret state', and with Steven Dorril continues to publish the investigative journal *Lobster*. His chapter in this collection presents a brief survey of what is known about the various plots against Wilson from those in the security services. Some have dismissed all talk of subversion at this time, but as Ramsay shows, there was a long-established campaign against Labour which reached a crescendo during the Wilson years. Moreover, some of the attempts at undermining the elected government proved potent: the Prime Minister found himself continually having to deflect and outwit smears, a situation that, at the very least, sapped energy and morale.[21]

The final two contributions examine various aspects of party performance between 1964 and 1970, and between them demolish the idea that Labour under Wilson was a discredited force after six years in power. Tiratsoo focuses on the still popular left-wing interpretation of the period – that Wilson 'betrayed' a popular radicalism – and shows it to be incorrect in almost every detail. Johnman provides a fascinating account of Conservative Party policy exercises in the second half of the 1960s, as the Party sought to find a winning formula. Both chapters reinforce an often forgotten truth, that the 1970 general election was narrowly lost and won, and can hardly, therefore, be presented as a resounding rejection of Wilsonism.

Each of the chapters in this volume attempts to take a more considered view of the 1964–70 Wilson Governments than has hitherto been the case. In many ways they are more positive in their approach to the Wilson years than the vast majority of those who have previously cast their gaze over the period. This is not due to any nostalgia for what was, in a number of respects, a more civilized phase of modern British history.[22] The collection forms part of a wider process of reassessment by historians and commentators sceptical that Wilson's premiership was as disastrous as has been suggested by earlier accounts.[23] The collection's ultimate conclusion is that Labour's period in office must still be broadly considered flawed. However, it at least offers different reasons for this failure and explains why it occurred in terms which do not suggest that Labour as a whole and Wilson in particular have to suffer our moral condemnation.

Notes

1. K.O. Morgan 'Symposium. The Labour Party's record in office' *Contemporary Record* Vol. 3 No. 4 (April 1990) 22.
2. D. Marquand *The Progressive Dilemma* (1991) pp. 155, 158. For an example of such disappointment, see T. Burgess et al. *Matters of Principle. Labour's Last Chance* (Harmondsworth, 1968).
3. See D. McKie 'Introduction' in D. McKie and C. Cook (eds) *The Decade of Disillusion: British Politics in the Sixties* (1972) pp. 1–3.
4. A. MacIntyre in the *Listener* 29/7/1971 and E.P. Thompson in *New Society* 29/7/1971. See also R. Williams (ed.) *May Day Manifesto* (Harmondsworth, 1968) pp. 151–61.
5. J. Saville *The Labour Movement in Britain* (1988) p. 133.
6. D. Coates *The Labour Party and the Struggle for Socialism* (Cambridge, 1975) pp. 97–129; J. Hinton *Labour and Socialism. A History of the British Labour Movement* (Brighton, 1983) pp. 189–92 and R. Miliband *Parliamentary Socialism. A Study in the Politics of Labour* (1972) pp. 350–69.
7. J. Callaghan *Socialism in Britain Since 1888* (Oxford, 1990) pp. 195–212; C. Ponting *Breach of Promise. Labour in Power, 1964–70* (1989) especially part 5; A. Sked and C. Cook *Post-War Britain. A Political History* (Harmondsworth, 1984) pp. 247–52.
8. P. Foot *The Politics of Harold Wilson* (Harmondsworth, 1968).
9. Ponting op cit. 405.
10. S. Haseler *The Tragedy of Labour* (Oxford, 1980) p. 27.
11. P.M. Williams *Hugh Gaitskell* (Oxford, 1982) pp. 447-51.
12. S. Haseler *The Death of British Democracy. A Study of Britain's Political Present and Future* (1976) pp. 61–2, 143; Haseler op. cit. 26, 108–14.
13. D. Healey *Time of My Life* (1989) p. 361.
14. B. Levin *The Pendulum Years. Britain and the Sixties* (1970) pp. 223–41.
15. C. Booker *The Neophiliacs* (1970) p. 258.
16. P. Einzig *Decline and Fall? Britain's Crisis in the Sixties* (1969) pp. 38–9, 228–30; R. Emmett Tyrrell (ed.) *The Future That Doesn't Work: Social Democracy's Failures in Britain* (New York, 1977); S. Haseler *The Battle for Britain. Thatcher and the New Liberals* (1989) p. xi.
17. A.E. Dyson 'Farewell to the left' in R. Boyson (ed.) *Right Turn* (1970) pp. 146–57.
18. *Guardian* 20/3/1989.
19. J. Dash *Good Morning Brothers!* (1970 edn) p. 132.
20. K. Livingstone *If Voting Changed Anything, They'd Abolish It* (1988 edn) p. 11.
21. Those seeking further details on these points should consult S. Dorril and R. Ramsay *Smear! Wilson and the Secret State* (1991).

22. For such an approach to the period, see K.O. Morgan *Labour People. Leaders and Lieutenants, Hardie to Kinnock* (Oxford, 1987) pp. 252–3.
23. For example, see Ross McKibbin's review article in the *London Review of Books* 24/10/1991, and articles in the *Guardian* (13/11/1991 and 18/11/1991), *Independent* (30/8/1991) and *The Economist* (1/6/1991).

1 Downhill all the way: thirteen Tory years 1951–64

Dilwyn Porter

Labour's narrow general election victory in October 1964 owed much to the way in which its propagandists had characterized the preceding Tory regime. The self-appointed natural party of government, it was suggested, had proved itself unfit to govern. Harold Macmillan and his colleagues were represented as a party of blimps, permanently stranded in Edwardian England, who had somehow contrived to miss the fast train into the second half of the twentieth century. As defenders of class privilege and purveyors of outmoded thinking, the Conservatives blocked the exit from the past, standing between the nation and its bright, technocratic future. The progress of science since the war, observed Harold Wilson in typical pre-election mode, promised 'to take mankind forward into a future which our fathers could not have dreamed possible'. But, in the 13 years since 1951, the Conservatives had demonstrated that they were 'incapable of mobilizing Britain to take full advantage of the scientific breakthrough'. They were, he added, 'fifty years out of date'.[1]

Blending naturally with this theme was the idea that the 13 years of Conservative government had been wasted. The details of this indictment were articulated in the Labour Research Department's handbook, *Twelve Wasted Years*, published in September 1963, which claimed that the Tories had presided over 'years of stagnation at home and lost influence abroad'.[2] Repeated references to 'thirteen wasted years' in the election campaign 12 months later served two important purposes. Voters were reminded of the sorry saga of missed opportunity and relative decline which was said to characterize the period after 1951. At the same time Labour's image of competence was enhanced. 'Thirteen wasted years' proved a powerful concept, influencing electors in October 1964 and beyond. Writing in 1966, just after Wilson's second victory, Shirley Williams noted that 'the whole election boiled down to one question – *their* thirteen years or *our* seventeen months'.[3]

Wilson's claim that the Conservatives were 50 or so years behind the times was more than a rhetorical flourish. The pre-First World War location was carefully chosen; the Edwardians, after all, had been another society heading for disaster. Moreover, the Conservatives had left themselves open to such an attack. As Prime Minister between 1957 and 1963, Macmillan cultivated a personal style often described by contemporaries as 'Edwardian'. Denis Healey has written recently that Macmillan's 'Edwardian langour' helped him 'to get away with innumerable deceptions and political somersaults'.[4] It also helped him to sustain comforting illusions about Britain's place in the world, a substantial political asset in the period of post-Suez trauma. Later, as the realities of reduced circumstances crowded in, Edwardianism was to prove a liability. The parallels with the years before 1914 were by then less than comforting, recalling the mood of mordant introspection which had followed military defeats in South Africa. As one broadcaster noted in 1963, there was 'a Crimean War or Boer War situation', albeit rather 'diffused and unemphatic'.[5]

Other commentators suggested that this mood was pronounced and more sharply focused. 'Self-examination', according to one contemporary historian, was the major theme of 1962, an exercise made more intense by the protracted and ultimately unsuccessful negotiations to join the Common Market. Heightened awareness of Britain's limitations rebounded on the Government. 'Economic failure, inconsistency and an apparent lack of leadership', observed Arthur Marwick, 'brought strong discontent with Conservative administration'.[6] The emergence of this discontent marked a critical stage in the development of a political climate favourable to advocates of economic and social modernization. Wilson's Labour Party, it will be argued, was a beneficiary of this new climate; the Conservatives were disadvantaged. 'Right through Britain', William Rees-Mogg has recalled, 'there was an oppressive feeling of there being an overload of people who were elderly and not competent'.[7] An analysis of the Conservative record between 1951 and 1964 will suggest how they came to be regarded as part of this problem.

Writing on the eve of the 1964 general election, Malcolm Muggeridge found little of note in the 13 years of Tory government which were drawing to an end 'except the Suez fiasco and the Profumo scandal; two episodes which they certainly would prefer should be forgotten'.[8] Such verdicts, fashionable at the time, were less than fair. The tenacity of Conservative administrations, stretching across three parliaments and four prime ministers, was in itself noteworthy. Winston Churchill had begun in October 1951 with a majority of only 15 and a less than perfect memory for ministerial names and faces. But by the time that Eden led the Party into the May 1955 election, increasing the majority to 58, the first instalment of post-war affluence had been delivered, notably by Macmillan at the Ministry of Local Government who encouraged an enormous expansion of new housing.

Despite the largely self-inflicted humiliation of Suez, Conservative prospects revived under Macmillan after 1957. Persistent Labour leads in the opinion polls throughout 1957 and the first half of 1958 were reversed. 'It was not just that the Government got the credit for the fact that electors were better off; it was because for many people the process of becoming better off led to a change in social values.' So ran the conventional political wisdom of the day.[9] Buttressed by the new consumerism Macmillan increased the Conservative majority to 100 in October 1959, prompting speculation that a permanent Tory hegemony had arrived. Even when Macmillan's government ran into acute difficulties after 1961 it proved remarkably resilient. To the young blades at *Private Eye* in 1963 'it seemed almost incredible that Harold Macmillan should still be Prime Minister'. 'We had done everything short of assassinating him', recalled Richard Ingrams.[10] And it should also be remembered that under Macmillan's controversial successor, the much-derided 'Fourteenth Earl', Sir Alec Douglas-Home, a recovery was staged which reduced Labour's majority to a whisker in October 1964.

Underpinning Conservative electoral success after 1951 was the Party's commitment to what has been identified as the post-war consensus. Though the extent to which right and left converged in the 1950s has sometimes been exaggerated, certain shared parameters were evident, marking out the middle ground in which social peace could take root. For Conservatives, who had been moving in this direction since the adoption by the Party of R.A. Butler's *Industrial Charter* in 1947, consensus politics required a commitment to full employment and the welfare state. It also embraced an acceptance of the mixed economy inherited from Attlee's government in 1951 and subsequently modified only by the denationalization of steel and road haulage in 1953. In addition, relations between government and the trade unions were to be characterized by consultation and conciliation, an approach pioneered by Sir Walter ('the oilcan') Monckton, Churchill's Minister of Labour.[11]

Commitment to this policy framework signalled a determination to shake off the legacy of the 1930s and, in particular, an association with 'devil take the hindmost' economics. 'The important thing in the 1950s', John Biffen has observed, 'was to live down the bad, black days of interwar Britain'.[12] Who better than Macmillan, who had once advocated the nationalization of the coal industry, to set the tone? A passionate exponent of *The Middle Way* since the 1930s, he often spoke with feeling of the pre-war unemployed and their plight. 'As long as I live', he declared, 'I can never forget the impoverishment and demoralisation which all this brought with it'. He was pledged 'never to allow this shadow to fall again upon our country'.[13] During the 13 years of Conservative government after 1951 unemployment remained low by inter-war standards. In 1955 the monthly average of registered unemployed dropped to 232,000, just over 1 per cent of the work-force. Only once, in 1963 when it reached 573,000, did the monthly average exceed half a million and even that figure represented a negligible unemployment rate of 2.6 per cent.[14]

Beveridge, in his famous 1942 report, had identified mass unemployment, or 'idleness', as one of five 'giant evils' which post-war governments would have to tackle. A little inflation, in Macmillan's view, was a small price to pay for its defeat. Neither did the Conservatives appear unwilling to work through the rest of Beveridge's agenda. 'Disease' was confronted through the agency of the National Health Service, now, as Kenneth Morgan has noted, despite its controversial origins, 'a favoured target for Conservative munificence'.[15] Consolidated current and capital expenditure almost doubled from £493.9 million in 1951/2 to £951.7 million in 1962/3, with an especially notable surge of hospital building initiated under Enoch Powell in the early 1960s.[16] Provision of resources on this scale seems likely to have influenced a steadily improving trend in key health indicators. The infant mortality rate, for example, recording the deaths of children under one year in each thousand live births, declined from 31.1 in 1951 to 21.7 in 1963.[17] 'Ignorance', another of Beveridge's demons, was subjected to similar treatment. Expenditure on education rose from £416.1 million in 1951/2 to £1,233.0 million in 1962/3, a significant increase even though about half its value was swallowed by rising costs.[18]

The main thrust of the attack on 'squalor' was initiated by Macmillan's success in mobilizing resources for housebuilding between 1951 and 1954. Completions, which peaked at 354,129 in 1954, exceeded both the achievement of the previous Labour Government and the ambitious target set by the Conservative Party Conference in 1951. Over the period 1951–63 the proportion of new homes built for the private sector increased, overtaking local authority completions in 1959. This and the steady expansion of owner occupation, comprising 42.3 per cent of all tenures by 1961, was suggestive of the burgeoning affluence which swept the Conservatives back into office in 1959.[19] In the 1950s, it has been argued, 'home ownership in the property-owning democracy . . . (helped) to cement the Tory vote and the Tory tradition', especially amongst the skilled working class.[20]

At the start of the 1960s most British people were healthier, better educated, better housed and more prosperous than they had been before. Poverty, the giant evil 'want', appeared to have been virtually banished from the land. Macmillan's celebrated boast was not without substance. 'Let's be frank about it', he had observed in July 1957, 'most of our people have never had it so good'. The extent to which Conservative policies were responsible for this happy situation is not easily determined. Britain, it could be argued, was simply carried along by a booming international economy after the end of the Korean War. Moreover, Britain benefited from a fortuitous shift in its terms of trade as prices of food and raw materials fell rapidly in the 1950s while manufacturing prices were stable or rising. By 1960, according to Graham Hutton, Britain's terms of trade had improved by about 30 per cent and the ratio of export to import prices had returned almost to its advantageous pre-war level.[21] Falling import prices significantly eased pressure on Conservative governments enabling them to pursue expansion without dire consequences for the balance of payments.

Terms of trade were especially favourable after 1957 and it is noticeable that consumer spending surged towards the end of the 1950s, encouraged by the easing of credit controls in 1958 and Heathcoat-Amory's pre-election budget which cut taxes by £300 million. Rising demand was attracted to durables which accounted for almost half the increase in real consumer expenditure between mid-1958 and mid-1959. Writing in June 1958 Mark Abrams suggested that the British market for durables was 'a very long way from saturated'. Recent survey evidence indicated that only 56 per cent of all households owned a television set; only 26 per cent owned a washing machine and 24 per cent a car.[22] By November 1959 he was reporting significant increases; 74 per cent now owned a television; the figures for washing machines and cars had grown to 40 per cent and 30 per cent respectively.[23] Abrams and other commentators argued that a significant watershed had been crossed especially for 'the more prosperous half of the working class'.[24] The arrival of 'gaudy prosperity' wrong-footed Labour which was slow to come to terms with the material aspirations of the working class. Whatever the underlying explanations the Conservatives appeared to have delivered these improvements. 'Once we made people think about pounds, shillings and pence', complained one Labour activist in 1959, 'they began to consider how well they'd done in the last few years and to decide that the Tories were doing all right by them'.[25]

It is, however, necessary to look beyond material progress and social welfare. They provide only part of an explanation for the longevity of Conservative administration after 1951. In twentieth-century Britain, as Robert Holland has argued, the art of the possible has usually involved juggling with both welfare and greatness. The pursuit of the latter, he notes, has at times obscured the domestic agenda, Britain's *ancien régime* measuring its success by 'achievements in war and diplomacy rather than by more complex and material criteria'.[26]

Judged on these terms the various Tory leaders after 1951 earn mixed reviews. Churchill's leonine instincts led him to seek a three power summit conference at which Britain could be seen rubbing shoulders with the new superpowers, thus signalling to the world and the electorate that 'Britain still counted'.[27] Eden, matinee idol turned 'benzadrine Napoleon', was determined to lay the ghost of appeasement, the other haunting shadow of the 1930s, seeing Nasser as a pocket Hitler or Mussolini. The consequence of this miscalculation was the Suez fiasco of 1956. 'In a matter of months', Muggeridge wrote later, 'he succeeded in reducing his country to a laughing-stock . . . his government to impotence, his party to confusion, and himself to a condition of nervous prostration.'[28] The trauma of Suez lay in the exposure of Britain's limitations. Nasser's nationalization of the Canal in July was, as Harold Nicolson noted, 'a pretty resounding slap in the face'. It soon became clear that Eden would have been well advised to turn the other cheek rather than run the risk of failure. 'We have shown that we have not a friend in the world', wrote Nicolson as the sorry episode drew to a close, 'our reputation is tarnished: and in the end, at the first serious threat from Bulganin, we have had to climb down'.[29] Suez was for Britain a painful lesson in the realities of the new world order.

At least it was over fairly quickly, allowing Britain's Conservative rulers to continue their reluctant adjustment to reduced circumstances. Within a few years Eden's successor was urging white South Africa to bend before the 'wind of change'. Macmillan, it seemed, had discovered that Europeans, rather than Africans, were the problem in Africa. The management of this denouement without, for example, the major carnage which attended the French retreat from Algeria became an achievement for which the British establishment congratulated itself. Even Andrew Shonfield, a trenchant critic of economic performance, gazed in wonder at 'the ease with which the British managed to divest themselves of the biggest and richest empire in the history of man'. Full marks, apparently, were due to the senior civil servants who had supervised this smooth transfer.[30] This version of contemporary history, in which new states were granted independence by the British rather than gaining independence from them, made a virtue of necessity. Macmillan was its principal source. The British, as he explained later, 'had not lost the will or even the power to rule . . . it was rather their duty to spread to other nations those advantages which through the long course of centuries they had won for themselves'.[31]

This gloss was necessary because of the tenacity with which the British electorate in the mid-twentieth century adhered to a vision of the nation which belonged to the past. 'This reluctance to escape from the tradition of greatness', observed one Tory MP in 1962, 'is, I think, common to all the social classes'[32]. It had, of course, been especially evident at the time of Suez. Public opinion, according to the polls, had been a little confused but, on balance, favourable to Eden. Bournemouth ladies, it seemed, did not like the Russians, the Americans or Nasser. Eden had struck a blow at all three; 'therefore Eden must be right'. Not for the first time, or the last, middle-class socialists recoiled when confronted with unsympathetic aspects of working-class culture manifested by labourers who backed Eden while 'talking of Wogs, Dagoes and Gyppies (sic) as vituperatively as they did when they were "seeing the world" in the Army'.[33] After Suez, as Britain's overseas possessions diminished year by year, these powerful instincts and the imperial nostalgia to which they related required careful management if the credibility of the Conservative elite was to remain intact.

Conservative defence policy, outlined principally in Duncan Sandys' White Paper of April 1957, indicated a reorientation of policy designed to preserve the illusion that Britain could still compete in the major league. Conventional forces, deployed expensively across the globe, were to be run down; national service was to be abandoned; defence expenditure was to be cut back and held to 7 per cent of GNP. But at the same time the Government committed itself to the development and maintenance of an independent nuclear deterrent which, it was suggested, would restore Britain's diminished international prestige at a stroke. It was all very reassuring, if you put aside the possibility that such a strategy might invite rather than deter Soviet aggression. Britain might be losing an empire but it had by 1958, as Randolph Churchill argued, acquired the ability to take out a dozen Soviet cities from bases in Britain and a further dozen from bases in Cyprus. 'We did not have that power at the time of Suez', he reflected. 'We are a major power again.'[34] There was the additional advantage that awkward customers, like Nasser, would, in future, have to think twice. Thus the old illusions became attached to the independent nuclear deterrent, the retiring emperor's suit of clothes which would ensure that Britain would arrive appropriately dressed in the conference chambers of world diplomacy.

Even some Labour critics of Conservative defence policy conceded that it had 'a wider value than the purely strategic'. It was undeniable, wrote Alistair Buchan in 1960, that Britain 'as an effective nuclear power, now occupies a position of confidence in Washington which no other country can attain in the forseeable future'. He also acknowledged 'that Britain had participated in certain special negotiations, such as those on nuclear testing, with the United States and Russia'.[35] The summit diplomacy to which Churchill had unsuccessfully aspired in the early 1950s was, it seemed, now within reach, allowing Conservative Party leaders to assume the guise of British statesmen as they flitted from capital to capital. Macmillan, noted Alistair Burnet of the *Economist*, had undertaken an overdue reappraisal of foreign policy commitments acquired 'when British governments believed they could still play a predominantly authoritative and energetic role throughout the world'. This subtle process was largely hidden from the British electorate which could draw the conclusion from Macmillan's well-publicized appearances in Moscow, New York and Washington that their leader still counted on the world stage. Macmillan and Home, Burnet suggested, offered an approximation of statesmanlike behaviour. 'This is the image that British opinion has seized upon'.[36]

And image was increasingly important in an era when 74 per cent of households owned a television set, supplementing the solid electoral advantages of affluence and the independent nuclear deterrent. In a perceptive article written after the 1959 election, Raphael Samuel, having interviewed working-class voters in Clapham and Stevenage, testified to the continuing mystique of the traditional governing class. It was significant, he argued, that the revival of Conservative prospects after Suez had been under Macmillan rather than the more prosaic Butler. Labour propagandists might mock 'his raffish and downbeat Edwardianism' but working-class deference voters, amongst others, grasped the point. 'A governing class', concluded Samuel, 'must look like a governing class. Its leader must always appear in the confident stance of that class, arrogant on occasion, but always unruffled.'[37] The essence of this stance, also the source of much of its appeal, was unflappability, a quality evidenced at the United Nations in September 1960 when Macmillan, his speech interrupted as Khrushchev banged on the desk with a shoe, inquired gently if 'perhaps we could have a translation'.[38] This was the patrician way with foreigners and a reassuring signal.

'The country', suggested a *Spectator* editorial after Macmillan's retirement, 'may well, some day, look back with regret to a man who knew how to give such style to the otherwise unglamorous politics of a prosperous Welfare State.'[39] There can be no doubt that Macmillan knew what he was doing. The grand Edwardian manner was carefully nurtured with a view to maximizing Conservative support. One party political broadcast before the 1959 election put on the country-house style, showing the Prime Minister and his colleagues at Chequers. 'How comfortable the ministers looked, ensconced in the seat of Authority', noted one wavering voter; 'how *obviously* at home'.[40] Narrower still and narrower were the bounds of empire set but there was some consolation to be derived from the knowledge that the right people were still in charge.

In a note to Conservative Central Office in July 1961 Macmillan developed his views on style and leadership. Hugh Gaitskell had accused him of 'Edwardian nonchalance – what others have called unflappability'. Picking up this tame half-volley he drafted a response with party Conference in mind or even 'some suitable garden party'. He suggested, with Olympian condescension, that if Gaitskell 'had a little more experience of life, he would know that sometimes in dangerous moments it is advisable, even if one feels alarm, to cultivate an outward show of confidence'. He had learned this 'in early youth under fire on the battlefield', an experience which 'for reasons which I wholly understand . . . was not vouchsafed to Mr. Gaitskell, Mr. Wilson, Mr. Brown, Mr. Jay and the other leading members of the Labour front bench'.[41] It has been argued that the foremost achievement of the Macmillan Government was 'to postpone the crisis of confidence in post-imperial Britain'.[42] For a brief period it seemed possible to balance the twin burdens of welfare and greatness, to aspire to affluence while retaining Britain's world role. After 1961 it became increasingly difficult for Britain's Conservative rulers to sustain this position and, in itself, 'an outward show of confidence' was not enough.

It was perhaps surprising that the Suez debacle failed to generate a crisis of confidence akin to that which had followed 'Black Week' in 1899. At the turn of the century what Sidney Webb had called 'a burning feeling of shame at the failure of England' had been sufficiently powerful to bring the issue of modernization onto the political agenda as the nation's economic and social efficiency was subjected to intense scrutiny.[43] Suez had supplied an external shock. 'Seldom', claimed Samuel from the perspective of the New Left, 'has the incapacity of the governing class to govern been more apparent'.[44] But Macmillan bought a breathing space and there was a time-lag of about five years before the Conservatives had to pay the price.

The impact of Suez, however, should not be underestimated. In Iain Macleod's judgement the unfortunate affair was 'the biggest factor in losing the "intellectual vote", which for whatever reasons the Conservatives certainly did lose in the early 1960s'.[45] The experience of Rex Malik, author of *What's Wrong with British Industry?*, published eight years on in 1964, is instructive here. He traced the origins of his book, a characteristic product of early 1960s self-examination, back to 1956 when the Suez affair had exposed 'the near-criminal stupidity, the bungling, the incompetence and general flabbiness' of the British establishment. An article in the *Spectator*, written just after the fiasco had caught his eye with its sombre observation that the country was ruled 'by a collection of chancers and *apres-moi le deluge* men'.[46] They had a few more years to run.

Macmillan, according to Bernard Levin, was in his element when 'avoiding conflict, postponing pain'.[47] But conflict could not be avoided nor pain postponed indefinitely. At the start of 1960 two-thirds of a Gallup poll sample believed that Britain 'would be the country with the most to offer ordinary people for happiness and contentment'. Over the next three years, however, this confidence was eroded and acute disenchantment with the Conservative Government was evident. 'Orpington man' surfaced to deliver a major blow to Tory morale at the celebrated by-election in March 1962 after which, Gallup suggested, support for the Party in the country was at only 33 per cent, the lowest level since 1946.[48] The Conservative economic record had been dented within a year of the 1959 election as the surge of expansion faded and a balance of payments problem emerged which demanded urgent attention. As 'go' turned to 'stop' affluent consumerism was checked, notably by Selwyn Lloyd's counter-inflationary budget of April 1961 and the emergency package which followed three months later. At the same time the fragility of Britain's claim to major power status was exposed not least because the much-vaunted independence of its nuclear deterrent proved somewhat illusory. Dean Acheson's often quoted remark that 'Britain had lost an empire and . . . not yet found a role', dating from December 1962, struck home. Its impact was significantly reinforced a month later when de Gaulle made it quite clear that there was little point, for the immediate future, in seeking a new leading role in Europe.

From the vantage point of 1962 the National Institute for Economic and Social Research reported that the significant break in recent trends had occurred in mid-1960 'when the short sharp burst of expansion in the British economy stopped'. Since then, it continued, 'there has been little further growth'.[49] This setback was compounded by a balance-of-payments crisis as the £132 million surplus of 1959 gave way to a £273 million deficit in 1960; the deficit on visibles, rising from £116 million in 1959 to £404 million in 1960 and remaining stubbornly high at £149 million in 1961, was a particular cause for concern.[50] Lloyd's emergency measures, prompted by pressure on sterling, were designed as a response to this situation and also to the re-emergence of price inflation after a period of stability. An influential OEEC report on *The Problem of Rising Prices*, published in May 1961, and the annual report of the Bank for International Settlements a month later both identified 'wage-push' as the immediate cause of inflation, indicating a problem which the British Government would be required to address. The United Kingdom's balance of payments predicament, in the Bank's view, arose from 'the almost continuous tendency of wage increases to exceed productivity gains, with consequent increases in costs and prices'.[51]

Lloyd's July 1961 package combined orthodox deflationary measures, such as a 2 per cent rise in bank rate, with a public sector 'pay pause' devised with a view to exerting downward pressure on private sector settlements. The idea was to provide an opportunity for productivity growth, currently lagging behind wages, to catch up. Though it could be argued, and it was certainly Macmillan's view, that the pay pause achieved its purpose, the political cost was considerable. 'The Pay Pause', wrote Macmillan after the Orpington defeat, '. . . has offended dons, schoolmasters, school-teachers, Civil Servants, clerks, nurses, public utility workers, railwaymen and all the rest'. It was, however, most resented by middle-class professionals and other white collar workers who saw their differentials eroded; those 'who feel that they are *relatively* ill-paid compared to the high wages which they hear about coming into the ordinary artisan's household'.[52] These concerns and irritation at intervention in pay bargaining, as when an award for teachers previously agreed was blocked, alienated significant numbers of the Conservatives' natural supporters amongst the electorate. It did seem unfair that industrial workers could use their union muscle to breach the pause while white collar workers were restrained. Thus the pause and the 2.5 per cent 'guiding light' which followed in February 1962 posed, as one member of the Cabinet noted, 'a tremendous problem of public relations'.[53]

Failure to resolve this problem satisfactorily helped to intensify developing criticism of Conservative economic management. To some extent this was externally generated, an OECD survey in March 1962 taking an especially pessimistic view of Britain's economic performance over the previous decade. 'The picture', it concluded, 'was, repeatedly, one of home demand rising faster than output, with exports insufficiently dynamic to look after the balance of payments and the authorities required to impose frequent measures of restraint'. In addition to the debilitating impact of stop–go there was the problem of Britain's 'relatively large burden of defence expenditure overseas'.[54] Such views augmented a home-grown chorus which was making itself heard by 1962, spreading doubt and destroying complacency. 'Anyone', wrote Graham Hutton in one particularly comprehensive survey, 'who can rest content with Britain's economic performance in the 1950s compared with those of other leading industrial nations must have set his sights desperately low in the late 1940s'.[55]

Hutton's comparative emphasis was typical of much of the economic criticism of the early 1960s. 'The grounds for disquiet at the present time', noted the Conservative MP and television journalist Christopher Chataway in 1961, 'are provided . . . by comparing our own economic performance with the rates at which the economies of various western European countries are growing'. Germany, he declared, was doubling its production every 10 years, France every 17, whereas Britain required 32 years to achieve the same increase.[56] The decision to apply for admission to the Common Market, announced in July 1961, encouraged the comparative approach. It was in the early 1960s that it became increasingly apparent that the only post-war economic miracle to be explained 'was the British failure to take part in the progress of the rest of the civilised world'.[57]

An abundance of statistical evidence from a variety of sources underlined the dismal story of the first industrial nation and its fall from economic grace. OEEC figures (summarized in Tables 1.1–1.3), for example, confirmed that the gap between Britain's performance and that of other developed nations had widened during the years of Tory stewardship. The Oxford economist, Sir Roy Harrod, returning from a meeting of the International Monetary Fund in October 1961 emphasized the message which such statistics conveyed. 'Britain', he informed the Prime Minister, 'is now universally regarded as a country of very low growth'.[58]

As awareness of Britain's comparative failure mounted there was an increasing tendency for commentators to question the extent of the material prosperity which had been achieved under the Conservatives. 'Facing up to

Table 1.1   *Volume indices of GNP at market prices (1953=100)*

Country	1951	1955	1960
OEEC (average)	92	111	137
Germany	86	120	161
France	93	111	137
United Kingdom	96	108	121

Source: OEEC *Twelfth Annual Report* (Paris, 1961)

Table 1.2   *Volume indices of GNP per capita (1953=100)*

Country	1951	1955	1960
OEEC (average)	94	110	129
Germany	87	117	148
France	96	109	128
United Kingdom	97	108	117

Source: OEEC *Twelfth Annual Report* (Paris, 1961)

Table 1.3   *General indices of industrial production (1953=100)*

Country	1951	1955	1960
OEEC(average)	94	119	155
Germany	85	128	180
France	99	117	166
United Kingdom	98	114	130

Source: OEEC *Twelfth Annual Report* (Paris, 1961)

the brutal facts of our position', wrote David Butler in September 1962, '(at a time, moreover, of domestic economic difficulty) has perhaps given some people a sense of having been tricked by the optimistic propaganda of 1959'.[59] This sentiment was manifested, amongst other ways, in growing concern regarding regional disparities. 'The idea', wrote Geoffrey Moorhouse a little later, 'that over the past few years two Englands have taken shape, one in the North the other in the South, unequal socially and economically, has become a major national preoccupation'.[60] Rising unemployment, even at modest 1960s levels, underlined the point. It seems likely that the economy began to expand again in the first quarter of 1963 though the turning point may have been obscured by the impact of the harsh winter. But unemployment, running nationally at 3.6 per cent in February 1963, the highest rate since the 1947 fuel crisis, remained persistently higher at 6.0 per cent in the Ministry of Labour's Northern region, 5.7 per cent in Scotland and 4.5 per cent in Wales, than in London and the South East where the rate

peaked at 1.8 per cent.[61] Contemporary research suggested other disquiet-
ing aspects of an affluent society in which not all were able to share. For
those receiving National Assistance payments the most that could be
claimed for the welfare state by 1962 was that it 'has been possible to build
a floor in real terms at a little above the subsistence levels of the 1930s'.[62]

There was, of course, a widely perceived connection between Britain's
economic performance and its ability to sustain a world role. 'Britain's
influence in the world', as the 1957 Sandys White Paper had recognized,
'depends first and foremost on the health of the internal economy and the
success of her export trade'.[63] The scope of Britain's defence commitments,
itself a reflection of continuing great power pretensions, was subjected to
renewed scrutiny. As one economist noted, we had a 'wrong image of
ourselves' which ensured that, Sandys notwithstanding, 'we are still trying
to do an impossible number of things within the limits of total military
expenditure'.[64] There was also the negative impact of Britain's external role
on economic performance to be considered.

Moreover, the credibility of the independent nuclear deterrent, centrepiece of the Sandys strategy, was increasingly suspect. Having abandoned its
prohibitively expensive commitment to a British-made surface-to-surface
missile, Blue Streak, in February 1960, the Government was forced to rely
on American technology in the dubious form of Skybolt. It was, as Robert
McNamara admitted, 'a pile of junk' but, the Government having pur-
chased it, 'it was "our" junk and as such capable of exercising talismanic
powers in British politics'.[65] When the United States cut its losses on Skybolt
in November 1962 the paucity of Britain's resources and the highly conditional independence of its nuclear force was apparent. The Polaris deal,
hastily struck a few months later, plugged the gap which had been blown in
Britain's defence strategy but dependence on American-made missiles
remained.

The satirical revue *Beyond the Fringe*, which began its West End run in
1960, capitalized on the Government's embarrassment, referring to a new
British missile, 'Greased Lightning', which could be carried into enemy
territory by highly trained athletes. More seriously the advantages derived
from possession of an independent deterrent were questioned. It had
secured a place at the top table but, as Alistair Buchan observed, there were
few illusions 'even in London and certainly none in Moscow or
Washington, about the fact that it is their own armoury and their own
attitude which is crucial'.[66] This uncomfortable reality was especially obvious after the 1962 Cuban Missile Crisis, a superpower confrontation in
which British interests were largely marginalized. The argument was also
developed, notably by Labour's Shadow Defence Secretary, that modern
long-range nuclear weapons 'put strategic independence beyond the reach
of medium powers like Britain'. Security, it was suggested, could best be
achieved through some form of 'interdependence' under the NATO
umbrella.[67] But this route was closed for those who resisted the idea that
Britain was simply one amongst a number of middle-ranking powers.

Within a few weeks of the Skybolt humiliation Macmillan's Government
suffered an even more crucial reverse when de Gaulle's veto dramatically

terminated Britain's negotiations with the Common Market. For many Conservatives, forced in the late 1950s and early 1960s into a reluctant reappraisal of Britain's world role, the prospect of EEC membership had come to represent the least worst outcome, the opportunity to assert British influence in a new sphere as the colonies retreated and the Atlantic axis wobbled. Also important was the idea that EEC entry would supply a necessary stimulus to economic modernization. The Common Market, as one committed advocate of entry argued, offered the nation 'not merely a way out of its economic difficulties but also a form of relief from the psychological pressure engendered by loss of power in the world'.[68] In these circumstances the French veto of January 1963 was a crippling blow, a savage exposure of the state of relative impotence to which Britain had declined. 'General de Gaulle said "No", and Britain's own views on her national destiny suddenly appeared absurdly irrelevant'.[69]

These circumstances help to explain the paranoia which gripped the Conservative establishment in the summer of 1963 as the Profumo affair ran its course. By then, the mask of unflappability, so important as Macmillan worked to postpone the post-Suez reckoning, had begun to slip. The Cabinet reconstruction of July 1962 when, as Jeremy Thorpe remarked, the Prime Minister 'lay down his friends for his life', hinted at panic. 'It astonished me', wrote one of its seven victims, 'that a man who had kept his head under the most severe stresses and strains should lose both nerve and judgement in this way'.[70] How different it all was from January 1958 when Macmillan loftily dismissed the resignation of his entire Treasury team as 'a little local difficulty'.

Loss of nerve and judgement were apparent to those close to Macmillan as the Profumo scandal generated a wave of rumours suggestive of decadence at the heart of the British establishment. In June 1963 Macleod discovered Macmillan 'in a terrible state, going on about a rumour of there having been eight High Court judges involved in some orgy'. He could just conceive of 'one, perhaps two . . . but eight, I just can't believe it'.[71] In this troubled state of mind he was unable to resist demands for an inquiry into the Profumo affair despite Macleod's advice that such a step would simply prolong the Government's ordeal by rumour. Macleod's judgement was probably correct. There was an inevitable element of high farce involved in Lord Denning's pursuit of, amongst others, 'the headless man', rumoured to be of Cabinet rank, who had been photographed doing something odd with the Duchess of Argyll.

In itself the War Minister's relationship with Christine Keeler, a woman whose calling Denning could readily infer from the cut of her bathing costume, was of little importance. But the Profumo affair mattered because it provided the electorate with an unusually intimate glimpse of the Conservative *ancien régime* at a point when its credibility was already severely stretched. The art of the possible, as Macmillan's government discovered, was more easily practised if one's trousers were not seen to be around one's ankles. It was important, as Samuel had observed after the 1959 election, for a governing class to look and behave like a governing class. The 51.6 per cent of NOP's sample who confessed in June 1963 that they were 'shocked' or 'horrified' by what had occurred suggested that confidence in the Conservatives as the natural party of government had been undermined.[72]

Macmillan, who in his prime had characterized the Labour Party as 'out-of-touch and out-of-date', now found the same labels attached to himself and his party. Edwardianism was a wasting asset as the Prime Minister was contrasted unfavourably with the youthful, dynamic Kennedy. Amongst younger Conservatives, Rees-Mogg recalled, there was an embarrassed awareness of being led 'by a figure from the past . . . [who] seemed to be running out of new ideas'.[73] When Macmillan finally gave way in October 1963 the outcome of the leadership contest disappointed those who had hoped that the Conservative Party would distance itself from what he had come to represent. To Anthony Sampson, whose influential *Anatomy of Britain* was published in 1962, the Tories showed an unhealthy inclination to retreat 'into an isolated and defensive amateur world, which cherishes irrelevant aspects of the past'.[74] Whatever the merits of Lord Home, who emerged from an arcane process of consultation conducted largely amongst prominent Old Etonians, it seemed unlikely that he would curb this tendency. 'Much depended on character', observed Butler, the disappointed candidate, but 'even if [Home] could get himself across to the public, the difficulties of the peerage remained and spoilt the image of modernization'.[75]

By 1963 'modernization' had come to imply a major reconstruction of British society, its institutions and its values, with a view to improving economic performance and reclaiming lost esteem. As Butler's comment indicated, leading Conservatives were very conscious of this agenda. It could hardly have been otherwise. Britain in the early 1960s has been likened to 'a patient undergoing psycho-analysis and reaching the stage of being brought by the therapist to face the truth'.[76] A sense of the sleeper awakening runs through the wave of modernization literature initiated by Michael Shanks's *The Stagnant Society* in 1961 and continued by, for example, Anthony Sampson's *Anatomy* and Nicholas Davenport's *The Split Society*, forerunners of the Penguin *What's Wrong?* series. Those, like Graham Hutton, who had come to a depressing view of Britain's situation, were much encouraged by this movement of opinion favouring 'a real overhaul of the government and the economy'.

The movement had taken root, he noted, amongst 'a rapidly growing minority of responsible people' who had experienced 'a feeling of belonging to the only nation without aim or inspiration; of being borne down by imposts, restrictions and hindrances'.[77] What H.G. Wells, in an earlier generation, had labelled 'the revolt of the competent' rippled through society, assisted by the Duke of Edinburgh's well-publicized observation in October 1961 that it was 'about time we pulled our fingers out'.[78] In this way, as the upward movement of material prosperity faltered and Britain's credibility as a major power was undermined, the crisis of modernization, delayed since the late 1950s, finally surfaced.

Protagonists varied both in their diagnoses and in their proposed remedies. Shanks, for example, focused on labour market rigidities and trade union reform. Davenport attacked what he regarded as the anachronism of a 'City-based moneyed ruling class' in whose interest sterling was bolstered 'at the cost of abnormally low growth and the alienation of the working masses'.[79] But some common themes emerged. Modernization, it was agreed, required the mobilization of a sense of national purpose overriding party politics and class interests. In Bulgaria, to Shanks' surprise, they did these things better. Whatever else Bulgaria lacked it was not short of national purpose, something conspicuously absent in Britain.[80] Davenport, impressed that almost as much was spent on gambling as on education, concluded that British society, 'though it is tolerant, liberal and decent by comparison with many others, has very little serious purpose'. He added: 'It is surely time that we got one'.[81]

Another persistent refrain was of the need to jettison outmoded ideas and institutions which blocked the route to modernization or, at least, to subject them to radical reform. The main targets here, clearly identified in Sampson's *Anatomy* were 'the old privileged values of aristocracy, public school and Oxbridge which still dominate government today'.[82] Arguments related to this theme tended to develop in two ways. Modern societies were assumed to be democratic and open; therefore, if Britain was to join them, privilege would have to be abandoned. Thus it seemed curious to Wilson that 'in this so-called opportunity state . . . no one in 1963 can become Conservative Prime Minister unless he has been to Eton'.[83] More telling, perhaps, were arguments linked to structural functionalism. The case against the public schools, noted Malik, was that 'on any realistic look at the evidence, they do not provide the elite we need'.[84]

It was assumed, of course, that the excess baggage of tradition would be traded in for a new set of ideas and institutions more appropriate to a scientific age. In Sampson's view the Conservative establishment was at fault here, clinging to power but failing to accommodate 'the vast forces of science, education and social change which (whether they like it or not) are changing the face of the country'.[85] Lord James, Vice Chancellor of one of the new universities, was not alone in complaining that Britain's 'top people' showed little interest in new technology. This would have to change if only to stem the outward flow of research scientists to the United States. At the same time it was recognized that the tasks of management in a modern industrial state were likely to be discharged more effectively by professionals than by amateurs, however gifted, or those who had reached their positions on seniority rather than merit.[86] Expertise rather than the correct old school tie were required not least for the complex task of planning the economy, preferably in the French indicative style which the modernizers so admired.

To some extent this preoccupation with modernization was to be found at the heart of the much-abused Tory establishment. Reginald Maudling, at the Board of Trade in 1960, supplied a confidential assessment of British industrialists in complacent pursuit of soft options which would not have been out of place in the published literature of the new movement.[87] 'We are suffering', he wrote, 'from the malaise of the affluent society without having the fundamental economic strength of the Americans. We still believe that the world owes us a living.' Maudling looked in vain for what Shanks or Davenport would have called 'a sense of national purpose', doubting whether the will to address Britain's problems could be generated until the country 'has been brought face to face with the realities of our economic position in the modern world'. All that he could offer in the meantime was a commitment to 'plug away', relying largely on 'exhortation' and 'cajolement'. The sense that something more was required inspired Maudling's subsequent 'dash for freedom' in his 1963 budget, a calculated gamble designed to banish stagflation and 'a break-out from the constrictions of the past'.[88]

There is evidence to suggest that the aborted Paris summit of May 1960 marked the point at which Macmillan 'suddenly realised that Britain counted for nothing'.[89] This was subsequently reflected in his important Cabinet memorandum, dubbed, 'half jokingly', the 'Grand Design', which indicated the direction of his thinking at the start of 1961. A concerted response from the West was required if communism was to be resisted but it was clear that Britain had 'neither the economic nor the military power to take the leading role'. Security, he argued, lay within a framework of 'interdependence' which might even be stretched to incorporate a deal on nuclear weapons with the French.[90] Such high level reappraisals were a necessary precondition for any modernization strategy which the Conservatives might develop. Within a short time it was clear that this would embrace both EEC membership and commitment to a series of wide-ranging investigations, spearheaded by professionals like Beeching and experts like Buchanan, into troubling aspects of the British economy and its infrastructure. At the same time economic planning was given circumspect encouragement. Macmillan's response to a suggested 'five year plan' in January 1961 was to indicate that such a scheme already had the Cabinet's tacit agreement. 'Of course the trouble is that we cannot say so – or perhaps we can?'[91] The establishment of 'Neddy' later that year seemed to signal that this Tory dilemma had been resolved.

Macmillan's initial hesitancy was indicative of a party uneasy with the new agenda of modernization. This was reflected later in the approach to the 1964 election campaign when the issue was at first highlighted and then nervously played down.[92] Many Conservatives, after all, were Conservatives because they liked things as they were. There was also an inconvenient short-term factor to be considered. Whatever long-term advantages might stem from a commitment to modernization, prospects for re-election were unlikely to be improved by persistent exposure of Britain's shortcomings. Sustaining the Tory hegemony after 1951 had involved sheltering the electorate from such awkward realities. A commitment to consumption, dating from Churchill's determination to 'let pork rip', was linked to the maintenance of a world role which nurtured imperial nostalgia. Modernization had taken a back seat as Britain, in Donald Macrae's words, 'resumed the easy road of long decline'. And, he noted, it was, under the Conservatives 'a comfortable road save that its surface seems more broken, its rewards of pleasant prospects less, as the *autobahnen* of other societies thunder by'.[93] An enhanced awareness that this road led to national humiliation was the legacy bequeathed to Labour as 'their thirteen years' gave way to 'our seventeen months'.

Notes

1 H. Wilson *The New Britain: Labour's Plan Outlined by Harold Wilson* (1964) p. 9.
2 Labour Party Research Department *Twelve Wasted Years* (1963) p. v.
3 *Spectator* 8/4/1966.
4 D. Healey *The Time of My Life* (1990) p. 192.
5 *The Listener* 21/2/1963.
6 A. Marwick *The Explosion of British Society 1914–1962* (1963) p. 153.
7 'Symposium. 1961–64: Did the Conservatives Lose Direction?' *Contemporary Record* Vol. 2 No. 5 (Spring 1989) 30.
8 *New Statesman* 6/10/1964.
9 *The Listener* 27/9/1962.
10 R. Ingrams (ed.) *The Life and Times of Private Eye* (1971) p. 15.
11 See A. Seldon 'The Conservative Party Since 1945' in T. Gourvish and A. O'Day (eds) *Britain Since 1945* (1991) pp. 243–5.
12 'The Postwar Consensus: John Biffen interviewed by Anthony Seldon' *Contemporary Record* Vol. 2 No.1 (Spring 1988)16.
13 H. Macmillan *The Middle Way: 20 Years After* (1958).
14 Central Statistical Office (hereafter CSO) *Annual Abstract of Statistics* No. 101 (1964) Table 143 p. 130; A.H. Halsey (ed.) *Trends in British Society Since 1900* (1972) Table 4.8 p. 119.
15 K.O. Morgan *The People's Peace: British History 1945–1990* (Oxford, 1992) p. 116.
16 CSO op. cit. Table 37 p. 42.
17 Ibid. Table 35 p. 36.
18 Ibid. Table 37 p. 42; see also the comments in Halsey op. cit. 158–60.
19 CSO op. cit. Table 56 p. 64.
20 J. Ramsden 'The Changing Base of British Conservatism' in C. Cook and J. Ramsden (eds) *Trends in British Politics Since 1945* (1978) p. 38.
21 G. Hutton 'The UK Economy 1951–61: Performance and Retrospect' *Lloyds Bank Review* No. 61 (July 1961) 3.
22 *Financial Times* 21/6/1958.
23 Ibid. 2/11/1959.
24 P. Crane 'Labour Its Own Worst Enemy' *Political Quarterly* (hereafter PQ) Vol. 31 No. 3 (July–Sept. 1960) 379.
25 See D.E. Butler and R. Rose *The British General Election of 1959* (1960) p. 70.
26 See R. Holland *The Pursuit of Greatness: Britain and the World Role 1900–1970* (1991) pp. 18–19.
27 Ibid. 250–51.
28 *New Statesman* 6/10/1964.
29 N. Nicolson (ed.) *Harold Nicolson: Diaries and Letters 1945–62* (1971) p. 291 Letter Harold Nicolson–Vita Sackville-West 7/11/1956.
30 *The Listener* 26/7/1962.
31 H. Macmillan *Pointing the Way 1959–1961* (1972) pp. 116–17.
32 *The Listener* 12/7/1962 (Aubrey Jones in conversation with David Lockwood).
33 Nicolson op. cit. 292–3 Letter Harold Nicolson–Vita Sackville-West 15/11/1956; M. Young *The Chipped White Cups of Dover* (1960) p. 6.

34 See A. Sked and C. Cook *Post-War Britain: A Political History* (Harmondsworth, 1990) p. 143.
35 A. Buchan 'Britain and the Nuclear Deterrent' *PQ* Vol. 31 No. 1 (Jan.–March 1960) 43.
36 A. Burnet 'Too Many Allies?' *PQ* Vol. 32 No. 2 (April–June 1961) 147.
37 R. Samuel 'The Deference Voter' *New Left Review* No. 1 (Jan.–Feb. 1960) 12.
38 See A. Horne *Macmillan 1957–1986* (1989) pp. 278–9.
39 *Spectator* 14/2/1964.
40 Samuel op. cit. 12.
41 Public Records Office (hereafter PRO) PREM 11/3479 Letter Harold Macmillan–George Christ 30/7/1961.
42 L.A. Siedentop 'Mr Macmillan and the Edwardian Style' in V. Bogdanor and R. Skidelsky (eds) *The Age of Affluence 1951–64* (1970) p. 52.
43 For a brief survey of this earlier modernization crisis see S. Newton and D. Porter *Modernization Frustrated: the Politics of Industrial Decline Since 1900* (1988) pp. 1–30.
44 Samuel op. cit. 13.
45 R. Blake *The Conservative Party from Peel to Thatcher* (1985) p. 279.
46 R. Malik *What's Wrong with British Industry?* (Harmondsworth, 1964) p. 10.
47 B. Levin *The Pendulum Years: Britain and the Sixties* (1970) p. 201.
48 R.J. Whybrow *Britain Speaks Out 1937–87: A Social History as seen through the Gallup Data* (1989) pp. 58, 64.
49 *National Institute Economic Review* (hereafter *NIER*) No. 19 (February 1962) 4–5.
50 CSO *Annual Abstract of Statistics* No. 102 (1965) Table 274 p. 236.
51 See T.L. Johnson 'Pay Policy after the Pause' *Scottish Journal of Political Economy* Vol. 9 (1962) 1–2.
52 H. Macmillan *At the End of the Day 1959–1961* (1973) p. 59. Diary entry for 24/3/1962; for the introduction of the pause see D.R. Thorpe *Selwyn Lloyd* (1989) pp. 326–7.
53 Earl of Kilmuir *Political Adventure: The Memoirs of the Earl of Kilmuir* (1962) p. 319.
54 Organization for Economic Co-operation and Development (hereafter OECD) *Economic Surveys by the OECD: United Kingdom* (Paris, 1962) p. 13.
55 Hutton op. cit. 1.
56 *The Listener* 5/1/1961.
57 S. Pollard *The Wasting of the British Economy: British Economic Policy 1945 to the Present* (1984) pp. 4–6.
58 PRO PREM 11/3287 Letter Sir Roy Harrod–Harold Macmillan 11/10/1961.
59 *The Listener* 27/9/1962.
60 G. Moorhouse *Britain in the Sixties. The Other England* (Harmondsworth, 1964) p. 13. Moorhouse dates the origins of this preoccupation to an article by George Taylor in the *Guardian* 15/8/1962.
61 See *NIER* No. 27 (Feb. 1964) 4; for regional unemployment figures see OECD *Economic Surveys by the OECD: United Kingdom* (Paris, 1963) Table 7 p. 19.
62 D.C. Wedderburn 'Poverty in Britain Today – the Evidence' *Sociological Review* Vol. 10 No. 3 (Nov. 1962) 279.
63 A.C.L. Day 'The Economics of Defence' *PQ* Vol. 31 No. 1 (Jan.–March 1960) 57.
64 Ibid. 65.
65 Holland op. cit. 311; see also D. Reynolds *Britannia Overruled: British Policy and World Power in the Twentieth Century* (1991) pp. 210–16.

66 Buchan op. cit. 43.
67 D. Healey 'Interdependence' *PQ* Vol. 31 No. 1 (Jan.–March 1960) 46–56.
68 A. Hartley *A State of England* (1962) pp. 236–7.
69 N. Beloff *The General Says No: Britain's Exclusion from Europe* (Harmondsworth, 1963) p. 7. See also Holland op. cit. 286–91 and Reynolds op. cit. 216–21.
70 Kilmuir op. cit. 324.
71 A. Howard and R. West *The Making of the Prime Minister* (1964) p. 51.
72 D.E. Butler and A. King *The British General Election of 1964* (1965) p. 20.
73 'Symposium' op. cit. 28.
74 A. Sampson *Anatomy of Britain* (1962) p. 633.
75 Lord Butler *The Art of the Possible* (1971) p. 248. For an especially hostile view of Home's appointment by the magic circle see R. Bevins *The Greasy Pole: A Personal Account of the Realities of British Politics* (1965) pp. 147–51; also *Spectator* 17/1/1964.
76 Levin op. cit. 87–8.
77 Hutton op. cit. 24.
78 See Sampson op. cit. 37.
79 N. Davenport *The Split Society* (1964) pp. 174–9.
80 M. Shanks *The Stagnant Society* (Harmondsworth, 1962) p. 15. For a brief survey of this literature see Newton and Porter op. cit. 136–9.
81 Davenport op. cit. 15.
82 Sampson op. cit. 637–8.
83 See R.S. Churchill *The Fight for the Tory Leadership: A Contemporary Chronicle* (1963) p. 146.
84 Malik op. cit. 118.
85 Sampson op. cit. 638.
86 *The Listener* 26/7/1962 (Lord James of Rusholme in conversation with Andrew Shonfield).
87 PRO PREM 11/2973 Minute for the Prime Minister from Reginald Maudling 10/10/1960 marked 'Personal and Confidential'.
88 R. Maudling *Memoirs* (1978) pp.113–16.
89 See Horne op. cit. 230–31.
90 PRO PREM 11/3325 Memorandum by the Prime Minister 29/12/1960–3/1/1961 marked 'Top Secret'. See also Macmillan *Pointing the Way* op. cit. 323–6.
91 PRO PREM 11/3293 Prime Minister's Personal Minute to the Chancellor of the Exchequer 178/61 5/1/1961. The five year plan had been suggested by W. Lionel Fraser in a letter to *The Times* 5/1/1961.
92 See Butler and King op. cit. 92–3.
93 *The Listener* 23/11/1961.

2 'White heat' and white collars: the evolution of 'Wilsonism'

Steven Fielding

About ten years ago when addressing a Youth Conference I used the phrase – Ask your dad – at that time it was relevant. Since that time vast changes have taken place. Nowadays dad [is] often regarded as [a] square. He should now consult Junior.

Morgan Phillips, Labour Party General Secretary, 1961[1]

"This is a technological age", he said. "You must modernise or get out! Modernise or get out!"

Frankie Howerd, comedian 1966[2]

After being elected leader of the Labour Party in February 1963 Harold Wilson announced his vision of the 'New Britain' and outlined the ways in which a future Labour government would ensure increasing national prosperity. Of those speeches which developed this theme, the most famous was delivered to the Labour Party Conference in October 1963. There Wilson tied his party's fortunes to the full development of the 'scientific and technological revolution'. Conference delegates allegedly gasped as their leader talked of 'the white heat of technological change' and were staggered by his description of the multifarious applications of computers and self-reproducing machine tools. Members of Wilson's audience considered that he had given them an entirely new vision of Labour's future. Indeed, both the right and left of the Party saw the speech in the same apocalyptic terms. Contributors to the Gaitskellite *Socialist Commentary* felt that Wilson had 'struck the essential theme of the times' and had spoken to the country 'in terms capable of gripping the imagination'. Bevan's former mouthpiece *Tribune* similarly thought it was 'an historic utterance which established Labour unchallenged as the party of Britain's destiny'.[3] Harold Wilson's leadership was deemed to have been dramatically distinct from that of Hugh Gaitskell, his late predecessor. Indeed, immediately prior to the general election of October 1964 some party enthusiasts considered that Labour had 'experienced a profound revolution in its traditions, its way of thought, its method of political attack'. Others considered that Labour had become a 'new party' since Gaitskell's death. What contemporaries came, albeit briefly, to describe as 'Wilsonism' had been born.[4]

Despite the superficially different tone, much of the analysis and vocabulary associated with Harold Wilson had, in fact, been adopted by the Party under Gaitskell. The same can be said of Labour's hitherto unprecedented concern with its 'image' and use of public relations experts, a feature which marked the party's pre-election campaigning during 1963 and 1964.[5] Wilson's ability to promote unity within the party certainly differentiated him from Gaitskell. His presentation of Labour's case was also much more incisive. However, fundamentally, Wilson's 'white heat' rhetoric in particular and his 'New Britain' speeches in general were the result of long-term planning within the party to construct a strategy which, it was hoped, would allow Labour to adapt to the politics of 'affluence'.

This chapter will examine the evolution of Labour's electoral strategy in the years between the 1959 general election and that held in 1964. It will outline the reasons for the change in outlook within the leadership as well as explaining why some in the Party opposed certain innovations. Finally, consideration will be given to the possible impact such a refashioning had on Labour's position within the electorate during the 1960s. Under both Gaitskell and Wilson the Labour leadership assumed that popular affluence had fundamentally transformed British society and, therefore, political attitudes. As a consequence, it was deemed necessary for the Party to change its message as well as its attitude to electioneering. Time will not be spent rehearsing arguments over the existence or otherwise of the 'affluent worker'.[6] Nor will the chapter highlight the internal party policy disputes, such as those over nationalization and nuclear disarmament, which followed the 1959 general election.[7] Instead, it will attend to Labour's perception – flawed or not – of the society in which it operated and the means it sought to employ in order to win support in such a context. This focus should not be taken to suggest that Labour's narrow victory in 1964, and the more substantial achievement of 1966, was solely due to changes in strategy. Many other factors need to be taken into account. For example, convention has it that the internal collapse of the Conservative Government after its failure to enter the Common Market in 1963 was important. It has also been suggested that a change in the national mood, from the optimism of the late 1950s to the cynicism of the early 1960s, helped undermine Conservatism. Moreover, after 13 years of Conservative rule, some electors are said to have felt that it was 'time for a change'.[8] However, as the result of the 1992 general election indicates, a government's troubles do not automatically rebound to the advantage of the Opposition. Therefore, it is suggested that without the changes described in this chapter, it is at least questionable whether Labour would have been able to exploit those opportunities granted by an ailing administration.

Contemporary commentators generally considered that the cause of Labour's third successive general election defeat in 1959 had been its failure to come to terms with the affluent society. Popular affluence was thought to have promoted a blurring of class differences and the dissemination of 'middle-class' values within the working class. The Conservatives had proved best able to take electoral advantage of these social changes.[9] Mark Abrams's 1960 study for *Socialist Commentary* further revealed the extent to which Labour was seemingly losing support among those working-class voters considered to be most susceptible to the politics of affluence – women and the young.[10] Moreover, on the eve of the 1964 election the alleged negative impact of the cultural and political 'convergence' of skilled manual and white collar workers on Labour voting was confirmed.[11]

Such analysis merely reinforced what some Labour revisionists, particularly on the Party's right and centre, had suspected since the late 1940s.[12] It underscored Gaitskell's contribution to the special debate on the election at the 1959 Labour Party Conference. The fundamental cause of defeat was, he asserted, the transformation of capitalism which, due to Labour's postwar reforms guaranteed future economic growth. The Party's task was to adapt to the fact that most workers were no longer poor and permanently free of the fear of unemployment. In particular, members had to appreciate that Labour's reliance on the 'instinctive loyalty' of the manual working class was insufficient to secure power. Moreover, this group was in relative decline and would eventually be outnumbered by those employed in white collar occupations. In fact, the manual working class was also undergoing transformation. According to Gaitskell:

the typical worker of the future is more likely to be a skilled man in a white overall, watching dials in a bright new modern factory than a badly paid cotton operative working in a dark and obsolete 19th-century mill.[13]

Numerous party reports, compiled in the aftermath of defeat, echoed these observations. They appeared to indicate that affluent manual workers were increasingly turning against Labour. In London especially, the swing against the Party was said to have been greatest in constituencies where factory workers were most concentrated. It was even suggested that some of those workers who voted Labour did so in the hope that the Conservatives would still be returned to office. Labour's inability to win many seats in the New Towns, despite their predominantly proletarian complexion, was taken to indicate the party's failure to win the 'new' working class. Workers living on recently established housing estates were deemed to have become 'isolated' from work-place loyalties, choosing instead to watch television and tend their own gardens. In this kind of social setting, a new type of individualism had emerged leaving many alienated from older forms of collective loyalty. Thus, affluent workers were considered to have become more open to the influence of 'middle-class' values, allegedly promoted through television and Conservative political advertising. Young married couples in their twenties, especially if both were in employment, were said to be particularly reluctant to vote Labour. Women were especially liable to vote Conservative, even if their husbands chose Labour. To such aspiring working-class voters, the party was supposedly associated with all that was old and unsuccessful. As one voter put it, 'Labour stands for the lowest'.[14]

Given the projected decline of the manual working class, revisionists felt that Labour had to make a special effort to win the support of the growing number of professional, white collared and other 'intermediate' social groups. These were voters who not only existed outside the trade union movement, Labour's 'traditional' electoral base, but were actively hostile to it. As Merlyn Rees, Labour's defeated candidate in Harrow, put it:

I was born the son of a coal miner, the grandson and great grandson of a coal miner. At my home the singing of the Red Flag, the Co-op, the trade union, are things that get an answer in the tingling of my blood. They get no answer in tingling blood in the suburbs of London.[15]

The doyen of revisionism, Anthony Crosland, considered that, living in 'atomized' suburbs, white collar workers were more family-centred and privately orientated. This meant that despite incomes not much different to those employed in manual occupations they, nevertheless, considered themselves to be of a higher social status. He felt that the contradiction between their 'objective' and 'subjective' class status meant that white collar workers were inherently politically unstable: they 'floated' between the parties more than any other social group. Furthermore, Crosland predicted that as class conflict became less violent voters as a whole would be less inclined to make an 'automatic' assessment of their political interests than hitherto. Instead, they would become more 'pragmatic' in their choice and be more amenable to 'rational persuasion' by the parties. Therefore, according to Crosland, affluence did not necessarily imply the demise of the Labour Party. However, it did mean that Labour had to concentrate on the way it presented 'itself and its policies to the public, to the tone and content of its propaganda, and generally to the impression which it makes on the voters'. In 1959 Labour had been identified with a 'sectional, traditional class appeal' and had relied on images associated with full employment and the welfare state. These had once served the party well, but by the late 1950s were taken for granted by most voters. To enable it to appeal to white collar workers Labour needed to present itself forcefully as 'a progressive, national, social-democratic party'.[16] Gaitskell was also concerned to change Labour's image and was especially keen that the party learn from the Conservative's pre-election poster campaign. He suggested that Labour needed to show such voters that it was 'a modern mid-twentieth-century party, looking to the future, not to the past'.[17] Labour's association with the 'have nots' was no longer enough: affluent manual workers and members of the intermediate groups were more inclined to vote for the party of the 'haves'. Labour needed to develop an image that would persuade these voters that it offered them scope and opportunity to develop.[18] Crosland suggested John F. Kennedy's evocation of the 'New Frontier' as an example of the kind of approach that could possibly mobilize such groups in Labour's favour.[19]

Despite dissenting from their politics, some on the emergent New Left and old Labour left agreed with the revisionists that the party was losing ground among women and working-class youth.[20] However, many on the Labour left were resolutely hostile to most, if not all, the manifestations of 'affluence' and opposed adapting themselves to it.[21] The Conservatives were said to have won in 1959 because they had appealed to human selfishness. If Labour emulated their tactics in any way the party would inevitably conclude by betraying socialism.[22] As Michael Foot put it, 'we have to change the mood of the people of this country, to open their eyes to what an evil and disgraceful and rotten society it is'.[23] It was not the Party's task to change itself, but to change society. A delegate at the 1959 Labour Party Conference advanced this perspective most forcefully by declaring that:

I have been appalled this afternoon to find that so many people at this conference, from the leader of the Party downwards, are concerned with satisfying and appeasing public opinion.

Instead, he suggested:

Let us show we are basically a moral Party, who believe in truth and believe in socialism! If we do that, it does not matter whether we become a Government in 1964, 1974 or 1984. When we do form a government, I know that we have something to offer the country. We have a new world to offer them, and a new society, not a botched-up old system. Let us go forward from this Conference! Let us go forward and not turn back![24]

The left considered Labour's policies to be fundamentally sound, as were the means it adopted to communicate them. Members simply had to be more enthusiastic in evangelizing the electorate. Discussions of 'image' and the need for political advertising were deemed immoral because of their associations with the Conservatives. Advertising was also seen to be a waste of national resources and the left was uneasy using methods employed by sellers of detergent.[25] As one party agent declaimed:

Ad men are no more interested in the Labour Party than they are in my Aunt Fanny . . . all they know about is appealing to people's greed, whereas we are trying to appeal to their ideals.[26]

Some, including Len Williams, the Party National Agent during the early 1960s, felt that commentators like Abrams had exaggerated Labour's position. Despite the 'prophets of gloom' he considered that the party's troubles could be overcome by better organization; party funds would be wasted if spent on advertising.[27] In an attempt to discredit its findings Abrams's *Socialist Commentary* study was also criticized for its small size and the unrepresentative nature of its sample. The left suspected that spuriously scientific surveys were being concocted to lend weight to Gaitskell's revisionist agenda.[28] Some also questioned the advisability of Labour accommodating itself to affluence, which they considered a passing economic phase. According to Richard Crossman Labour needed to become a 'Fighting Socialist Opposition' and wait for the inevitable crisis in capitalism. Only this, he wrote, would bring the party back to power.[29]

That Labour could not afford to wait for the conversion of society to socialism or the demise of capitalism was suggested by the threat posed by the Liberal revival of the early 1960s. For a time at least Jo Grimond's attempt to realign the non-socialist left seemed more than a possibility. The spectacular Liberal victory in the normally Conservative stronghold of

Orpington in the 1962 by-election confirmed Labour's failure to attract skilled and white collared workers residing in the suburbs.[30] Even voters disenchanted with the Conservative government seemed unwilling to turn to Labour. Whilst white collar suburbanites saw Labour as the party of the organized working class a fourth election defeat in 1964 remained a distinct possibility. Given the party's inability to win over former Conservative voters the right-wing Labour MP Woodrow Wyatt even proposed an electoral pact with the Liberals. Whilst this was never likely, the Campaign Committee did consider the most appropriate means of persuading young industrial workers on new housing estates to vote Labour rather than Liberal.[31]

Thus, a dissenting element concentrated on the left apart, there was widespread agreement within the party about the underlying cause of Labour's 1959 defeat. There was also general accord as to the best means of recovering from it. Yet, the existence of this consensus was obscured by the bitter internal divisions which followed Gaitskell's attempt to revise Clause Four of Labour's constitution. This clause committed the Party, in theory at least, to extending nationalization, something which Gaitskell felt contributed to Labour's unpopularity.[32] Despite the passions aroused on both sides of the argument this was ultimately seen as, at best, an irrelevant and futile campaign by a number of revisionists. Crosland, for example, thought that Labour could transform its electoral fortunes without changing principles. He considered that, in any case, most voters were left unmoved by new and detailed policies. Harold Wilson accepted much of the social analysis which underpinned Gaitskell's attack on Clause Four. However, like other members of the Shadow Cabinet, he opposed his leader's assault on what amounted to no more than political 'theology'. Others, within the Transport House bureaucracy, agreed that it was unnecessary to embark on new policy initiatives, like those which followed defeat in 1955.[33]

Therefore, instead of support for substantially new policies, attention was focused on the maxim that: 'Elections are won by the picture the party, whether nationally or locally, has presented over a period of time prior to the election.'[34] Morgan Phillips, the Party General Secretary, was especially determined that at the next election Labour would 'project a clearer image of our party'.[35] Others agreed about the need to focus on a particular theme which would lend coherence to Labour's programme in order to facilitate its communication to the electorate, especially the new social groups.[36] Recognition grew for the proposition that if such work was to be successfully executed it had to be informed by research into voters' attitudes.[37] This was in contrast to opinions expressed during the 1959 campaign when those in charge of Labour's organization fought shy of innovative publicity methods. Matching Conservative advertising was deemed financially impossible, so party members were exhorted to take their message to the factories and doorsteps.[38] Even those who accepted the need to 'capture the imagination of the public' and appreciated the importance of image considered that it was not Labour's role to 'descend' to the level of the 'Tory tricksters'. They were confident that such American techniques would be rejected by the allegedly more sophisticated British electorate.[39] When this proved not to be the case it became the convention to point to such methods as one way of explaining defeat. Thus, whereas in 1955 Labour's organiz-ation was deemed culpable, the villain of the piece in 1959 became Conservative posters, especially those bearing the legend 'Life's better under the Conservatives. Don't let Labour ruin it.'[40] Such propaganda was deemed to have been especially effective due to those social changes pro-moted by affluence outlined above. Many in the party came to accept that most uncommitted, affluent voters preferred watching television to attend-ing public meetings. Thus, the only way of influencing such volatile electors was considered to be a national advertising campaign. As one agent claimed, 'a growing number of agents and active workers are, like me, beginning to wonder if some of our more traditional activities are not just a sheer waste of time and energy'.[41] It was accepted that most voters were not interested in politics whilst the vital uncommitted were considered to be especially fickle and likely to be swayed by comparatively unimportant influences. Thus, candidates were advised to acquaint themselves with the name of the favoured football team's centre forward and ensure their own ruby wedding anniversaries were reported in the local press. Activists were exhorted to 'TELL AND SELL' party policy to the don't-knows and floaters.[42] Labour could ill afford to refrain from competing with the Conservatives.

Yet, even the most enthusiastic advocates of modern forms of electioneer-ing felt that the role of local Labour members was still potentially decisive in influencing the attitudes of uncommitted voters.[43] A national competition was held to encourage improvements in the physical condition of local party offices because it was felt they influenced the way people thought of Labour. Members were asked of the passing public: 'Do they, from looking at YOUR premises, get the idea that Labour is finished, down at heel, out of date, or do they get an impression of a modern forward looking Party, clean, efficient and belonging to the space age?'[44] Leaders particularly hoped to increase membership among those groups which seemingly remained impervious to Labour's charms. Any resentment of middle-class newcomers among existing members was recognized as a possible impedi-ment which had to be overcome. One way of attracting such people was felt to be special occupational interest meetings for doctors, teachers, managers and the like in local hotels where cocktails could be served.[45] However, no special recruitment campaign was undertaken for non-manual workers. It was optimistically assumed of white collar workers that 'the very nature of their occupations causes them to recognise the restrictive nature of the capitalist system and to appreciate the virtues of a planned economy'. Thus, the dominant view remained that involving such workers in Labour politics was the concern of the appropriate trade union.[46] Because many white collar workers enjoyed incomes not much better than unionized industrial workers it was felt that, if encouraged by interested union leaders, they would soon realize that their economic interests were the same as the rest of the working class. This under-estimation of the true nature of the task was compounded by the fact that few union leaders wanted to increase the political interest of non-manual workers.[47]

Increasing the number of women members was also a priority for those concerned with modernizing the party's appeal, because of the aged composition of most Women's Sections. Young married women living on new housing estates were a particular target in view of their alleged vulnerability to Conservative propaganda. In some constituencies 'neighbourhood' groups were formed by existing members as a way of recruiting friends. Neighbours would be invited round for a regular coffee morning or sherry party. In such an informal atmosphere an attempt would be made to influence the turn of the conversation towards subjects like food prices. Wisbech members even held a fashion show to gain favourable press coverage for their Section.[48]

One of the more imaginative initiatives undertaken by a local party was at Gateshead. There the Party introduced a social club for pensioners, a coffee bar for adolescents decorated by themselves and a 'space-age club' for all members' children. This was intended to make Labour more attractive and accessible to the local community. For its pains Gateshead activists were criticized for promoting 'a load of gimmick-dressed tripe' by an anonymous agent. He bemoaned the fact that 'traditional working-class solidarity' had been replaced by 'petty bourgeois wine bibbing'. Compared to the long hard slog of canvassing and getting the vote out, such efforts were considered a waste of time.[49] Other members were frustrated by similar obstructionist attitudes. One asked: 'Why should our party surroundings and, indeed, the mode of the pleasurable activities we arrange have less well-being than our comfortable modern homes?' Another announced that members were no longer prepared 'to spend their leisure time in cold, dismal rooms, drinking tea out of cracked cups and discussing what happened 30 years ago'. There was, some felt, no reason why socialists in an affluent society could not host sherry evenings, attend the theatre and form luncheon clubs.[50]

Despite kindred efforts, the attempt to increase membership among women was only a partial success (see Table 2.1). More generally, although the years 1962–3 saw individual membership rise by nearly 80,000, this failed to take the total to that of 1959. Such an increase was admittedly modest, but it can at least be quantified unlike changes in the social composition of the Party which remain largely obscure. Regardless of this, at the end of the decade, some suggested that Labour members were increasingly middle class. This was a controversial claim. Certainly Tony Benn felt in 1964 that Labour remained composed of ageing manual workers who met in dilapidated premises.[51] In contrast, there is no doubt that the proportion of women members remained at virtually the same level as it had done in 1959.

As the election approached the emphasis shifted away from increasing membership and towards winning support amongst the electorate as a whole. The purpose of Labour's pre-election campaign was decided during 1962 and 1963 in consultation with Mark Abrams who conducted a survey of fifty constituencies to inform discussion. It was decided that it would appeal to the 'middle majority', that third of voters who were felt to have no fixed political allegiances. The assumption was that these electors were mostly either white collar or skilled manual workers. The campaign would focus on their concerns and seek to convince them that only Labour could

Table 2.1   *Individual Party Membership, 1959–66*

	Men	Women	Total	Change +/–	% Women
1959	492,213	355,313	847,526	– 41,429	41.9
1960	459,584	330,608	790,192	– 57,334	41.8
1961	434,511	316,054	750,565	– 39,626	42.1
1962	444,576	322,883	767,459	+ 16,894	42.1
1963	480,639	349,707	830,346	+ 62,887	42.1
1964	478,910	351,206	830,116	– 230	42.3
1965	475,164	341,601	816,765	– 13,351	41.8
1966	454,722	320,971	775,693	– 41,072	41.4

Source: Labour Party Annual Conference Report (1967)

further increase national prosperity and expand their own individual opportunities. Such voters were not considered to be 'profound students of politics and policies. They decide on the basis of impressions and instincts. It is *their* idea of what kind of party we are that matters, and they will not read long statements of policy.' Therefore, in order to facilitate the projection of the Labour message it was determined that the Party needed a phrase and symbol which would encapsulate all that it stood for. It was hoped that this would impart a positive, optimistic impression that would eventually have some 'psychological effect on the electorate generally'.[52]

These considerations informed Labour's six month press and poster campaign which was launched in May 1963 at a cost of over £100,000. The campaign's logo was a cheerful thumbs up symbol which was accompanied by the slogan 'Let's Go with Labour and we'll get things done'. The message of the series of press adverts was summed up in the first which comprised a dominant picture of Harold Wilson and a brief explanation of Labour's case under the legend 'Harold Wilson explains Labour's New Plans for making Britain Dynamic and Prosperous Again'.[53] Although nationally directed, it was hoped that the campaign would become a focal point for local activities. Members were encouraged to purchase and use 'Let's Go' window posters, envelope stickers and car stickers. In Doncaster activists produced 'Let's Go' balloons and proceeded to have a balloon race. Mothers were also encouraged to have their children wear 'Let's Go' badges.[54]

Wilson's use of the rhetoric of science was intended to achieve the same ends as the 'Let's Go' campaign. It was designed to present Labour in a dynamic light and appeal explicitly to those social groups who hoped to prosper most within a vibrant economy. Although his emphasis on the scientific revolution marked Wilson off from Gaitskell, others in the Party had made the call to 'Ally socialism with science' more than three years before his famous 1963 speech. A pamphlet on the subject, with an introduction by Wilson, had also been published in 1961.[55] Thus, although more willing to open Labour to scientists than his predecessor, Wilson had by no means created the sense that this was desirable.[56] The use of a science-glorifying rhetoric partly originated from those around Morgan Phillips rather than Wilson himself. Phillips hoped to use science as a device for drawing members away from their bitter internecine warfare over Clause Four. He intended it to restore a sense of unity around a grand and inspiring vision during a difficult time.[57] As General Secretary he considered it his duty during such a crisis to raise morale by giving members a 'confident and forward looking lead'. In particular, Phillips wanted to assert that, despite appearances, socialism was more than relevant in the era of prosperity because of the way planning rather than the market could exploit the potentialities of scientific endeavour.[58] It was with this in mind that he presented a special National Executive Committee (NEC) meeting with a document on 'The state of the party' in July 1960. This was subsequently expanded and given the more optimistic title of 'The future of the party' and eventually became *Labour in the Sixties*. It was to be later elaborated into the series *Signposts in the Sixties* and subsequently became the basis for Labour's 1964 manifesto.[59] The NEC commended *Labour in the Sixties* to the 1960 Party Conference although it did not, as was usual with such a document, formally endorse it. Instead it was officially designated as 'the work of the General Secretary'. This unusual formula was the result of divisions on the NEC between Gaitskellites and their opponents. Each side was unwilling to endorse all the document, yet neither wanted to dismiss it out of hand.[60] Despite this, *Labour in the Sixties* won the approval of Conference. Introducing the document, on behalf of the ailing Phillips, Ray Gunter confirmed its intention as helping to 'project our thoughts away' from Labour's present troubles. In an anticipation of Wilson's 1963 speech Gunter affirmed that 'never in history have Socialist principles been more relevant than they are in the 60s' due to the need for the state to direct the scientific revolution.[61] Harold Wilson closed the debate by hoping that the document marked the end of 'sterile' arguments over nationalization. Henceforward, he hoped that the Party would face the future rather than dwell on the past.[62]

After his election as leader, the reforging of Labour's image went hand-in-hand with the projection of the personality of Harold Wilson. This may have been partly because Wilson needed to be quickly established in the public mind in what was possibly an election year. He certainly had to overcome initial doubts that Gaitskell was irreplaceable.[63] However, even if Gaitskell had lived it seems likely that a similar projection of the Labour leader would have occurred. The dramatization of Harold Macmillan's personality was seen as one of the strengths of the 1959 Conservative campaign. As a consequence, Hugh Gaitskell was urged to 'give his own personality a face-lift, so that his political radicalism and personal charm replace the present reputation for chill caution.' Unfortunately, his public persona – in contrast with that of the then Shadow Chancellor Harold Wilson – was considered an impediment to winning popular support.[64] Thus, by the time of Wilson's election it was an assumption behind the 'Let's Go' campaign that, if it was to win the support of uncommitted electors, Labour required personification. This was why Wilson was featured so prominently in press advertising.[65] There was an additional reason: Wilson embodied Labour's modernizing message in a way Gaitskell never could. Moreover, the contrast between Wilson and the increasingly embattled

Macmillan was especially useful to Labour. Wilson wanted the Conservatives to retain Macmillan as leader because as an 'old, effete, worn out . . . cynical dilettante' he was an ideal foil. This contrast was actually reinforced when Alec Douglas-Home, the epitome of upper-class ennui, became Prime Minister. On the eve of the 1964 election Wilson was felt to be a 'good' leader of his party by 67 per cent of Gallup respondents. In contrast, there was an even split between those who thought it best that Douglas-Home resign as Prime Minister in favour of another Conservative and those who wanted him to remain in office. Those who formed part of Wilson's inner circle had feared the possible consequences if the seemingly more modern and egalitarian figures of Iain MacLeod or Reginald Maudling had been selected. They would have made it more difficult for Wilson's attack on indolent, upper-class Conservatism to seem credible.[66]

Thus, the emphasis on dynamism, science and his own personality which defined 'Wilsonism' had been established in the years prior to Wilson's election as Labour leader. In fact, Wilson's radicalism – at least in relation to his predecessor – was largely due to the fact that he simply emphasized parts of Labour's programme previously left unmentioned.[67] Even so, it was still up to Harold Wilson himself to put the final touches to the process of adapting Labour to 'modern' developments and attempt to win over the new social groups. He did this in a series of speeches made between January and April 1964 which were collected together and published in a Penguin paperback for mass circulation.[68] These took as their theme the hope for a 'New Britain', which deliberately echoed Kennedy's 'New Frontier' rhetoric.[69] Despite this, his speeches essentially developed and underlined issues and proposals established by previous campaigns. Wilson linked the increasingly obvious relative national decline to the failure of the aristocratic Conservatives to fully utilize the talents of new social groups. Only Labour, he claimed, could liberate the latter's energies and grant them the social status they deserved. By making such an emphasis Wilson was attempting to exploit any status discontents within the new rising classes. He hoped to direct their frustrations against their social superiors, something which had been suggested by Crosland.[70] In these speeches Labour emerged as a modern party which represented the entire working population, including members of the new social groups: their aspirations were linked to national recovery under the auspices of an interventionist state. Only Labour could help them expand the possibilities of individual development. 'I am', Wilson is said to have conceded, 'making myself acceptable to the suburbs.'[71] Indeed, such was his flight from associating with specifically 'traditional' working-class concerns that, during the 1964 campaign, a party official expressed discontent with a Daily Mirror 'shock issue' on housing because it seemed to associate Labour with slums.[72]

Wilson chose to focus on the fact that the British economy was lagging behind a world 'rushing forward at an unprecedented, an exhilarating speed'. As a consequence, for the first time since the seventeenth century, German workers enjoyed a better standard of living than their British counterparts. Moreover, within ten years it was likely that British workers would have fallen behind those in Japan, France and Italy. The problem was that 'too much of British industry . . . [was] officered from the pages of Debrett' to the exclusion of better qualified, if socially more humble, personnel. As Wilson had suggested earlier in 1963:

We need a shake-up in industry. There's still too much dead-wood – too many directors sitting in boardrooms not because they can produce or sell, but because of their family background. To make industry dynamic we need vigorous young executives, scientists and sales experts chosen for their abilities – not their connections.[73]

He stated that the forthcoming election would be fought over this economic issue: who would best 'galvanize our sluggish, fitful economy' and promote sustained growth? Wilson's contention was that the Conservative Party was, by its very nature, unable and unwilling to accomplish this task. This was because it was a sectional party which identified with finance not industry, that is with those who made money by speculation, not with those who earned it through work. The Conservatives represented the interests of a 'closed, exclusive society', not those of the majority.

The Conservative reluctance to abandon free market principles was deemed to be an 'abdication of responsibility for the nation's well-being' and an indication of their acceptance of 'this grovelling, this defeatist doctrine of humiliating impotence'. If Britain wanted to avoid becoming a second-class economic power and its population ensure their continuing well-being Labour offered the only hope. A Labour government would employ state planning as a means of actively stimulating and encouraging the modernization of industry. However, it would also faithfully represent the 'thrusting ability, even iconoclasm' of grammar and comprehensive school pupils. It would remove any impediments to initiative endured by scientists, technicians, craftsmen and skilled workers. Whilst the Conservatives allowed 'the spiv, the speculator, the take-over bidder, the tax evader, the land grabber' to prosper, Labour would promote 'the useful people', 'who earn money by useful service to the community'.

Wilson's egalitarian rhetoric was reflected elsewhere in society. Just as Labour, the party of the 'traditional' working class, was attempting to revive its fortunes by modifying its appeal to newly affluent and more educated workers, so were ailing newspapers of the left. Shortly before being sold by the Trades Union Congress to IPC the *Daily Herald*, with a readership mainly composed of ageing working-class men, was remodelled to appeal to women and those educated in grammar schools. This transformation was completed on the eve of the 1964 general election when the *Herald* re-emerged as the *Sun*.[74] A similar transformation had also been experienced by *Reynold's News*, the Co-operative-owned Sunday paper. This had broadly appealed to the same constituency as the *Herald* and now also hoped to attract younger, more affluent, readers. In the autumn of 1962 it was translated into the *Sunday Citizen* promising to be more 'dynamic' and be about 'people who are electrifyingly alive to the challenge and opportunities of our times'. It would be an 'old progressive newspaper in a new, dynamic, compact garb'.[75]

On its launch, the *Sun* was broadly sympathetic to Labour, although the first few issues were criticized by those close to Wilson.[76] In its first editorial the *Sun* announced its credo and the type of reader it hoped to attract:

It is an independent newspaper designed to serve and inform all those whose lives are changing, improving, expanding in these hurrying years.
    We welcome the age of automation, electronics, computers. We will campaign for the rapid modernisation of Britain – regardless of the vested interests of managements or workers. But we will crusade against any Government which drives the evolution forward without far-sighted schemes for retraining and generous compensation where unemployment arises.
    The Sun is a newspaper with a social conscience. A radical newspaper ready to praise or criticise without preconceived bias. Championing progressive ideas. Fighting injustice. Exposing cruelty and exploitation.

It explicitly appealed to those who went on holiday abroad, were under 35 and to married women who worked; people who ate steaks and had come into recent possession of cars, houses, refrigerators and washing machines.

For all these millions of people with lively minds and fresh ambitions the Sun will stimulate the new thinking, hoping to produce among its readers the leaders of tomorrow, knowing that they are more likely to emerge from a college of advanced technology than from Eton or Harrow.[77]

The early 1960s was, then, a period when it seemed to some on the political left that such people were potential recruits to the cause of progress – whether they expressed their affiliation in politics or in the market.

Having explained the rationale behind Labour's electoral strategy between 1959 and 1964, we continue with a brief survey of the effect of this strategy on the voters. In 1964 Labour was returned to office after conducting a much praised campaign. However, as the Party was to discover in 1987, pleasing journalists and commentators does not necessarily translate into winning support in the country as a whole. In fact, in 1964 the margin of victory was slight; Labour actually won a smaller percentage of votes cast than in 1955. The most significant factor was a rise in support for the Liberals among disenchanted Conservatives, which, more than anything, denied Douglas-Home continued tenure in Downing Street.
    Yet, Labour's campaigning should not be simply dismissed: one can only speculate what success the Party would have enjoyed had it followed the path advocated by left-wingers such as Crossman and Foot. Moreover, it is unreasonable to suppose that Labour could have fully recovered from three successive defeats in just one election. This was especially the case in 1964 because, despite their numerous problems, the Conservatives could still claim credit for ever-increasing, if slowly decelerating, standards of living. Public faith in the Government's economic competence might have diminished since 1959, but it had not completely evaporated. When asked by Gallup if the election slogan, 'It's your standard of living – keep it with the Conservatives', applied to them, 38 per cent of respondents felt it did not but, 46 per cent thought that it did. Moreover, on the eve of the campaign

47 per cent considered the Conservatives better able to guarantee continued prosperity as opposed to only 34 per cent who thought the task best entrusted to Labour.[78] Thus, 1964 was a preliminary stage in the improvement of Labour's public image. This process was only consummated in 1966 after Wilson's performance as Prime Minister had overcome deep-seated doubts about his Party's competence to govern.

As already established, the avowed intention of the Labour leadership after 1959 was to win over women, the young, affluent skilled manual workers and sections of the lower-middle class. This was because both Gaitskell and Wilson took on trust surveys conducted by academics and market researchers which seemingly pointed to such a strategy. However, such studies were fallible and increasingly subject to different forms of interpretation. Thus, although Labour had been all but discounted by the authors of the 1959 Nuffield election study, by 1966 these same authorities had substantially revised their analysis. As Richard Rose wrote in 1964, 'many socio-economic trends which in 1959 were credited with "inevitably" resulting in a Conservative victory still continue. . . . Today, the really interesting question is why the simple sociological or economic explanation is incomplete.'[79] The 1966 Nuffield study rejected 'affluence' as the decisive factor in determining political allegiance and focused instead upon parental influence. This newly discovered force was said to favour Labour as the number of electors raised by Labour-voting mothers and fathers grew. By 1966, therefore, the Conservatives – lauded seven years before as the 'normal' majority party – were said to be in danger of remaining in opposition in perpetuity.[80]

Notwithstanding the fickleness of contemporary psephology, the effectiveness of Labour's attempt to win support needs to be determined. The evidence, unfortunately, is limited but does indicate that the Party's revived image enjoyed some – albeit uneven – success. With regard to younger voters, Labour seemed to have largely achieved its objective (see Table 2.2). Those under 35 consistently voted Labour more than the average throughout the three elections of 1964, 1966 and 1970. During the 1964 campaign the *Sun* invited first time voters to explain why they favoured a particular party. By no means all chose Labour, but a clear majority did: given the political inclination of the *Sun* this was no revelation. However, the reasons proffered by readers indicate the extent to which Labour's arguments and Wilson's rhetoric had been accepted as common sense by some young electors. One correspondent stated that he would vote Labour 'Because I believe a vast amount of talent and energy, especially among the young, will be released if we give Labour a chance to make a new Britain.' Another suggested that, under Wilson 'the Britain of the future shall be a classless one, where all petty snobbisms of accent, dress, education will be defunct . . . [it will be a] a society which seeks to harness the talents of all in the best possible manner'. A third reader stated that 'I shall vote for the party of teachers and trained economists, the Labour Party; not the party of company directors and blimps.' A fourth noted of Labour that it 'had acquired a new, modern approach to every aspect of life in Britain . . . They appear to be bursting with ideas for "putting Britain back on the map" again, and this infectious zeal has spread throughout their party.'[81] Thus, at least in relation to that tiny minority of young voters in the habit of writing letters to national newspapers, Labour had left its mark.

Given the tone of the *Sun* correspondence it is perhaps not surprising that Labour also made a number of converts among the 'affluent'. The emphasis on the liberation of energies and talents allegedly held in check by aristocratic indolence was intended to appeal to the young as much as to the suburbanites. Table 2.3 indicates the scale by which the Party won over white collar (social category C1), skilled manual (C2) and most spectacularly middle class (AB) voters, between 1964 and 1966. Furthermore, despite the difficulties which faced Labour in government, the Party retained some of these gains even in 1970. This was especially the case in relation to white collar workers. Ironically, the Labour vote declined proportionately between 1964 and 1970 in only one occupational category: the unskilled working class (social category DE). In contrast to the young and affluent taken as a whole, women remained unmoved by Labour's message. As with its failure to increase the proportion of female members, Labour was unable to close the gender gap within the electorate during the 1960s. In fact, the evidence available suggests that, relatively at least, Labour lost support among women more than men once installed in office with a clear majority after 1966 (see Table 2.3).

In the longer term, the changes in emphasis which culminated in 'Wilsonism' were inconclusive. By the 1980s, as Labour suffered a run of election defeats which surpassed even those of the 1950s, psephologists once again declared Labour finished as an electoral force. The Party was seemingly doomed to remain trapped within its old bastions in Scotland, Wales and the North of England. Labour's fourth consecutive defeat in 1992 was said to have been at the hands of 'Essex man', an ideal-type suburban, affluent but nevertheless working-class, figure. Within the Party came calls, familiar to those with memories of the 1959 inquest, to transform Labour's 'old fashioned' image and distance itself from the 'traditional' working class.[82] Despite its undoubted electoral success in the 1960s, it was as if 'Wilsonism' had never existed.

The principal reason for this was that Wilson was less concerned with transforming the character of his party than winning power. In this, he was a victim of the timing of his election as leader and then his success in achieving a Commons majority so soon afterwards. Gaitskell had died on the eve of Labour's pre-election campaign and his successor was therefore faced with the prospect of an imminent General Election. Like Gaitskell, Wilson found it more convenient to side-step party bureaucrats who were often hostile to new campaigning methods. Len Williams, one of the most vocal of Mark Abrams's detractors within the Party, was Labour's General Secretary during the 1964 campaign. As a result Wilson formed his own 'caravan' of advisers, recruited mainly by Gaitskell, and conducted his own campaign independent of Transport House.[83] Once established as Prime Minister, Wilson had little reason to recast Labour's internal structure, confident in the assurance that by 1966 Labour had become the 'natural' party of government. As a result he did not feel it necessary to confront

Table 2.2 *Age structure of the Labour vote, 1964–70*

	All	21–24*	25–34	35–44	45–54	55–64	65+
1964	44.8	48.8	48.2	48.4	43.8	43.5	37.8
1966	48.7	51.2	54.6	51.2	47.0	45.9	43.2
1970	43.8	47.2	45.8	40.6	49.1	43.7	37.1

Notes: Figures refer to the percentage in the relevant age group which voted Labour
* in 1970 the voting age was lowered to 18
Source: Nuffield Election Studies of 1964, 1966, 1970

Table 2.3 *Gender and social composition of the Labour vote, 1964–70*

	All	Men	Women	AB	C1	C2	DE
1964	44.8	48.3	41.7	8.9	24.8	54.4	59.1
1966	48.7	52.4	45.4	15.5	29.9	58.5	65.2
1970	43.8	47.3	40.6	10.4	30.5	55.4	57.3
1964–70	−1.0	−1.0	−1.1	+1.5	+5.7	+1.0	−1.8

Notes: Figures refer to the percentage in the respective gender social group which
        voted Labour
Source: Nuffield Election Studies of 1964, 1966, 1970

Labour's deteriorating relationship with the electorate. This problem caused individual party membership to fall by nearly 150,000 or just over 18 per cent between 1964 and 1970.[84] Whilst in government such a decline seemed relatively unimportant. Thus, although the projection of Wilson's 'dynamic' and 'modern' image held numerous temporary advantages, in the long-run it obscured the existence of Labour's deep-seated problems. Despite all the talk, the party which returned to Opposition in 1970 was very similar to the one that had failed to win the 1959 general election.

That which culminated in what was somewhat inaccurately known as 'Wilsonism' was part of a general acceptance of 'affluence' on the part of the Labour leadership. This was no craven collapse in the face of rampant consumerism, as some on the left feared. It was, instead, a calculated attempt to redefine the meaning of social change and locate it within a more politically favourable framework. Instead of seeing 'affluence' as something of which to be afraid, a force which needed to be attacked, the implications of the term were appropriated and used to criticize Conservative shortcomings. From cowering before increased television ownership and the like, the Party began to use such new realities to advance its own arguments. Under Wilson especially, the decline of the 'traditional' working class and rise of the 'affluent' worker was seen as less of a problem and more of an opportunity to construct a new electoral alliance across the classes. Those interested in the plight of the present-day Labour Party need to explain why, along with the early *Sun*, this approach faltered, only to be successfully adopted by radical Conservatives in the late 1970s.

Notes

1 Labour Party Archive, National Museum of Labour History, Manchester (hereafter LPA), GS/PCONF/25, Notes for the press conference introducing *Labour in the Sixties*.
2 Quoted in a BBC *Arena* programme, 'The Frankie Howerd Story', 25/4/1992.
3 H. Wilson *Purpose in Politics* (1964) pp. 14–28; *Socialist Commentary* (November 1963) p. 3, 12; *Tribune* 4/10/1963 and *The Times* 2/10/1963.
4 T. Nairn 'Hugh Gaitskell' *New Left Review* No. 25 (May–June 1964) 63–8; P. Hall 'Labour's hundred days' in P. Hall (ed.) *Labour's New Frontiers* (1964) p. 1; G. Fanti 'The resurgence of the Labour Party' *New Left Review* No. 30 (March–April 1965) 27 and P. Anderson 'Critique of Wilsonism' *New Left Review* No. 27 (Sept.–Oct. 1964) 3–27.
5 For more on these innovations, see J. Pearson and G. Turner *The Persuasion Industry* (1965) pp. 257–66 and R. Rose *Influencing Voters. A Study of Campaign Rationality* (1967) pp. 60–86.
6 For a critical view of the implications of this term, see N. Tiratsoo 'Popular politics, affluence and the Labour party in the 1950s' in A. Gorst, L. Johnman and W.S. Lucas (eds) *Contemporary British History, 1931–61* (1991) pp. 44–53.
7 For a survey of these issues, see D. Howell *British Social Democracy. A Study in Development and Decay* (1980) pp. 221–43.
8 D.E. Butler and A. King *The British General Election of 1964* (1965) pp. 30–34, 97, 145.
9 D.E. Butler and R. Rose *The British General Election of 1959* (1960) pp. 196–201.
10 Collected together in M. Abrams and R. Rose *Must Labour Lose?* (Harmondsworth, 1960).
11 *New Society* 16/4/1964.
12 For example, see various contributions to R.H.S. Crossman (ed.) *New Fabian Essays* (1970 edn).
13 *Labour Party Conference Annual Report* (hereafter *LPCAR*) 1959 pp. 107–9. See also, C.A.R. Crosland *The Conservative Enemy* (1962) pp. 145, 151, 159–60, and *Forward* 23/10/1959.
14 LPA, National Executive Committee (hereafter NEC) minutes 28/10/1959, Election Sub-Committee (hereafter ESC) minutes 28/10/1959, National Labour Women's Advisory Committee minutes 5/11/1959; *Labour Organiser* (hereafter *LO*) Vol. 38 No. 449 (Oct./Nov. 1959) 211–12, Vol. 38 No. 450 (Dec. 1959) 220; C. Rowland 'Labour publicity' *Political Quarterly* Vol. 31 No. 3 (1960) 348; M. Rees 'The social setting' *Political Quarterly* Vol. 31 No. 3 (1960) 292 and J. Morgan (ed.) *The Backbench Diaries of Richard Crossman* (1981) p. 786.
15 *LPCAR* 1959 pp. 116, 123; Rees op. cit. 290–94.
16 Crosland op. cit. 116, 144, 145–6, 149, 150, 152, 157, 161, 162.
17 *LPCAR* 1959 pp. 106, 109.
18 P. Crane 'What's in a party image?' *Political Quarterly* Vol. 30 No. 3 (1959) 233–5.
19 Crosland op. cit. 7.
20 For example, see D. Potter *The Glittering Coffin* (1960) pp. 36–51 and Morgan op. cit. 786.

21 Tiratsoo op. cit. 54–8.
22 *Tribune* 16/10/1959.
23 *LPCAR* 1959 p. 122.
24 *LPCAR* 1959 pp. 126–7.
25 Rowland op. cit. 349–50 and *LO* Vol. 39 No. 458 (August 1960) 147–8.
26 *LO* Vol. 42 No. 488 (Feb. 1963) 32.
27 *LO* Vol. 39 No. 459 (Sept. 1960) 174–6, Vol. 39 No. 462 (Dec. 1960) 225–6 and Vol. 41 No. 486 (Dec. 1962) 225–6.
28 R. Samuel 'Dr. Abrams and the end of politics' *New Left Review* No. 5 (Sept.–Oct. 1960) 3. See also the correspondence in *Socialist Commentary* (August 1960) 24–7, (Sept. 1960) 25–6 and (Oct. 1960) 28–9.
29 R.H.S. Crossman, *Planning for Freedom* (1965) pp. 86–112.
30 See J. Grimond *The Liberal Challenge* (1963); M. Young *The Chipped White Cups of Dover* (1960) and K. Young 'Orpington and the "Liberal revival" ' in C. Cook and J. Ramsden (eds) *By-Elections in British Politics* (1973) p. 199.
31 D. Marquand 'Can Labour recover?' *Encounter* Vol. XIX No. 4 (Oct. 1962) 57–8 and his 'Has "Lib–Lab" a future?' *Encounter* Vol. XVIII No. 4 (April 1962) 63–5; letter in the *Guardian* 23/11/1961 and LPA, Campaign Committee (hereafter CC) minutes 5/4/1962.
32 P.M. Williams *Hugh Gaitskell* (Oxford, 1982) pp. 314–34.
33 Williams op. cit. 329–30 and LPA, Home Policy Sub-Committee (hereafter HPSC) minutes 11/1/1960.
34 LPA, HPSC minutes 11/1/1960.
35 LPA, NEC minutes 28/10/1959.
36 Rowland op. cit. 351.
37 LPA, HPSC minutes 9/11/1959 and ESC minutes 28/10/1959.
38 *LO* Vol. 38 No. 448 (Sept. 1959) 163–4.
39 E. White 'Putting ourselves across' *Fabian Journal* No. 26 (Nov. 1958) 1–3.
40 *LO* Vol. 38 No. 449 (Oct./Nov. 1959) 183–5 and Vol. 39 No. 451 (Jan. 1960) 5–6.
41 *Labour Woman* Vol. 47 No. 10 (Dec. 1959) 130 and *LO* Vol. 39 No. 458 (July 1960) 130–33, Vol. 39 No. 459 (Sept. 1960) 173–4 and Vol. 42 No. 489 (March 1963) 57.
42 *LO* Vol. 39 No. 451 (Jan. 1960) 13–14, Vol. 41 No. 486 (Dec. 1962) 225–6 and Vol. 43 No. 501 (March 1964) 45–6 and 48.
43 M. Abrams 'Opinion polls and party propaganda' *Public Opinion Quarterly* Vol. 28 No. 1 (Spring 1964) 16.
44 *LO* Vol. 40 No. 467 (May 1961) 95.
45 *LO* Vol. 40 No. 463 (Jan. 1961) 5 and Vol. 40 No. 468 (June 1961) 109.
46 *LO* Vol. 39 No. 459 (Sept. 1960) 163 and Vol. 40 No. 467 (May 1961) 83–5.
47 *Tribune* 23/10/1959; *Labour Woman* Vol. 50 No. 7 (July 1962) 4–5 and LPA, Organisation Sub-Committee minutes 22/2/1961 and 19/9/1961.
48 *LO* Vol. 39 No. 458 (August 1960) 150–52, Vol. 39 No. 460 (Oct. 1960) 187–8 and Vol. 40 No. 463 (Jan. 1961) 12–13.
49 *LO* Vol. 40 No. 464 (February 1961) 25–6 and Vol. 40 No. 465 (March 1961) 54.
50 *LO* Vol. 40 No. 470 (August 1960) 150–52 and Vol. 40 No. 472 (Oct. 1960) 187–8.
51 B. Hindess *The Decline of Working-Class Politics* (1971). For a different view to this, see D. Berry *The Sociology of Grass Roots Politics* (1970) and T. Benn *Out of the Wilderness. Diaries, 1963–67* (1987) pp. 35, 65, 84, 136, 142.
52 LPA, CC minutes 22/1/1962, 19/7/1962, 11/3/1963 and 13/5/1963, *'Let's Go'*

Campaign Guide Pamphlets and Publications Collection 1963; Socialist Commentary (July 1963) 10–12; LO Vol. 42 No. 493 (July 1963) 130–32 and New Society 6/6/1963.
53 Daily Mirror 21/5/1963.
54 LO Vol. 42 No. 491 (May 1963) 90, Vol. 42 No. 492 (June 1963) 107–8, Vol. 42 No. 496 (October 1963) 186–8 and 195–6, Vol. 43 No. 499 (January 1964) 9 and Labour Woman Vol. 51 No. 6 (June 1963) 7.
55 Forward 22/1/1960; Labour Party Science and the Future of Britain (1961).
56 A. Howard Crossman. The Pursuit of Power (1990) p. 248.
57 Morgan op. cit. 811–12.
58 LPA, Publicity and Political Education Sub-Committee minutes 20/6/1960.
59 Morgan op. cit. 860–61.
60 LPA, NEC minutes 27/7/1960; Morgan op. cit. 863.
61 LPCAR 1960 pp. 133–4.
62 LPCAR 1960 p. 149.
63 New Society 31/1/1963.
64 Rowland op. cit. 358–9.
65 Abrams op. cit. 17.
66 G.H. Gallup (ed.) The Gallup International Public Opinion Polls. Great Britain 1937–75 Vol. 1 (New York, 1977) pp. 761–2; Benn op. cit. 70 and Morgan op. cit. 1005.
67 Morgan op. cit. 987.
68 Unless otherwise stated, references for the next three paragraphs are taken from, H. Wilson The New Britain (Harmondsworth, 1964).
69 Benn op. cit. 81.
70 Crosland op. cit. 161–2.
71 A. Watkins 'Labour in power' in G. Kaufman (ed.) The Left (1966) p. 176.
72 R. West 'Campaign journal' Encounter Vol. XXIII No. 6 (Dec. 1964) 19.
73 National Union of Sheet Metal Workers and Coppersmiths Quarterly Journal (July 1963) 25–6.
74 J. Curran and J. Seaton Power Without Responsibility. The Press and Broadcasting in Britain (1991 edn) pp. 108–11.
75 LPA, GS/RN/93, standard letter sent to local Labour parties announcing Reynold's News's change of title and format.
76 Benn op. cit. 144.
77 Sun 15/9/1964.
78 Gallup op. cit. 762–3, 768.
79 New Society 5/3/1964.
8o Butler and Rose op. cit. 197; D.E. Butler and A. King, The British General Election of 1966 (1966) pp. ix and 267.
81 Sun 30/9/1964, 6/10/1964, 2/10 /1964.
82 See, for example, Guardian, Independent, Financial Times 11/4/1992 and Observer, Sunday Telegraph, Sunday Independent 12/4/92.
83 Benn op. cit. 87, 151.
84 LPCAR 1970 p. 62.

3 The road to Scarborough: Wilson, Labour and the scientific revolution

David Horner

Given their absolute centrality to contemporary, personal, social and economic life, it is a worrying phenomenon that science and technology have rarely been exposed as important issues in mainstream national politics. An exception to this was Labour's campaign and electoral victory of 1964 which promoted the idea of a 'white hot' scientific and technological revolution which would forge a new Britain. The rhetoric of this revolution had been expertly unfolded in Harold Wilson's famous Labour Party Conference speech in October 1963. In the words of Tony Benn, writing in 1968 as Minister of Technology:

It was a theme that caught the mood of the moment, captured the imagination of engineers and scientists and became the symbol of a new approach which a Labour government was making which was distinctive and different from that which had characterised the period of Conservative rule.[1]

In the popular imagination the technological 'white heat' has come to characterize that historical moment.

However, Labour's commitment to Britain's transformation through science and technology has frequently been explained away as a mere rhetorical device to set against the senescence of a lacklustre Tory Party. Political opportunism has been seen as the key to unlocking this particular turn in the party's policy and ideology. There are, of course, some elements of truth in these charges since all politics involves the recognition and exploitation of the opportune moment. Nevertheless, as this chapter will argue, the deployment of 'the scientific revolution' as the keynote of the Labour campaign was rooted in a longer running discourse on the social relations of science which had been developed by radical socialist and communist scientific intellectuals in the 1930s and 1940s.

The dominant self-interpretation for Labour's adoption of a 'scientific' platform, argued for example by R.H.S. Crossman, was that it was both politically unifying and politically relevant.[2] The rhetoric of linking planning, science and socialism was embodied in Harold Wilson's 1963 Conference speech. The practice was embodied in the creation of the Ministry of Technology in the aftermath of Labour's election victory of October 1964. This chapter attempts to explore the role of left-wing scientists in the process which brought this about and to explore the continuities and discontinuities with the earlier efforts to formulate socialist policies for science and technology. Wilson was to draw on this tradition and its leading figures and was, paradoxically, the ultimate beneficiary of a Marxist vision outlining the social and economic transformation of society through the planned application of science and technology. However, the groundwork for this had been laid in the mid-1950s by Wilson's predecessor as leader of the Labour Party, Hugh Gaitskell.

A distinctively Marxist analysis and vision of science as an agent of social transformation was given in J.D. Bernal's seminal book, *The Social Function of Science* (1939). Bernal, an eminent crystallographer and prominent supporter of the Communist Party of Great Britain (CPGB), had a major influence on a generation of left-wing scientists particularly those involved in the Association of Scientific Workers (AScW). During the Second World War the AScW grew rapidly and became an important focus for the advocacy of the centralized planning of scientific research and the fullest utilization of science and technology for social welfare (after the model of planning in the Soviet Union). The AScW was strongly influenced by the CPGB and directed its energies not only towards influencing the wartime Coalition Government but also the labour movement.

In the context of post-war reconstruction the AScW produced a comprehensive blueprint for the reformation of Britain's science, *Science and the Nation* (1947).[3] This prefigures many of the ideas and themes that would re-emerge in Wilson's modernization policies of the early 1960s. *Science and the Nation* criticized the lack of co-ordination and planning by the state and advocated the establishment of a central body to plan scientific effort across the whole economy and society. It attacked the technical backwardness of much of British industry and highlighted the range of new scientific and technological opportunities which needed to be exploited to sustain Britain's social and economic development. A corollary of these arguments was the increasingly important role of scientific and technical experts in social and economic life and particularly the need to incorporate scientific expertise and planning in government. Patrick Blackett, one of Britain's leading physicists and an expert on atomic energy, was President of the AScW at the time of publication of *Science and the Nation*. Blackett was to play a prominent role in the formation of Wilson's scientific platform of 1964. He had become a Labour Party Fabian in the 1920s while at work in the Cavendish Laboratory and in the 1930s and 1940s emerged as a leading figure of the scientific left.

The AScW campaigned vigorously for a major shift in emphasis from military to civil research and development, again a theme which was to emerge strongly in the policies of the Ministry of Technology in the 1960s. Blackett, for example, had lost his position as an adviser to the post-war Labour Government on atomic energy because of his opposition to its commitment to its military rather than civil development. In the immediate post-war period left-wing scientists had succeeded in achieving a certain dominance in the discourse on science, society and the state. However, the Cold War led to the depoliticization of science and the marginalization of the scientific left.[4]

The defeat of the Labour Party in the general election of 1955 generated a period of intense discussion within the Party in the search for modernizing policies. Labour had evinced little interest in science since the modest reforms enacted by the Government of 1945–51, which included, for example, the creation of the National Research and Development Corporation (NRDC) under the auspices of Harold Wilson at the Board of Trade.

The Labour leadership's renewed interest in science provided opportunities for a revival of the politics of science and for interventions from socialist scientists outside the formal arena of Labour Party politics. The nature and form of these interventions, however, were to be limited by the relative informality of the arrangements by which advice on science policy was mobilized by Gaitskell. Those involved in these informal science advisory groups represented a cross-section of the scientific left from the Fabian socialism of Blackett to the communism of Bernal. The groups also involved less eminent participants such as R. Innes and R.G. Forrester who had played active parts in the science policy work of the AScW.

The discussion of Labour policy for science and technology took place amidst the internal party conflict between the 'revisionists' and the 'traditionalists'. These arguments were expressed in the debates around Clause Four of the Party's constitution relating to social ownership and around the issue of unilateral nuclear disarmament. They also intersected with the growing external controversies about Britain's economic performance and the relationship of investment in scientific research and development to economic growth.

An informal group of scientists sympathetic to the Labour Party was brought together in 1956 to advise the new Labour leader, Hugh Gaitskell, on scientific matters. This group was to remain in existence in various forms for the next seven years and was to play a significant role in alerting the Labour Party to the increasing political importance of the state's involvement in scientific and technological development.

Gaitskell had previously encountered many of those who were to play a part in the group when, in the late 1930s, he had regularly attended the Tots and Quots Club. This informal dining club, formed by G.P. Wells and Solly Zuckerman, had met regularly to discuss the social aspects of scientific affairs from a broadly left-wing perspective.[5] Gaitskell was one of a number of leading Labour politicians to have joined the AScW in the immediate aftermath of the Second World War. His post as Minister of Fuel and Power in the post-war Labour Government also brought him into contact with the political dimension of scientific and technical developments.[6]

However, following his election to the leadership of the Labour Party, in 1955, his objective was to shift the political philosophy of the Party in the direction of 'revisionism'.[7] Thus in the wake of Labour's election defeat of 1955 a whole series of study groups had been established to re-examine the Party's policies.[8] However, the Party's engagement with science arose in rather less formal circumstances. The formation of the Gaitskell Group of scientific advisers owed much to the activities of Marcus Brumwell, a long-standing member of another Labour Party informal advisory group, the 1944 Association of businessmen. Brumwell organized a dinner on 17 July 1956 for a number of eminent scientists sympathetic to Labour and some prominent members of the party. Those present at what was to prove to be the inaugural meeting of the 'Gaitskell Group' included Austen Albu MP, Professor P.M.S. Blackett, Dr J. Bronowski, Marcus Brumwell, James Callaghan MP, George Dickson, R.G. Forrester, David Ginsburg, Professor David Glass, Rt.Hon. J. Griffiths MP, Sir Ben Lockspeiser, Professor D.M. Newitt, Morgan Phillips and Professor Sir Solly Zuckerman.[9]

Brumwell had sought Bernal's support in his effort to incorporate science more prominently into Labour Party policy.[10] Quite independently Bernal had been conducting his own survey of the views of eminent scientists and politicians on the funding and organization of British science.[11] Brumwell drew upon Bernal's work in the drafting of a background document, 'The Labour Party and Science', for the July meeting. He reiterated Bernal's criticisms of the funding of fundamental research in Britain and highlighted the gross imbalance between the resources devoted to civil research and development and those available for military purposes which, according to Brumwell, amounted to 86 per cent of government expenditure on science. The document laid out a set of national objectives for science and possible steps for their realization: the improvement of existing scientific and technical resource utilization through the diminution of industrial secrecy and overlapping research efforts; the transfer of scientific workers from military to civil research; strategic planning which would identify and emphasize the growth points of science; and the remodelling of the education system both to extend provision and to improve the scientific content of education. The need to link the planning of science to the major economic needs of the country was recognized but no proposals were offered as to what changes in the government machinery for science would be required.[12]

At the July meeting, Callaghan, as Labour's spokesman for science, wanted to know what the deficiencies were in the present state of British science and what could be done to remedy them. Blackett, whilst supporting the view that the present capitalist system encouraged unplanned and overlapping types of development, felt that 'the country at large was not in a revolutionary mood' and advocated the use of existing structures (especially the University Grants Committee (UGC)) as a means of channelling more money into basic research. In order to pursue the question of a science policy for Labour more concretely it was decided to focus on key issues. Blackett and Glass were to produce a report on what might be required as far as changes in the education system were concerned. Zuckerman would look at the best use of scientists in industry, whilst Bronowski, Newitt and Albu would collaborate on the changing character of industry.[13]

This established a pattern of relatively informal discussions between important Labour politicians and scientific experts which were to continue for the next seven years and promoted the view that scientific advice for the Labour Party was the prerogative of semi-independent but sympathetic experts.

The Gaitskell Group met for a second time at an informal dinner at the Reform Club organized by Brumwell on 8 July 1957.[14] The potential significance of these discussions was now signalled by the presence of Gaitskell himself. Callaghan had been replaced by Alfred Robens MP as Labour's shadow spokesman for science. Robens had been closely associated with the revisionist publication *Socialist Commentary* and was a supporter of the 'consolidationist' approach to public ownership and of the Bevinite approach to foreign policy.[15] He was assisted by Arthur Skeffington MP, who had a long association with AScW as a parliamentary contact. The expert side of the group was strengthened by the addition of Professor B.R. Williams, an economist concerned with technical change.[16]

Robens and Brumwell had met in May 1957 to discuss the role of the science advisory group. The tasks given to the group included the preparation for the National Executive Committee (NEC) of a policy statement, 'The Labour Party and Science' and the provision of information for headquarters staff at Transport House and the constituency parties. Organizationally, Robens suggested setting up a working party of six scientists who, with the assistance of Skeffington, H. Mitchell (Labour Party House of Commons Research Staff), Brumwell, Dickson and Forrester, would be responsible for drafting the policy document.[17]

In the event, at the meeting of the group in July, it was agreed to establish a two-tier organization stratified between so-called 'senior' and 'junior' scientists. Gaitskell had suggested that what was required was one basic policy document, principally for circulation to the parliamentary party, with a second document for wider public circulation. A working party of 'less' senior scientists (who, it was felt, would be able to spend more time on the project than their more eminent colleagues) was established to draft a basic document which would serve as a policy resource. This group met for the first time on 23 July 1957 under the chairmanship of Alf Robens and was responsible for drafting 'Science and the Labour Party' completed in April 1958.[18]

The working party reflected a relatively wide range of opinions and sections of the labour movement including the Association of Scientific Workers and the Institution of Professional Civil Servants (IPCS). However, the TUC was not directly represented. The retention, at least to a limited extent, of 'organic' links between the political and trade union wings of the movement and the presence of members who had been active on science policy issues in the 1940s had a significant influence on the final shape of the policies. The thrust of the analysis took it beyond the 'revisionist' framework. The final document bears comparison with AScW's policies of a decade earlier in its comprehensive approach and commitment to a strongly interventionist role for the state, especially with regard to industrial research. It discusses in detail specific sectors such as fuel and power, agriculture, transport and health, with a strong emphasis on national co-ordination and planned investment policies.[19] Large increases in scientific manpower and government civil research and development were proposed. These quantitative changes would be paralleled by qualitative changes in the type of research supported by government. A massive shift of resources was proposed from military to civilian research, hinged around the creation of a mechanism for the central co-ordination of all research.

'Science and the Labour Party' revived the concept of a 'Scientific and Technical Planning Board', first proposed by the AScW, which would be responsible for all aspects of the strategic planning of defence and civil research. The board would be placed under a senior cabinet minister and would be assisted by a high-powered secretariat. For research in the private sector the document advocated direct methods of forcing technological innovation including the setting up of 'mixed' and state corporations.[20] In terms of existing Labour Party policy for science, for example as expressed in *New Deal For Science* (1949), this represented a radical programme.[21]

The draft statement was subsequently reviewed at a dinner given by Brumwell at Brown's Hotel on 27 June 1958. Those present included the 'senior' scientists and politicians (Blackett, Bronowski, Brumwell, Dickson, Forrester, Gaitskell, Ginsburg, Lockspeiser, Mitchell, Newitt, Robens, Snow and Williams).[22] Robens appeared keen to get the Party to adopt a scientific platform, arguing that the preparation of a co-ordinated policy for science was especially important for Labour since 'they are the only party that believes in thorough planning'. Similarly Snow, in an almost 'Bernalist' vein, expressed the view that 'science is now specially a part of and compatible only with the socialist conception of life'.[23] In spite of the 'revisionist' context, a radical discourse linking science, planning and socialism seemingly retained a significant resonance.

Gaitskell's revisionist intentions of removing the Labour Party's commitment to state control of industry and his suspicion of large-scale planning led him to be wary about the general prescriptions offered by the Robens' working party. In particular he was unsympathetic to the proposals for reductions in defence expenditure and the imposition of direct controls on industry. At his request a briefer set of 'Cabinet Papers' were to be drawn up by a group of the 'senior' scientists for circulation to the Shadow Cabinet in order to present a 'frank statement of what a Labour Government should do about science'.[24] At the same time the main document, 'Science and the Labour Party', was to be revised and a more popular version produced for public consumption. The informal status of the Robens working party meant that the document did not get formal consideration by the NEC. The shorter version of 'Science and the Labour Party' was prepared by Nigel Calder, based on the work of the 'junior' scientists group. This was published in March 1961 as *Science and the Future of Britain* but did not become official Labour Party policy.[25]

Bernal gave a favourable reception to 'Science and the Labour Party', commenting that it was a report of 'excellent quality but lacking a quantitative approach'.[26] Bernal again stressed that any major expansion of government input into civil research would have to be predicated on a severe cut in military research spending. He emphasized the necessity of linking the planning of science with economic planning, particularly in the case of industrial research. Unplanned private industry governed only by the market would continue to be restrictive of scientific development even under a Labour government. The theme, that scientific progress should be 'planned in relation to a rapid expansion of production and its transformation to a modern, fully automated industry', would be central to Wilson's Scarborough speech of five years later. However, Bernal warned of the dangers of an 'over-organized' science under the control of the civil service bureaucracy and was keen to see scientists themselves in executive positions.

Bernal was included in the group of 'senior' scientists who were to be responsible for the production of the 'Cabinet' discussion papers for Gaitskell. Others in the group included Blackett, Snow, Williams and Dickson, with Brumwell as the unofficial organizer. This group met seven times between September 1958 and July 1959 to discuss the various drafts produced by its members.[27] It was also responsible for monitoring the revision of 'Science and the Labour Party', supervising the production of a discussion pamphlet once this revision had taken place and preparing a set of speakers' notes for use at constituency level.

The drafting of the 'Cabinet Papers' was tied more closely into the emerging 'revisionist' framework. This was evident in a widening gap between the views of Blackett and Bernal.[28] Blackett increasingly moved from his espousal of a radical socialism to an accommodation with the social democratic revisionism of Gaitskell's Labour Party. The major area of debate in the compilation of the papers arose around policy for civil research and development, which was increasingly seen as the key to economic success for any future Labour government. Blackett argued that:

excluding nationalisation on a big scale, the Government has two possibilities open to it; to leave things as they are or to buy itself a position of influence in industry by offering financial help for research and development projects.[29]

He identified a number of reasons for the technological inefficiency and backwardness of some British firms: an inadequate supply of qualified personnel; inadequate financial resources; inadequacies in top management; the inadequate size of firms; and too many firms competing in too small a market. His recommendation was that government should aim to put money (estimated at £10 million per annum) into private firms to underwrite R & D projects considered of particular importance. Organizationally this could be done through an expanded National Research and Development Corporation (Blackett had been head of the NRDC throughout the 1950s) and through research and development contracts placed by the research councils, primarily the Department of Scientific and Industrial Research (DSIR), and by appropriate ministries. Only if industry did not respond adequately to these offers of financial help should the government take the initiative to form new companies or buy existing ones.

Bernal was opposed fundamentally to this approach which appeared to leave 'many of the problems of administration . . . of government control of science untouched'. He wrote of Blackett's contribution that it brought out 'the logical consequence of a Labour Party policy which refuses to extend nationalisation or to plan industry', cutting down direct government applied research to a minimum. Bernal argued that planned civil research would be an absurdity in an industry where all the main sections remained under the control of private interests.[30]

Bernal saw that Blackett's approach was modelled on contract research as it was conducted in the defence sector. Bernal had technical as well as political objections to make of this idea. The crucial technical difference was that in the civil sector the government was not necessarily the final purchaser of the product. Lack of control of the product would aggravate unsatisfactory features such as competition leading to duplication of research, the holding back of research workers to prevent rivals using them and the proliferation of commercial secrecy which could be as damaging as military secrecy.[31] Blackett's paper was critical of the DSIR research stations and the research associations, arguing that they were unsuitable instruments for stimulating civil research. Bernal was inclined to blame faults on the use of 'unsuitable civil service methods, bad liaison with industry due to ignorance, prejudice or supposed "self-interest" '. Bernal was critical also of government agencies such as the NRDC and the DSIR because 'many of these bodies have representatives of industry in them and have never shown any inclination even to criticise much less transform the industries that they represent'.[32] He was in favour of a more radical examination of the dilemma posed by the desire for a strong central organization for science combined with the existing structure of distributed departmental scientific concerns. The decentralized approach to governmental organization of science, adopted after the Second World War, had failed largely because of the 'embittered opposition of the non-scientific civil service'.

However, in spite of such criticisms of Blackett's proposals they were included in the final set of 'Cabinet Papers' forwarded to Gaitskell, 'A Labour Government and Science'. The final collation was the work of Snow with the topics covered including the need to increase scientific and technical manpower; the expansion of fundamental science; the need to improve the efficiency of industrial research; and the improvement of government co-ordination of scientific resources.[33] The document set out priorities for the implementation of policy by a future Labour government whilst recognizing that this would be affected by decisions on disarmament and defence policy.[34]

Three phases of implementation were outlined, beginning with government appointments; the launching of a crash programme for science teaching; initiation of plans for new universities; increased expenditure on fundamental research; and consideration of proposals to subsidize industrial civil research. The second phase of implementation would involve the setting up of the Scientific and Technical Planning Board and a new Fundamental Science Research Council; the expansion of research into management structures and processes; and the expansion of the Production

Advisory Section of the Board of Trade. The third phase was to be geared almost exclusively to the development of new industries on the basis of technological innovation and the modernization of traditional industries. The two principal industries singled out for direct stimulation were electronics and precision metallurgy in relation to atomic energy.

Brumwell organized a further informal dinner on 27 August 1959 at which the 'senior' scientists met Gaitskell and Wilson to discuss their efforts.[35] Gaitskell remarked that the document was precisely what he had asked for and was prepared to accept it as the basis for his policy on science if returned to power. This was particularly significant in view of the impending October general election. Wilson endorsed Gaitskell's remarks and suggested that science should receive 'a section or two in the election manifesto'. Science was to make an important contribution to providing the Labour Party with the right image as modern and forward looking:

It was agreed that an imaginative and contemporary attitude to the use of science today well becomes the Labour Party who believe in planning, and might provide an encouraging sign of alertness and pioneering spirit to the electorate.[36]

A short leaflet, drafted by Snow and Bronowski, was to be issued to show that the Party intended to 'plan a full use of science to hasten the good and peaceful life'.[37] This statement based on the 'Cabinet Papers' was issued in the midst of the election campaign on the 1 October under the title *A New Deal for Science*.[38] The statement promised the appointment of a senior minister with general responsibility for scientific affairs, the expansion of scientific and technological education and 'the more rapid application of the latest scientific knowledge to industry'. This latter goal was to be achieved through an increased number of civilian research and development contracts given by the government, individual firms receiving grants for approved long-term research projects and the amalgamation of smaller firms to produce enterprises of a size to support major research programmes. A scientific and technical planning board would advise the government on the direction of industrial R & D, on the awards of research contracts and on the grants to individual firms.

Despite these efforts of the scientists and Gaitskell's commitment, science policy issues were not a marked feature of the 1959 election campaign. There were pledges from both main political parties to appoint a Minister for Science. Science and technology were emerging onto the political agenda. A more full-blooded adoption by Labour of science as a key election issue remained inhibited by the tensions between right and left and Gaitskell's suspicions. Nevertheless Labour's proposals represented a far greater degree of interventionism than the Conservative Lord Hailsham's laissez-faire approach to science policy. The work of the Gaitskell Group had provided the groundwork for the Labour Party to exploit the breakdown of the post-war consensus on science policy.

In the aftermath of its defeat at the polls in 1959 the Labour Party was again convulsed by fundamental debates over Clause Four of the Party's constitution and the issue of unilateral disarmament. The endeavour to create a distinctive policy for science and technology provided common ground for the various political tendencies within the Party. As Vig has argued the espousal in the period 1959–64 by Labour of a 'scientific image' satisfied both the interventionist aspirations of the left and the electoral ambitions of revisionists.[39]

Building upon the revisionist analyses of the mid-1950s Gaitskell argued that the Party needed to revoke its constitutional commitment to massive nationalization and reassure the electorate that Labour had accepted the modern age. By projecting an image of a modernized party he hoped to build a broad-based appeal to newly emerging social and professional groups. At the post-election special Labour Conference in November 1959 he faced bitter opposition and accusations of 'betraying socialism'. Opposition came not only from the left (for example, Barbara Castle and Crossman) but also from the 'pragmatic right' including Wilson.[40]

Wilson felt that Gaitskell had unnecessarily brought the issues into self-destructive prominence, when the fundamentalism of the left could be dealt with in a more pragmatic and subtle way. For the left public ownership remained a precondition for the planning of science. Barbara Castle, chair-woman of the Conference, told its delegates that:

We can no more win the battle of nuclear power, electronics and automation on the principle of *laissez-faire* than we could have won the last war on the same principle.[41]

However, these various streams of thought were to some extent merged and unified through the policy statement, *Labour in the Sixties*, produced for the next Conference in 1960. This statement presented a blueprint for party policy in the coming decade and stressed the relevance of the 'scientific revolution' to modern social and political development. It signalled the arrival of science and technology as key political issues for Labour.

The Conference debate on the statement was overshadowed by the defeat of the leadership on the issue of unilateral disarmament. However, Wilson's speech recommending the document was a major landmark and anticipated his famous speech of three years later when as Leader of the Party he placed the 'scientific and technological revolution' at the centre of his political campaign. Wilson urged the Party to make a specific appeal to scientists and advocated the harnessing of science and socialism. He stated:

This is our message for the 60s – a Socialist inspired scientific and technological revolution releasing energy on an enormous scale and deployed not for the destruction of mankind but for enriching mankind beyond our wildest dreams.[42]

Over the next three years a whole series of initiatives unfolded which would attempt to translate this rhetoric into policy.

In addition to the centrality given to the scientific revolution by *Labour in the Sixties*, a number of other developments had taken place to reinforce Labour's interest in science policy. Robens had founded a new parliamentary group, the Labour Party Science Group, which had begun to meet to discuss in detail the existing policy documents.[43] This followed on from Robens' appointment as Shadow Minister for Science in opposition to Hailsham.

In December 1960 a science and industry subcommittee of the NEC was established to give substance to the strategy outlined in *Labour in the Sixties*. This group met for over two years under the chairmanship of Wilson and kept him in touch with this increasingly important field of policy formation. The subcommittee included left-wing MPs such as Castle and Peter Shore together with Skeffington. At its first meeting it was agreed that Wilson and Shore should consult the informal groups of scientists who had previously been advising the Party 'with a view to coordinating their work with that of the committee'.[44] Wilson was increasingly to take responsibility for soliciting advice from the Party's scientific supporters whilst Gaitskell, preoccupied with the threats to his leadership, seemed to lose interest in this aspect of policy.[45]

The election defeat had left the future role of Gaitskell's scientific advisers in doubt. However, Brumwell organized an informal meeting of the 'senior' group of scientists (now also referred to as the 'VIP group') during June 1960. In a background document prepared for the meeting, 'Progress Report on Labour and Science', he outlined a possible future programme of work. The 'senior' scientists group would continue to meet to give advice and policy guidance and it was proposed that a full-time officer should be employed at Transport House to co-ordinate the supply of information on science to the Party. The working party of 'junior' scientists had already agreed to continue to meet to produce a popular version of the draft statement 'Science and the Labour Party'.[46]

At the meeting in June 1960 it was Wilson not Gaitskell who was present as the senior politician. He strongly supported the continued existence of the VIP group and hoped in particular that it would be able to provide ammunition for a parliamentary attack on Hailsham's passive role as Minister for Science. In addition, Wilson wanted the group to provide guidance and policy for the long term to the Shadow Cabinet. Bronowski argued that the Conservative Government had shown two great weaknesses: Hailsham seemed to have taken little action in the scientific field and the Government's new education plans carried 'no teeth'. Thus, there was scope to develop a debate to the Government's disadvantage. Newitt, however, was disappointed that the Labour Party was, apparently, playing down the role of a Shadow Minister for Science. Robens had been removed and no replacement had yet been appointed. Similarly Dickson was concerned that no steps had been taken to inform or involve the trade union movement.[47]

It was in the context of Wilson's support for the informal science advisory groups that Brumwell, in May 1961, circulated fresh proposals on the Party's need for scientific advice. However, Peart, Wilson's new Shadow Minister for Science was suspicious of the role of the informal science advisory groups. For example, he was 'quite clear that it is the official Parliamentary Scientific Committee which must and will make arrangements for the briefing of MPs'.[48]

Nevertheless, Wilson as chairman of the Science and Industry Subcommittee was anxious that the VIP group should turn its attention to examining the role of the Ministry for Science as well as Britain's future

participation in space research. On the key question of government intervention and science and industry Wilson felt that the group should await the
forthcoming document from the Home Policy Subcommittee. The policy
document, *Signposts for the Sixties*, produced for the 1961 Conference,
argued that the stimulation of scientific and technological innovation in
industry should be based on an enlarged and restructured NRDC.[49] The
new body would be authorized to initiate its own science-based production
or engage in joint ventures with private firms. It was to encourage R & D in
the private, civil sector by placing research contracts. Examples of promising areas for the stimulation of new advances included textile machinery,
shipbuilding techniques, machine tools and electronics. Rather than
embarking on a programme of large-scale nationalization, the NRDC
would also have a role in revitalizing and modernizing industry by the
setting up of new, publicly owned plants. The aim would be to fill specific
'technology gaps' in particular industries.[50]

Despite this continuing emphasis on the role of science and technology,
the members of the Gaitskell Group were increasingly to experience a sense
of frustration. In the autumn of 1961 the Shadow Minister for Science was
again changed, with Hugh Mitchison replacing Peart. Brumwell wrote to
Bernal following the appointment of Mitchison about changes that had
taken place on the Science and Industry Subcommittee:

the most exciting feature to my mind however, was that Frank Cousins has now
joined this sub-committee. I have never met him before but regard him as outstanding. Obvious are the implications if we can get some science-mindedness into the
TUC through him.[51]

The Science and Industry Subcommittee had been discussing topics such as
space research, technical aid to the Commonwealth, the balance of Britain's
research effort and the Government's role in civil research and development.
Following the publication of *Signposts for the Sixties* it was to concentrate
its energies on the proposals to revitalize the NRDC and the expansion of
public investment in private industry. The other focus of its attention was to
be an appraisal of national scientific and technical manpower needs.

The Conservative Government's creation of the Trend Committee in
March 1962 to enquire into the organization of civil science provided
renewed political motivation for the discussion of science policy issues. At
Wilson's instigation an informal dinner of the VIP group was held in June
1962. Brumwell prepared a summary of existing Labour Party proposals on
government organization for science.[52] Wilson's immediate concern was
with the possibility of an early general election in May or October 1963. He
wanted a succinct statement of priorities for science, to provide the Party
with a 'science plank for the election platform'. In addition he suggested a
statement for the public (possibly drafted by Bronowski and Snow) outlining Labour's policy. The original document, 'Science and the Labour Party'
and the 'Cabinet Papers' were also in need of revision.[53]

The meeting was well attended and included Bernal, Blackett, Bronowski,
Brumwell, Carter, Dickson, Forrester, Glass, Lockspeiser, Millwood,
Mitchison, Newitt, Skeffington and Wilson. The discussion ranged over

much of the ground that had been covered at previous gatherings. Newitt criticized the frequent changes of the Labour Shadow Minister for Science which suggested that the post lacked status. His comments reflected a growing sense of frustration and dissatisfaction felt by the scientists at the apparent sclerosis which now seemed to have overtaken the Party with regard to science policy. Forrester was also concerned that opportunities were being lost by the parliamentary party for pressing the case that the National Economic Development Council (NEDC) should be taking full account of scientific and technological possibilities. These criticisms were reflected in a memorandum drafted by Bronowski, 'Handling of Scientific Affairs by the Labour Party', which precipitated a crisis between Gaitskell and his senior scientific advisors.[54]

Bronowski's criticisms were circulated in September and the VIP group met in October without any politicians present. There was general agreement that a trenchant letter should be sent to Gaitskell signed by all the senior scientists expressing their frustration with the present situation. However, it was also agreed that it would be politic to get Wilson's approval of the letter which was to be drafted by Brumwell.[55] Wilson subsequently gave his approval to Brumwell's draft which strongly criticized the Party's failure and in effect delivered an ultimatum to Gaitskell. The letter argued that:

Science and technology are today an essential part of our culture and our economy. The Party needs to take this into account. The Government is failing to do so and we should focus our fire on this weakness . . . We believe there is a great public interest in science . . . which the Party has not yet found how to tap and harness. We are convinced this is an important task ahead of us.[56]

Attached to the letter was a two page account which summarized the group's activities and catalogued a series of criticisms including the frequent changes in the Shadow Minister; the infrequent meetings of the Science and Industry Subcommittee; the inadequate preparation for and co-ordination of the science debates; the failure to mount a continuous attack on Government science policy; the very few MPs involved in the presentation of Labour's policy on science; the fact that the NEC's Report to Conference in 1962 lacked appreciation of the scientific aspects of other fields of policy; and the inadequacy of the secretariat in this field both in the House and at Transport House.[57]

The document concluded that science in fact was being accorded a low priority and that this position needed to be radically transformed if there was to be any value in the continued work of the informal science advisory groups. The immediate changes being sought included the appointment of a Shadow Minister with no other responsibilities than science supported by a secretariat also with no other responsibility.[58]

Gaitskell's reply on 8 November was non-committal, promising only to write again shortly after further consideration.[59] Gaitskell had privately established his own working party on science, government and industry under Robert Maxwell.[60] Although Wilson's Science and Industry Subcommittee had made little headway in contributing to policy it provided him with a useful base. In contrast to Gaitskell, Wilson's continued courting of sympathetic scientists was evident, for example, by his attendance at a private dinner party held at Brown's Hotel on 16 November 1962. The guests invited by Brumwell on Wilson's behalf included Sir Howard Florey, President of the Royal Society, Frank Cousins, General Secretary of the Transport and General Workers Union, and Bernal.[61] Wilson's subsequent assumption of the leadership of the party, following Gaitskell's sudden death in January 1963, transformed the prospects for its scientific supporters. Modernization was to be the distinctive theme that would characterize Wilson's leadership. Brumwell circulated a letter to members of the Gaitskell Group at Wilson's election which expressed great satisfaction with this turn of events: 'in the new situation it appears that the whole activity of pepping up the Labour Party's attitude towards science has taken a violent and admirable step forward'.[62]

Wilson appointed Crossman as Shadow Minister for Science and Higher Education. Crossman saw clearly the potential of using the discourse of modernization as a means of forging Labour Party unity. He wrote later: 'we realised that here was the new, creative Socialist idea needed to reconcile the Revisionists of the Right with the Traditionalists of the left'.[63]

Blackett emerged as Crossman's principal adviser on scientific matters. Blackett had a number of discussions with Crossman and Brumwell concerning the 'next steps in helping to formulate a set of briefs on Science Policy for future Labour ministers' which called into question the continued existence of the old Gaitskell Group. Blackett's reasons for the dissolution of the existing group were based on the need to bring 'new blood' into the process of policy formation. He felt it was imperative to involve more MPs and younger scientists, a possible source being the recently created Fabian Science Study Group.[64]

The conclusion was that Crossman should at once establish a science working party (with himself as chairman), reporting to the Science and Industry Subcommittee, and drawing its membership from that body, the Fabian Study Group and the Gaitskell Group. Blackett saw the main tasks of such a working party as bringing up to date the documents prepared for Gaitskell in the late 1950s, commenting on the Labour Party report on 'A Policy for Higher Education' and producing studies of other fields where a Labour government would have to take immediate action.[65]

The Science and Industry Subcommittee, now under the chairmanship of Crossman, was given the task of making proposals on the work of the Ministry for Science under a future Labour government; the work of the state research organizations; the NRDC; and the research effort of private industry. The sub-committee was considerably enlarged (from a membership of 10 to 20) with its personnel overlapping Crossman's science advisory group which was constituted in March 1963. However, despite its apparently wide remit, its main focus of attention was on the issue of industrial training though it also served as the official channel for the submission of reports from other groups on science policy to the NEC.

A further resource in the new moves by Wilson and Crossman to give science a high political profile was provided by the (already mentioned)

Fabian Society Science Study Group, formed as a result of a weekend school on science policy in November 1961. This group consisted of a number of MPs including Albu and Bray together with some junior research workers and civil servants. Stanley Mayne ambitiously claimed in some introductory notes for the group that its purpose was to provide 'a blue print for the next Labour Government'. Mayne's principal proposal was for some kind of 'scientific parliament' or council which would be representative of the interests of science and technology at a national level. However, the group was 'too divided on organisational questions to issue a collective report'.[66]

Following Blackett's advice Crossman held a meeting at the House of Commons on 13 March designed to co-ordinate the various groups working on science policy issues. The meeting was chaired by Crossman and attended by a range of interested scientists and MPs: Albu, Blackett, Dr B.V. Bowden, Bray, Brumwell, Carter, Tam Dalyell, Forrester, Dr J.R. Godfrey, Judith Hart, Posner, Lord Shackleton, J. Maynard Smith, and Terry Pitt. The latter had recently been appointed to the Labour Party's Research Department (partly as a result of the earlier criticisms of the 'senior' scientists – Pitt had a Dip.Tech. degree from the Birmingham College of Advanced Technology) and was to act as secretary to what would be known as the Crossman Group. He was to play a key role in maintaining links with Transport House and the Science and Industry Subcommittee.[67]

The Crossman Group in fact took the form of three separate working parties, on scientific manpower, government machinery for science policy, and civil research and development. These working parties were to be responsible for the drafting of reports which were to form the basis of the first major science conference organized by the Labour Party at the Bonnington Hotel in July 1963.

The agenda of the Crossman Group was the creation of policies based on the 'new case for socialist planning' but in terms which would appeal to the broadest constituency within the Party. In addition Wilson's electoral strategy was partly based on winning the support of new professional groups for the Party. Wilson was concerned with the possibility of an early general election and was anxious to get the scientists renewed support in raising Labour's profile as the party of science. An informal dinner involving the core of the old Gaitskell Group, Blackett, Bronowski, Brumwell, Dickson, Forrester, Lockspeiser, Newitt, Snow and Williams, met to discuss amongst other things a proposal for a major conference in July 1963 to canvas the views of all the various science policy groups.[68] Wilson and Crossman agreed to the holding of the Labour Party and Science Conference; the production of a set of 'Cabinet Papers' to be ready by mid-July; the launching of an Association of Labour Scientists; the drawing-up of an 'electioneering manifesto' (perhaps to be signed by 12–20 distinguished scientists); the formation of various working parties; and giving consideration to the status of appointments to the Ministry for Science.

The conference on science was held at the Bonnington Hotel on 20 and 21 July 1963. The conference was sponsored jointly by the Labour Party and the Fabian Society and was designed to bring together the various groups (the working parties of the Crossman Group, the Science and Industry

Subcommittee, Robert Maxwell's Group, the Fabian Society Science Study Group and the Fuel and Power Group) to forge a coherent scientific platform.[69]

Three of the discussion papers stemmed directly from the work of the Crossman Science Group. These included 'Civil research and development' (by Carter and Williams), 'The expansion of higher scientific and technical education' (by Blackett), and 'Science and government: some key questions' (by Crossman). Two further papers, 'An immediate programme of civil R & D', and 'New public enterprise', dealt with aspects of the problem of encouraging technological innovation through new forms of public ownership, reflecting some of the Party's 'revisionist' thinking. The essence of the short-term proposals on civil R & D was the setting up of four full-time, high-powered planning teams designed to press forward technical programmes of development in four specific industries. A further paper, 'Expansion of the arts and social sciences', advocated the setting up of a new research council for the social sciences. In common with Blackett's paper on scientific and technical education the central theme was of the state's role in initiating programmes of expansion. A final background paper from the Maxwell Group presented a broad discussion of the problems of government organization and science.[70]

Crossman's proposals on government machinery had been discussed by his group as early as April. Blackett had written:

The central need is for a strong Ministry of Planning which will absorb the NEDC and plan the broad outline of national production and investment.[71]

In this context science and technology would be principally the responsibility of two ministries, a Ministry of Industry and a Ministry of Universities and Science, which would execute the strategic directives of the Ministry of Planning. The Ministry of Industry would incorporate the industrial department of the Board of Trade, the NRDC, the civil side of the Aviation Ministry and the development functions of the DSIR. The Ministry of the Universities and Sciences would be responsible for supervising the UGC and the research councils through a Civil Science Board. (Defence research would remain the responsibility of the service ministries).

In addition to these institutional arrangements Crossman's broader preoccupation was with the means by which the Whitehall establishment in general might be made 'responsive to technological and social change'. As he wrote, 'the problem we have to solve is how to marry a permanent civil service with outside expertise'. Thus, he was concerned not only to extend state support for the planning of science and technology but also to extend the application of science in government so that ' "planning is science based", and that Cabinet decisions are arrived at on the basis of a scientifically assessed intelligence'.[72]

The Bonnington Conference also discussed the organizational form by which Labour might continue to develop the support of scientists and technologists and foster expert advice to the Party. The idea of an Association of Labour Scientists (ALS) had been suggested as early as 1958 by Cecil Gordon in an informal paper submitted to the Gaitskell Group.[73]

Such an association would have institutionalized what had hitherto been an informal and *ad hoc* approach. The idea of setting up an ALS (modelled on the Socialist Medical Association and the Socialist Educational Association) was discussed again briefly at a meeting of Labour's NEC in June 1963 and at the dinner of the 'VIP Scientists' in the same month.[74] Crossman had considered that Tam Dalyell, the MP for West Lothian, might become secretary to the new organization. Dalyell had reservations which were strengthened by objections from other quarters. The proposal was discussed at the Bonnington Conference and appeared to have considerable support. However, Bowden had written to Crossman privately during the conference expressing his doubts about the 'proposed society of Labour Scientists'. Bowden's principal concern related to possible Communist domination of any such organization. He wrote: 'I spent years trying to keep the Socialist Medical Association straight' though this body was still 'more concerned with the adoption of the current CP line on "Peace", Cyprus etc. than with the health service or medicine'.[75]

Bowden also argued that, in general, scientists' principal loyalty was to science and they were not naturally socialists or loyal party supporters, although they might vote Labour if the Party appeared to be advancing policies favourable to science. Bowden's alternative to an ALS was the setting up of a 'standing conference' on the lines of the Bonnington event. Working parties could be established to deal with specific issues; and large private meetings could be held to which non-Labour scientists could be invited. Organized on this basis, there would be 'little danger of its being dominated by a small non-representative group'.[76]

Crossman was apparently persuaded by the critics of the plan to found an ALS and advanced the alternative idea of a standing conference at Labour's NEC meeting on 24 July. The nucleus of the standing conference would be constituted by those attending the Bonnington gathering. A small standing committee would be co-opted to run what was to be called the 'Standing Conference on the Sciences'. Dalyell would act as secretary and liaise with Terry Pitt at Transport House. The proposal was accepted by the NEC as the one which was likely to give more closely circumscribed political control.

Crossman had been closely in touch with Blackett over these developments and wrote to him following the NEC meeting reporting the 'favourable reaction to the idea of a standing conference on the sciences rather than an association along the old lines'.[77] Subsequently Crossman circulated a memorandum to those who had taken part in the Bonnington Conference to outline the new proposals regarding the question of organization and generally to indicate the next steps.[78] Thus, the final phase in the relationship between the Labour Party and its scientific constituency was encompassed by the 'Standing Conference on the Sciences'. However, the pressure to finalize party policy was eased as the prospect of an early general election in 1963 receded.

The main policy outcome of the Bonnington Conference had been limited to publicizing the proposal to establish a Ministry of Higher Education and Research. The wider aspects of Labour's policy would not emerge until the following year and the second Bonnington Conference in February 1964. In the interim, under the auspices of the Standing Conference on the Sciences a series of meetings and discussion groups were organized. These meetings were largely undertaken by Crossman, Dalyell and Bowden in universities and colleges. This canvassing of a largely academic constituency neglected industrial scientists and technologists and highlighted the failure to involve the scientific and technical trades unions. Nevertheless it served to promote Labour's scientific image amongst a growing section of scientists and technologists.

Despite the continuing internal party discussions and lack of a sharply focused public policy, the centrepiece of the Party Conference in October 1963 was Wilson's speech on the policy statement *Labour and the Scientific Revolution*.[79] The statement had been drafted by Crossman and Terry Pitt in the light of the discussions of the Science Group. Crossman had written in August to participants of the Bonnington Conference about the NEC's agreement to produce a draft policy on science for submission to September's Home Policy Committee meeting in preparation for the Labour Conference. He noted that the statement was to be:

suitable to form the basis for an Executive speech at conference introducing a major debate on Labour and the Scientific Revolution . . . Harold Wilson thinks it of the highest importance that the activities of the working parties should widen and deepen this winter.[80]

Thus, Wilson's first speech as Labour leader to the annual conference, with Blackett at his side, echoed his speech of three years earlier, merging the rhetoric of socialism with the argument for science and technology as the instruments of social progress. His central theme was that free enterprise in an unregulated economy would lead to the introduction of new developments in science and technology in a haphazard and socially divisive way. A Labour government, by contrast, would ensure their introduction in a purposeful way through social and economic planning. Wilson stated that:

The problem is this. Since technological progress left to the mechanism of private industry and private property can lead only to high profits for a few, a high rate of employment for a few, and to mass redundancy for many, if there had never been a case for Socialism before, automation would have created it. Because only if technological progress becomes part of our national planning can that progress be directed to national ends.[81]

Wilson's four-point programme for scientific development reflected some of the discussions of the Crossman Group. First, Wilson included a demand for a massive expansion of higher education under a new ministry to ensure adequate supplies of scientific and technical manpower. In addition this was to have the aim of preventing loss of talent through inequalities in educational opportunity between the different social classes. Secondly, Wilson argued for determination of priorities by a 'full Ministry of Science', to ensure that scientific resources were deployed in productive sectors rather than on 'prestige' defence projects and 'consumer gimmicks'. Thirdly, he proposed the promotion of economic growth and industrial efficiency through the use of civilian research and development contracts, the creation of new state industries based on government-sponsored research and the location of such industries in areas of high unemployment. And, fourthly, Wilson referred to the need to provide the status and facilities for British scientists which would halt their increasing tendency to seek work abroad. However, Wilson was vague about the kind of institutional framework which would be required to implement the programme which he had outlined. Thus, in the aftermath of the Scarborough speech policy discussions were preoccupied by the need to formulate a plan for the reorganization of government bodies responsible for science and technology especially given the publication of the Trend Report in October 1963.

Wilson called together some of his senior advisers for a meeting at the end of October to discuss the Trend Report and consider policy for a future election campaign.[82] Although Blackett and a number of the other 'senior' scientists were present, Bernal was deliberately not invited. Brumwell wrote to Bernal: 'I personally put the cause as Blackett's sort of excessive intellectual jealousy and Dick's . . . political sensitivities'.[83] Bernal's exclusion from any further direct participation in Labour Party policy discussions was confirmed at the time of the final meeting of the Standing Conference. Crossman issued an invitation to Bernal to attend but then had to hastily retract having found that he had 'exceeded my powers and issued my invitation without proper authorisation'.[84]

The Trend Report had proposed the setting up of an Industrial Research and Development Authority to co-ordinate existing government agencies responsible for civil R & D. This had been adopted by the Conservative Government. However, Blackett's proposal was for a new Ministry of Industry and Technology (MOIT) which would pursue a more interventionist role in attempting to steer industrial research and modernize manufacturing industry. Blackett wrote to Crossman that:

It is obvious, even if paradoxical, that if the Labour Party is to be able to carry out a substantial part of its social programme, it must ensure that private industry functions better than it has done under recent Tory governments. I remember Stafford Cripps in 1943 emphasising that any Labour government which leaves, as it must, most of manufacturing industry in private hands must provide the conditions under which it can be efficient. This may be emotionally distasteful at times but the challenge must be faced.[85]

The final meeting of Labour's Standing Conference on the Sciences was held in February 1964 to attempt to resolve some of the remaining dilemmas for the Party particularly around the issue of the form and function of Blackett's proposal for a Ministry of Industry and Technology.

It was Crossman, Blackett and Bowden who appeared at the press conference to outline the course of the discussions. The Conference had decided upon an increased level of support for civil research of £50 million in line with the recommendations of a recent influential FBI report. An enlarged role for the NRDC was proposed under a Ministry of Industry and Technology which would support development in private manufacturing industry not already under the remit of other government departments. The meeting had rejected the various proposals which had seen the civil side of the Ministry of Aviation (MoA) as the basis of the new ministry. The Ferranti scandal had evoked powerful hostility to any new ministry based on the MoA. The MOIT was to carry out its work in the light of objectives decided by a Ministry of Production – a planning department for economic development. The MOIT would use a variety of mechanisms including R & D contracts, the formation of consortia with state participation, assistance in new public enterprises, the use of its purchasing power, influence with the Board of Trade and tax incentives.

Blackett was enthusiastic and optimistic concerning the gains that could be made:

> On the scale envisaged . . . such a programme of government investment in industry, tied to research and development and new science based products would be something quite new in Britain. It could quickly bring about an important change of opinion in industry and in the world of technology generally, and within some years it should begin to make an impact on the commercial success of industry.[86]

However, the practical political imperative for a Labour government to achieve rapid results was instrumental in further changes to the concept of the MOIT. In September 1964, on the eve of the general election Blackett elaborated a leaner version of the MOIT in his key paper 'The case for a Ministry of Technology'. Blackett argued that:

> the best hope for the Labour Party to quickly make a definite impact on the technological level of manufacturing industry, would be to create immediately on taking Office, a *new* and *small Ministry of Technology* (MT).[87]

The core of the new ministry would be the enlarged NRDC with responsibility for increased investment in civil research and development. This would be supported by a technological and commercial intelligence division with 17 sections corresponding to the industrial sectors covered by the Sector Working Parties of the NEDC. Blackett's amended proposals were adopted by Wilson and Labour's election manifesto promised a 'Ministry of Technology to guide and stimulate a major national effort to bring advanced technology and new processes into industry'.

The precise institutional forms proposed by the Party in the 1964 election were less important than the fact that Labour had secured a 'modernizing' image which had displaced its traditional identification (and preoccupation) with public ownership. This chapter has attempted to trace the intellectual and political roots of Wilson's programme for modernizing Britain. There were clear continuities with the approach of an earlier generation of left-wing scientists (for example, the AScW's 1947 *Science and the Nation*) and Labour's programme in 1964. This was evident in the emphasis on the planning of civil science and its co-ordination with national social and economic goals. Wilson stressed the limited capacity of an unregulated private enterprise economy to innovate on a scale which would balance technological unemployment with the creation of new productive opportunities. He clearly acknowledged the leading role of the state in fostering technological innovation and the creation of the Ministry of Technology was to provide the general instrument for state intervention. The social status and economic function of scientists and technologists were recognized in the programme of expansion of science education in schools and universities. Education and training coupled with increased investment in research and development would create a new breed of science-based industries.

However, there were also considerable and important elements of discontinuity which partly reflected the fact that in its later stages the process of Labour's policy formation derived from a narrowly based political pragmatism. Though Blackett played an important role at this stage it was increasingly in isolation from his left-wing antecedents. Blackett's very success as Wilson's chief scientific adviser (and in subsequent posts as Deputy Chairman of the Advisory Council on Technology and Scientific Adviser to the Ministry of Technology) reflected his changed political perspective from the days of his prominence in the radical AScW of the 1940s. If the rhetoric of Wilson's Scarborough speech revealed its indebtedness to Bernal's ideas of a 'scientific and technological revolution', the underlying policies owed more to Blackett's pragmatic reformism.

Notes

1 *New Scientist* 26/9/1968.
2 See R.H.S. Crossman 'Scientists in Whitehall' in R.H.S. Crossman *Planning for Freedom* (1965) pp. 134–47. This interpretation is also adopted by N.J. Vig *Science and Technology in British Politics* (Oxford, 1968) pp. 81–103 and S.P. Wolff 'Politics and Industrial Science Policy: a study of the 1964–70 Labour Government' (unpublished MSc thesis, University of Sussex, 1975) pp. 48–59.
3 Association of Scientific Workers *Science and the Nation* (Harmondsworth, 1947).
4 G. Jones *Science, Politics and the Cold War* (1988).
5 See M. Postan 'Political and Intellectual Progress' in W.T. Rogers (ed.) *Hugh Gaitskell 1906–1963* (1964) pp. 49–66. Postan remarks that Gaitskell 'was at that time passing through a phase in which Marxists and their talk drew him irresistibly by the very provocation they caused' (p. 53).
6 Anon. 'Scientists in the Government' *Scientific Worker* Vol. 2 (Dec. 1947) 27. Gaitskell had joined the AScW in 1945. Harold Wilson, President of the Board of Trade and formerly parliamentary secretary, the Ministry of Fuel and Power, was a member of the AScW's Fuel and Power Committee. E.F.T. Durbin MP, Attlee's personal assistant during the war, had also joined the AScW in 1945.
7 For an account of this 'revisionist' trend within the Labour Party and Gaitskell's role in it see S. Haseler *The Gaitskellites: Revisionism in the British Labour Party 1951–1964* (1969).
8 Ibid 107.
9 Blackett Papers (hereafter *Blackett*), The Royal Society Library, Folder E24 'Minutes of a meeting at the Reform Club, 17 July 1956'. Lovell inaccurately states that 'since 1950 Blackett had been the senior member of a group of scientists who held occasional meetings with the aim of evolving a scientific and technology policy for the country'. See B. Lovell *P.M.S. Blackett: A Biographical Memoir* (1976) p. 76.

10 Brumwell had originally been introduced to Bernal by Herbert Read around 1930. Bernal Papers (hereafter *Bernal*), Cambridge University Library, Correspondence Box 80 Letter Brumwell–Anita Rimel 11/7/1971.
11 *Bernal* F.1 J.D. Bernal 'The Finance of Fundamental Research in Britain' Jan. 1956; F.1.5 Bernal 'Reconsideration of the Problem of the Finance of Fundamental Research in Britain in the Light of Replies to the Memorandum of that title circulated on 25 January 1956', May 1956; and F.2 Bernal 'Memorandum for Mr. Brumwell' May 1956.
12 *Bernal* F.2 M. Brumwell 'The Labour Party and Science' 17/7/1956.
13 *Blackett* E.24 Minutes of a meeting at the Reform Club, 17/7/1956.
14 *Bernal* F.2 'Discussion on Labour and Science at a dinner given by Marcus Brumwell at the Reform Club on 8th July 1957'.
15 See Haseler op. cit. 68–80.
16 The Science and Industry Committee of the British Association had initiated in the early 1950s studies of 'what determines the speed of application of new scientific knowledge in British industry' with a view to making proposals for improvements. Carter and Williams were responsible for the empirical work and analysis for the Committee. Their subsequent publications included B.R. Williams and C.F. Carter *Industry and Technical Progress* (Oxford, 1957); *Investment in Innovation* (Oxford, 1958); and *Science in Industry* (Oxford, 1959).
17 *Bernal* F.2 Letter Brumwell–Bernal 12/8/1957; and 'Note of conversation with Alfred Robens, 30 May 1957'.
18 Labour Party Archive Manchester (hereafter *LPA*), Draft Statement of a Working Party under the Chairmanship of A. Robens 'Science and the Labour Party', April 1958.
19 Compare, for example, Association of Scientific Workers *Science and the Nation* (Harmondsworth, 1947).
20 *LPA* A Report of a Working Party under the Chairmanship of A. Robens 'Science and the Labour Party' April 1958 revised 1959 p. 123.
21 *New Deal for Science* (1949).
22 *Blackett* E.26 'Discussion on "Science and the Labour Party" at a dinner given by Marcus Brumwell at Brown's Hotel on 27th June 1958'.
23 Ibid 2.
24 Ibid 4.
25 Labour Party *Science and the Future of Britain* (March 1961).
26 *Bernal* F.3 Bernal 'Notes on Draft Statement "Science and the Labour Party" ' 15/9/1958.
27 *Blackett* E.27 Senior Scientists Group minutes.
28 *Bernal* F.5 Letter Brumwell–Bernal 26/6/1959.
29 *Blackett* E.28 'Civil Research and Development' in 'A Labour Government and Science' (Unpublished 'Cabinet Papers' for Gaitskell) 31/7/1959 p. 19.
30 *Bernal* F.5 Typescript notes by Bernal 'Cabinet Papers' 1/9/1959.
31 Ibid.
32 Ibid.
33 *Bernal* F.5 Letter Brumwell–Bernal 25/5/1959.
34 *Blackett* 'Civil Research and Development' and 'General Machinery to Co-ordinate Scientific Resources and Activities' in 'A Labour Government and Science', op. cit. 16–24 and op. cit. 22–7, respectively.
35 *Blackett* E.28 'Discussion on "A Labour Government and Science", a document produced by a group of scientists for Mr. Gaitskell at his request, at a dinner given by Marcus Brumwell at Brown's Hotel on 27 August 1959'.

36 Ibid. See also Haseler op. cit. 143–9.
37 *Bernal* F.9 Letter Brumwell–Bernal 10/9/1959 and Letter Brumwell–Bernal 1/10/1959.
38 The Labour Party *A New Deal for Science: A Labour Party Policy Statement* (October 1959).
39 Vig op. cit. 81–3.
40 A. Sked and C. Cook *Politics in Post-War Britain* (Harmondsworth, 1979) p. 207.
41 Barbara Castle quoted in Vig op. cit. 82.
42 Harold Wilson quoted in Haseler op. cit. 243.
43 *Blackett* E.30 Letter Brumwell–Blackett 8/4/1960.
44 *Blackett* E.38 Labour Party Science and Industry Sub-committee minutes 20/12/1960.
45 Haseler op. cit. 237.
46 *Blackett* E.30 Brumwell 'Progress Report on Labour and Science' April 1960.
47 *Bernal* F.8 'Discussion on Labour and Science at a dinner given by Marcus Brumwell at the Reform Club on Monday 27 June 1960'.
48 *Bernal* F.8 Letter Brumwell–Bernal 22/3/1961.
49 The NRDC had been established under Harold Wilson when he was President of the Board of Trade in 1948. See S.T. Keith 'Inventions, Patents and Commercial Development for Governmentally Financed Research in Great Britain: The Origins of the National Research and Development Corporation' *Minerva* Vol. XIX No. 2 (Spring 1981) 92–122.
50 Vig op. cit. 84–5.
51 *Bernal* F.8 Letter Brumwell–Bernal 28/12/1961.
52 *Blackett* E.32 Brumwell 'Co-ordination of Scientific Activity' June 1962.
53 *Bernal* F.9 'Discussion on Labour and Science at a dinner given by Marcus Brumwell at Brown's Hotel on Tuesday 5 June 1962'.
54 *Blackett* E.32 Letter Bronowski–Brumwell, 'Handling of Scientific Affairs by the Labour Party' (no date).
55 *Bernal* F.9 VIP Scientists Meeting minutes 17/10/1962.
56 *Blackett* E.33 Draft letter to Gaitskell 1/11/1962.
57 *Bernal* F.9 Bernal 'Science and the Labour Party' 1/11/1962.
58 Brumwell wrote that 'we sent an ultimatum to Gaitskell saying that we were fed up and wouldn't lift a finger unless he showed some sign of taking action': *Blackett* E.33 Letter Brumwell–Blackett 27/2/1963.
59 *Blackett* E.33 Letter Gaitskell–Brumwell 8/11/1962.
60 Haseler op. cit. 237.
61 M. Goldsmith *Sage: A Life of J.D. Bernal* (1980) pp. 140–41.
62 *Bernal* F.9 Letter Brumwell–Bernal 27/2/1963.
63 Crossman 'Scientists in Whitehall' op. cit. 139.
64 *Blackett* E.49 Letter Blackett–Crossman 22/2/1963.
65 Ibid. Blackett suggested to Crossman that 'I think it might be a pleasant gesture if Harold Wilson and you took an early opportunity to arrange a dinner for all the older Members of the Gaitskell Group. They could then be thanked for their work.'
66 *Blackett* E.35 Fabian Society Science Group 1962–63.
67 *Blackett* E.41 Labour Party Science Group minutes 13/3/1963.
68 *Bernal* F.9 'VIP' Scientists Dinner 24/6/1963.
69 *New Scientist* 25/7/1963.
70 *Bernal* F.10 Typescript copies of the background papers to the July 1963 conference.

71 *Blackett*, E.42 Science Group, 'Organisation of Civil Research and Development' RD 457 April 1963.
72 Crossman 'Scientists in Whitehall' op. cit. 146.
73 *Blackett* E.26 Cecil Gordon 'Science and the Labour Party', 18/9/1958 p. 2 fn.
74 *Times* 4/6/1963.
75 *Blackett* E.46 Letter Bowden–Crossman 21/7/1963.
76 Ibid.
77 *Blackett* E.46 Letter Crossman–Blackett 24/7/1963.
78 *Bernal* F.9 Letter Crossman–Brumwell 2/8/1963.
79 *Bernal* F.9 Labour Party 'Draft Science Policy statement', RD 518, August 1963 and *Labour and the Scientific Revolution*, A Statement of Policy approved by the Annual Conference of the Labour Party, Scarborough 1963.
80 *Blackett* E.46. Crossman Memorandum 2/8/1963.
81 H. Wilson *Labour's Plan for Science* (1963) p. 2.
82 *Bernal* F.9 'Report of a dinner held 29 October 1963 at Brown's Hotel'.
83 *Bernal* F.9 Letter Brumwell–Bernal 28/10/1963.
84 *Bernal* F.10 Letter Crossman–Bernal 11/2/1964; Letter Bernal–Crossman, 20/2/1964; Letter Crossman–Bernal (no date).
85 *Blackett* E.49 Letter Blackett–Crossman 23/2/1964.
86 Ibid 2.
87 *Blackett* E.49 Blackett 'The Case for a Ministry of Technology' September 1964 (typescript).

4 Labour's economic performance, 1964–70

Nicholas Woodward

The Wilson years are a fascinating period for the economic historian.[1] Not only was it a time of rapid policy change, but it was also one when macroeconomic performance started to wane. When judged against the standards of the 1970s and 1980s, of course, performance was fairly satisfactory. Similarly when Labour left office it could argue that over the preceding six years there had been a reduction in economic inequality, a narrowing of regional disparities, a marked improvement in the balance of payments situation and a slight improvement in Britain's productivity performance. Nevertheless, against this a critic could point to the fact that both unemployment and inflation were higher in 1970 than in 1964 and rising, growth performance had failed to live up to expectations, and that it had only proved possible to rectify the balance of payments by adopting a more deflationary stance than any previous post-war government.

Further, more than one author has suggested that poor economic performance contributed to Labour's electoral defeat. Certainly economic issues figured prominently in the campaign, although judging from the various autobiographies and diaries there is not much agreement about which were most crucial. Harold Wilson, for example, has blamed the rise in prices, while Barbara Castle refers to the 'freak trade figures', which presumably opened up memories of the earlier balance of payments traumas, a view which has been endorsed by Roy Jenkins. Richard Crossman, by contrast, mentions both rising prices and the trade figures, while George Brown cites both the trade and unemployment figures.

But why was performance disappointing? Was it due to a changing economic environment, one in which it was more difficult to succeed? Or was it due to government policy, to errors of commission and omission? It is the aim of this chapter to answer these questions. The scheme will be as follows. After a brief survey of the economy and Labour's basic economic strategy in 1964 we turn to the balance of payments and how it influenced economic policy. We then look at why Labour failed to have a marked impact on productivity growth. The remaining two sections examine why unemployment and inflation rose in the late 1960s. Limitations of space, however, preclude much discussion of the Government's supply-side policies, which are, in any case, examined in more detail in the next chapter.

Our first task then is briefly to review the state of the economy in 1964. Overall the picture that emerges is that, although the economy seemed to be fairly healthy, the true position in fact was more delicate than the bare figures suggested. This is brought out, first, by the underlying rate of growth. In the first half of the 1960s (using the peak years 1960 and 1964) the economy was growing at about 3 per cent with labour productivity improving at just over 2 per cent. As Table 4.1 shows, moreover, these growth rates compare favourably with earlier experience. Nevertheless, although respectable by historical standards, they were much less so when compared with the other Western countries.[2] Of course, there was nothing new about this relative decline; it goes back to the late nineteenth century, and its causes have been a continuous source of debate ever since. Nowadays most economists would probably subscribe to the view that this reflects a range of supply-side failures, including perhaps weak management, poor industrial relations, low levels of training and education, misallocated research and development expenditure, and a financial system that places too much emphasis on short-term results.[3]

Table 4.1 *Growth of GDP and GDP per man year: United Kingdom* (%)

Period	GDP	GDP per man year		GDP	GDP per man year
1856–73	2.2	1.3	1951–55	2.8	2.0
1873–1913	1.8	0.9	1955–60	2.5	2.1
1913–24	2.2	1.0	1960–64	3.1	2.3
1924–37	2.2	1.0	1964–68	2.6	2.7
1951–73	2.8	2.4	1968–73	2.1	2.5

Source: R.C.O. Matthews, C H. Feinstein and J.C. Odling-Smee *British Economic Growth, 1856–1973* (Oxford, 1992); and *Economic Trends Annual Supplement* (1987)

When we turn to unemployment the situation again looked quite good. In 1964 the economy was at the top of the cycle and unemployment stood at 1.7 per cent, low even by the standards of the early 1960s (Figure 4.1). The immediate reason for this was the 'Maudling Boom' of 1963, when, in an attempt to engineer an improvement in the underlying growth performance, a reflationary package of tax cuts was introduced. Whether long-run growth could be stimulated so easily now seems rather doubtful, but the effect of the package was to push the economy into a strong boom with the result that unemployment came down from its 1963 peak.

Figure 4.1 Unemployment rates 1948–73

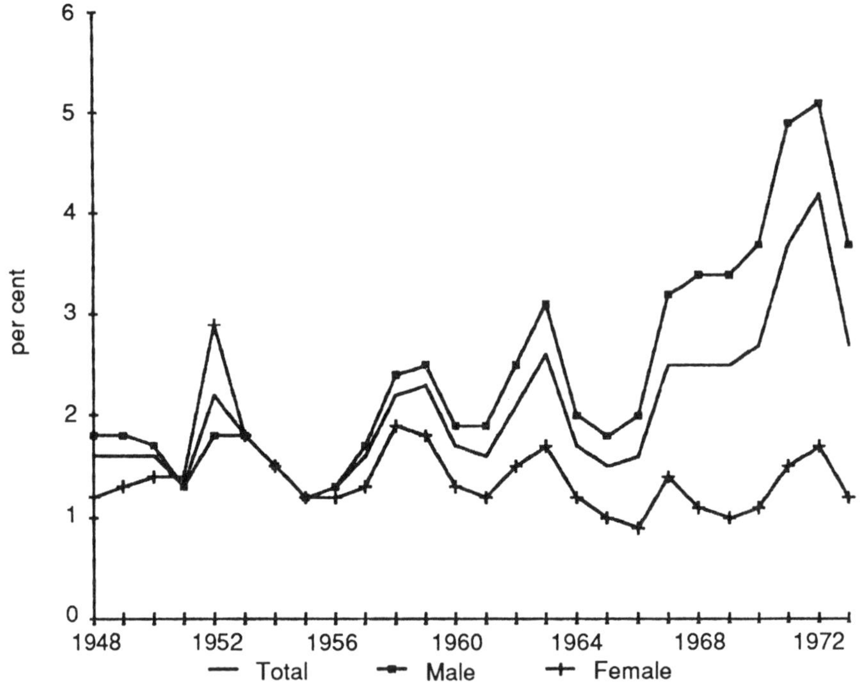

Source: Department of Employment *British Historical Abstract*;
Employment Gazette, various issues

The main point to make about unemployment in 1964, however, is that a rate of 1.7 per cent could not be sustained. The economy, in other words, was overheating and this made it inevitable that economic difficulties – in the form of inflation and balance of payments problems – would re-emerge. Thus, for example, it has been estimated that to prevent inflation accelerating in the years between 1960 and 1968 unemployment would have had to be somewhere between 2.5 and 2.7 per cent.[4] Similarly, to run a small current balance surplus in the early 1960s it was necessary to have an unemployment rate of about 2 per cent. With the benefit of hindsight, therefore, it seems that a rise in unemployment in the mid-1960s was unavoidable (see Figure 4.5 below).

Another reason for suggesting that employment prospects were not that good in 1964 is that company profitability was lower than it had been a decade earlier. High profitability has sometimes been singled out as one of the key features of the 1950s and 1960s. It is evident, however, that starting from the mid-1950s there was a tendency for wages to increase slightly faster than productivity while producers were unable to fully pass on the increase in costs because of an intensification of international competition.[5]

Figure 4.2 UK profit share and rate, corporate sector

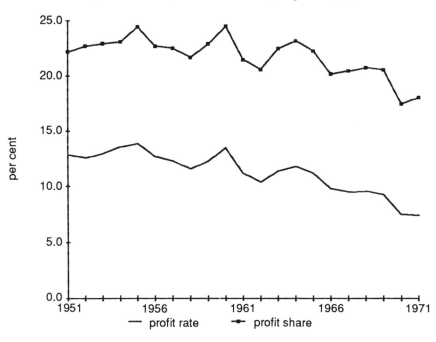

Source: S.A. Marglin and J. Schor *The Golden Age of Capitalism* (Oxford, 1990)

The result was, as Figure 4.2 shows, that profitability started to decline. This was an ominous development in that it threatened the long investment boom, which had started in the late 1940s and had been one of the main reasons for low unemployment; there was also the danger that it might encourage producers to economize on the use of labour.[6]

In 1964 inflation was fairly low. In that year retail prices increased at 3.7 per cent (Figure 4.3). Nevertheless it is noticeable that in response to the Maudling Boom the inflation rate had started to rise, with the result that in both 1965 and 1966 it was fairly high and threatened Britain's overseas competitiveness. This again points to the excess demand pressures and to the fact that corrective action would be necessary after the 1964 election.

The remaining aspect of performance – the balance of payments – was perhaps the most worrying feature of the economy in 1964. As Figure 4.4 shows, in most of the years between 1951 and 1963 the current balance had been in surplus. However, in 1964 a large deficit of £373 million (equivalent to 1.1 per cent of national income) emerged, which obviously would have to be corrected. This deficit was a consequence of both long- and short-term developments. The obvious short-term factor was the Maudling Boom, which sucked in imports while diverting potential exports to the home market. However, as Figure 4.5 suggests, the underlying payments position had deteriorated quite markedly since the mid-1950s in the sense that it now

Figure 4.3 Retail inflation rate 1950–73

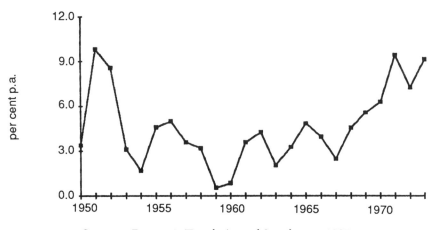

Source: Economic Trends Annual Supplement 1987

Figure 4.4 Current balance 1950–70

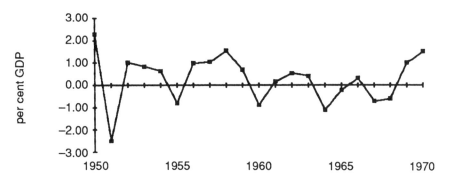

Source: Economic Trends Annual Supplement 1987

required a higher level of unemployment to maintain a given current balance.

What were the causes of this deterioration? No doubt a number of factors played a part. For example, high and rising military expenditure, trade liberalization and an inability to compete in non-price terms have all been cited. Decolonization may also have worked marginally to Britain's disadvantage.

There is also the obvious possibility that it was due to a loss of price competitiveness, itself a consequence of over-ambitious employment targets. The available evidence certainly points to some loss of price competitiveness in the decade before 1964, although this was very modest in the first half of the 1960s (Table 4.2). However, it would be wrong to attribute the

Figure 4.5   Current balance and unemployment 1955–72

Source: *Economic Trends Annual Supplement* 1987

whole of the deterioration to this. For one thing, sterling was probably undervalued in the mid-1950s owing to the devaluation of 1949.[7] For another, the poor trade performance – as measured by the share of world trade – continued through to the 1980s even at times when British manufactures had no difficulty in competing in price terms.

Table 4.2   *Indicators of Competitiveness* (average annual percentage changes)*

	1950–54	1954–59	1959–64
Relative wage costs	na	−2.6	1.0
Relative export prices	−1.4	−1.3	−0.8
* a negative value indicates deterioration			

Source: M. Surrey 'The United Kingdom' in A. Boltho (ed.) *The European Economy* (Oxford, 1982)

This suggests perhaps that a more fundamental cause of the problem was Britain's relatively poor growth performance. Post-war experience suggests that countries which sustain rapid economic expansion invariably enjoy rapid trade growth and are usually free of balance of payments problems. Rapid growth, it seems, not only equips those concerned with the requisite supply capacity but, on the demand side, forces them to become competitive in either price or non-price terms.[8] Interpreted in this light it is not difficult to see why Britain's balance of payments looked weaker in the mid-1960s than in the mid-1950s. In the latter period, following an early and relatively successful reconstruction, British producers faced a seller's market. Yet by the mid-1960s, following a decade of rapid growth amongst its competitors, British producers faced what was essentially a buyer's market and one in which they were ill-equipped to compete.

Whatever the cause, there is no doubt that the weakness in the payments position was a major reason for the other economic problem in 1964: the susceptibility to sterling crises. Such crises had been a periodic feature of the 1950s and early 1960s because sterling had been retained as both a reserve and a trading currency. The result had been a build-up of short-term funds in London. Furthermore, because the payments position looked somewhat fragile and because Britain had failed to accumulate a large volume of reserves, sterling was perceived as a prime target for devaluation. The result had been a series of sterling crises – in 1951, 1956, 1957 and 1961 – which had invariably been triggered off by the rumour of an impending devaluation.

These suspicions were strengthened by other developments. For one thing the policy stance in the early 1960s probably convinced holders of sterling that British governments were becoming increasingly reluctant to adopt stern financial measures in the interests of protecting sterling.[9] In addition, the reserve position was weaker owing to the deterioration in the balance of payments of the Overseas Sterling Area.[10] There is no doubt, therefore, that in the early 1960s the Government should have looked seriously at the role of sterling, particularly in light of Britain's changing position in the world economy. It is perhaps inevitable that such a review was not carried out until the late 1960s, by which time it was recognized that the City's prosperity depended less on sterling and more on its role in the Eurodollar market.[11]

Despite the relatively positive economic record during the 1950s and early 1960s, there had been a good deal of disappointment with Britain's economic performance. In part this was due to the low level of reserves and the weak payments position. At the same time there was some discomfort about inflation. More than anything else, however, there was a sense of concern about Britain's relative growth performance. It was in response to this that the Macmillan–Home Governments of 1959–64 adopted a more interventionist supply-side approach.

Labour's reaction was that, although these measures were moving in the right direction, they did not go far enough. Judging from the writing of Thomas Balogh, Wilson's economic adviser, the basic explanation for Britain's relative decline was a balance of payments constraint, underlying which was a weak uncompetitive industrial sector. Britain, it was argued, could not sustain rapid growth because she ran into balance of payments problems which, in turn, necessitated the introduction of deflationary measures. Such measures undermined investment and the introduction of new techniques, and precluded the exploitation of scale economies, which simply aggravated the lack of competitiveness. Thus Britain was caught in a vicious circle of low export growth and low investment.[12]

The long-run solution, therefore, was a strategy of state-led modernization. In his Swansea speech of January 1964, for example, Wilson drew attention to the need for a range of structural changes, including support for exporters; selective encouragement for industrial investment; state involvement in restructuring and the formation of new industries; extension of the regional programme; and investment in education and training. At the heart of the strategy, however, was to be the extension of indicative planning coupled with policies to promote modern technology.[13]

Another aspect of the strategy was a determination to discontinue 'stop–go' demand management in favour of planned expansion. By early 1964, moreover, it was vaguely recognized that Labour's resolve not to deflate might be tested on assuming office. At this time, with the economy in the midst of the Maudling Boom, a large payments deficit had begun to emerge. To deal with this it was proposed that in place of a traditional deflation the reserves would be allowed to decline whilst an incomes policy would be used to contain inflation. This would give the economy a temporary breathing space until the modernization programme had time to take effect. It already seems that a tentative decision had been made not to devalue.[14]

In drawing up this strategy there is no doubt that Wilson and his colleagues were strongly influenced by Labour's achievements between 1945 and 1951, but this may have led to unwarranted optimism about the potency of some of their instruments. The emphasis on a state-led modernization programme, for example, was undoubtedly influenced by the success of the reconstruction export drive. Similarly, the decision to implement an incomes policy in 1964 was no doubt determined by the effectiveness of Stafford Cripp's policy between 1948 and 1950. But obviously in the intervening years the economy had undergone quite radical structural change and there was no guarantee that industrial and incomes policies would prove equally effective in the 1960s.

It is also evident that Labour did not have well-considered financial policy in 1964, which reflects its failure to discuss such matters in Opposition.[15] The result was, for example, that it had no long-run conception of the role of sterling. Similarly, there had been no serious consideration of exchange rate policy, and how the Government would react if its financial policies came up against credibility problems. Labour was thus clearly unprepared for the financial crises of the mid-1960s. As much was admitted by James Callaghan when he wrote:

one field of experience was not included amongst my advisers, namely a first hand knowledge of how the City of London works; its strengths and weaknesses. Like most Chancellors, I did not learn the ways of the City until I had held the post for some time.[16]

Nevertheless, judged *ex ante*, Labour's strategy in broad terms was a sensible one. By the mid-1960s it was evident that the British economy had under-performed; the liberal policies of the 1950s had not worked well and demand management had been destabilizing. What was required, therefore, was a strategy in which there was more emphasis on long term issues and on supply-side policies, coupled with greater financial stability. This the Wilson Government aimed to provide. But the success of the policy would depend

Figure 4.6   Actual and constant employment budget (per cent GDP)

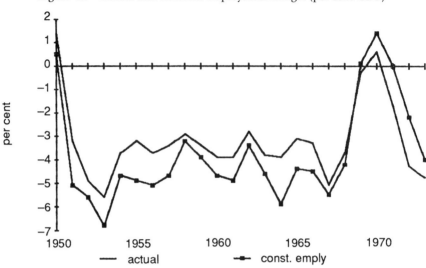

Source: T.S. Ward and R. Neild *The Measurement and Reform of Budgetary Policy* (1978)

upon two things: the effectiveness of the specific supply-side measures and whether the payments position could be corrected relatively easily.

It was, of course, the payments position which dominated the financial history of the Wilson Government. No sooner had Labour taken office than the Government was presented with the forecast of a payments deficit of £800 million. This was then followed by the first of a series of speculative crises in November 1964.

There are a number of excellent histories of Labour's financial policies,[17] and all that is necessary here is to provide a summary. Briefly, the story falls into three main phases. In the first, which runs between the autumn of 1964 and July 1966, the Government tried to secure a strong payments position through a series of *ad hoc* measures. It figured that in the long run its structural policies would effect an improvement. In the short term, however, other measures were required. Deflation and devaluation were ruled out. So the Government chose to borrow overseas, whilst introducing a host of changes which would act directly on the balance of payments. Of these the most important were an incomes policy, which was introduced in 1965, and an import surcharge. The latter proved to be effective, but, because it was in contravention of Britain's international obligations, the Government was obliged to phase it out by November 1966.

Over this period it was the intention to ease the pressure of demand somewhat to make way for exports and for this reason demand management was marginally contractionary (Figure 4.6). However, a rapid growth of private expenditure ensured that the pressure of demand remained high.

Even so, there was a slight improvement in the payments position, with the current balance moving from a deficit of £373 million in 1964 to a small surplus of £127 million in 1966. Unfortunately, the improvement was not sufficiently impressive to convince the markets that sterling was immune from devaluation and consequently there were two further sterling crises – in July 1965 and again in July 1966.

Following the second crisis there was a re-evaluation of policy. For the first time the devaluation option was discussed in Cabinet, although – largely under Wilson's influence – rejected. It was decided, therefore, that the economy should be run with a larger margin of spare capacity. So the famous July Measures of 1966 were introduced, which principally involved a tighter monetary and fiscal stance coupled with a 'hard' incomes policy. The July Measures mark the beginning of the second phase which lasted until the devaluation of November 1967.

The July Measures have often been presented as exceptionally severe. Judging from the full-employment budget, however, this view seems somewhat exaggerated. In any event the policy stance relaxed again in the spring and summer of 1967. Furthermore, despite a temporary improvement in the second half of 1966, the payments position returned to deficit in the early part of 1967 and pressure on sterling resumed. This presumably was partially due to the stance of policy and the disappointing improvement in the balance of payments. However, the markets' perceptions were also influenced by a readiness of the press to openly discuss for the first time the possibility of devaluation. This, together with a whole string of adverse news,[18] then helped to create the sterling crisis of the autumn of 1967. Faced with this crisis Callaghan and Wilson were tempted to play for time. However, it soon became evident that any international support for sterling would be highly conditional and they were thus forced to devalue.

The third policy phase then runs through to the election of 1970, by which time the balance of payments was back in surplus. The turnaround, however, did not appear quickly or painlessly. In part this was due to the usual J-Curve effect, but the late 1960s was also a time when import growth accelerated. Unfortunately, the slow progress convinced the markets that a second devaluation would be necessary. Indeed between devaluation and the spring of 1969 there were a further four sterling crises, all of which were checked by deflationary packages. By the summer of 1969, however, with the improvement in the payments position, the pressure was off sterling.

Ultimately, therefore, the devaluation was successful, although the improvement was also partly due to an upturn in world trade and, in particular, to the deflationary measures. These were concentrated into 1968, when sterling crises forced Roy Jenkins to put together two deflationary packages in addition to the usual spring budget, with the result that the policy stance became highly contractionary (Figure 4.6). This contractionary stance, moreover, continued into the spring of 1969. However, by the spring of 1970, with the payments strong, an election imminent and unemployment rising, it might have been expected that Jenkins would introduce a giveaway budget. In fact the budget was at best mildly expansionary. Jenkins's rationale was that Labour's electoral chances would be best served by sound economic management. But, with Britain in the midst of the first post-war wage explosion, there was every danger that reflation would aggravate the situation.[19]

A number of issues arise from this brief survey. The first concerns the question of whether or not the Government should have deflated and/or devalued much earlier than it did, the traditional view being that Wilson failed to act decisively, especially over devaluation.

Given the benefit of hindsight it can be seen that it was a mistake not to have deflated in either 1964 or 1965. By the autumn of 1964 the economy was clearly overheating (Figure 4.5) and this had been an important cause of the balance of payments deficit.[20] Furthermore a sharp deflation would clearly have established the Government's credibility in financial markets as well as providing a sound basis from which to mount an expansion and test the strength of the supply-side policies in the late 1960s. The Government, in other words, could have done worse than to generate another stop–go cycle. Deflation, however, was never seriously considered in 1964.[21]

As a result the Government started with one hand tied behind its back. The high level of demand in the economy ensured that there were persistent inflationary and balance of payments problems in the mid-1960s. Thus the success of the Government's strategy depended on the incomes policy, which was never likely to be effective in the tight labour markets of the mid-1960s, and the other structural measures, of which too much was expected.

Eventually – in 1966 – the Government was finally obliged to deflate. One of the victims of this, of course, was the National Plan, although there was no reason why the planning experiment should have been completely unhinged by the July Measures. However, in view of the deterioration in the balance of payments in 1967, there must again be doubts whether the deflation went far enough. Nevertheless, it is difficult to make judgements about the July Measures, because, with the slow-down in world trade in 1967, conditions did not favour a rapid improvement.

Devaluation might also have been seriously considered in 1964. This option, however, was immediately rejected. Wilson[22] and Callaghan[23] have since provided a series of economic rationalizations for this decision. Yet we can be fairly sure that the major considerations were political. A devaluation, by reducing living standards, would have been inadvisable with an another election imminent. There was also the risk of being labelled the 'party of devaluation', although whether that would have mattered very much is questionable.[24]

Nevertheless it needs to be stressed that the *ex ante* case for devaluation was not very strong in 1964, and indeed a respectable case against it could be (and was) made up to the summer of 1967, although with diminishing conviction.[25] Some reasons for suggesting this are as follows:

(a) Economists up to 1967 were divided over the issue, and this includes the Government's prominent economic advisers. Of the latter, for example, it appears that Kaldor favoured floating and Neild and MacDougall favoured devaluation from October 1964, but Balogh and Cairncross were initially opposed and changed their allegiances slowly.

(b) Up until 1966, or even possibly 1967, there were grounds for questioning whether sterling was overvalued. The available indicators suggested that export competitiveness had at worst deteriorated marginally in the early 1960s (Table 4.2), although it clearly did worsen again in the mid-1960s.

(c) Given the uncertainties about the export and import price elasticities in the 1960s, it was sometimes asked whether devaluation would actually work. Furthermore, it is worth mentioning that as late as the summer of 1969 there were doubts whether devaluation had been effective.[26]

(d) It was sometimes argued that, whether it worked or not, devaluation would have some undesirable side effects. For example, it was claimed, with some justification, that devaluation would signal the authorities' willingness to tolerate inflation; would tend to ossify the existing industrial structure; and encourage manufacturers to concentrate on down-market products, for which demand was increasing relatively slowly.

(e) The argument was widely used that the underlying cause of the problem was not so much price competitiveness as a failure to match the productivity performance of overseas countries. This could only be corrected by long-run industrial policies.

By July 1966 there was, of course, a stronger case for devaluation. By then it was (or should have been) evident that sterling faced a credibility problem and it probably would have been prudent to accept the market's judgement and devalue. But it was still possible to make a reasonable economic case against devaluation, although again this was rejected largely for political reasons. By now the political reputations of Wilson and Callaghan had come to depend on maintaining the $2.80 parity, although Wilson was reluctant to contemplate devaluation because of an agreement with President Johnson during the 1965 sterling crisis. Furthermore, support for devaluation in Cabinet was undermined when George Brown, its leading advocate, made a bid for the leadership during the July crisis.[27]

These arguments suggest, therefore, that the Wilson Government would have been well advised to change the direction of its financial policy much sooner than it did. But its mistake was primarily a failure to deflate; the case for devaluation was weaker than has generally been supposed. Behind the slow response, however, lay a range of economic and political considerations, not least a mistaken belief in the potency of its structural reforms.

Leading on from this we also need to raise the issues of whether the failure to act decisively in the mid-1960s seriously compromised macroeconomic performance, especially in the late 1960s, and whether policy mistakes in the mid-1960s contributed to the election defeat in 1970?

Two sets of claims have been made. The first is that by failing to act decisively in the early years the Wilson Government was at least partly responsible for the rise in inflation and unemployment in the late 1960s. This is rationalized on the grounds that when the decisive deflation eventually came, in order to restore credibility and repay international debts, the Government was obliged to restrict the growth of consumer spending more stringently than if firm action had been taken earlier. The result was that both unemployment and, because of a build-up of consumer frustration, inflation were higher than necessary.[28]

There are two points to be made about this claim. The first, which is to anticipate the arguments in later sections, is that, regardless of the policies adopted, it was probably inevitable that there would be some deterioration in the inflation–unemployment situation in the late 1960s, given the changes taking place both in Britain and in the world economy.

Even so, it is likely that the Government's financial policies marginally aggravated the deterioration. In support of that it is worth drawing attention to the study edited by Michael Posner in 1978.[29] This used the services of three of the leading UK academic economic forecasting bodies together with a smaller monetarist model devised by David Laidler. One of the issues the forecasters were asked to consider was a rerun of the macro-history of the 1964–9 period using their preferred counterfactual policy stance. One of the forecasters – the London Business School – did not consider deflation–devaluation as part of its preferred strategy. The other three, however, although adopting different strategies, favoured an earlier shift towards deflation and devaluation. Their policy simulations in general pointed to a better performance outcome, either lower inflation or lower unemployment (and both in the case of the National Institute). However, as Posner reminds us, the simulations do not suggest that the improvement in performance would have been that dramatic.

In the sense discussed, therefore, financial policy was misguided. There is, however, a second claim. This is the contention that the failure to act decisively in the mid-1960s undermined the government's growth strategy, and it is this which accounts for the disappointing productivity performance. This, in turn, is based on two other assumptions: that the deflationary measures from 1966 inhibited investment and structural change, while at the same time preventing the Government from fully introducing its supply-side strategy. Typical of this position was Tony Crosland, who wrote:

[The failure to devalue] constrained public expenditure. It antagonised the trade unions and alienated large groups of workers. It killed the National Plan and it frustrated policies for improving the industrial structure.[30]

These arguments, of course, are extremely plausible. No doubt if there had been a steady expansion in the latter half of the 1960s conditions would have been more conducive to long-run growth and it would have been possible to concentrate more on growth-promoting policies. Nevertheless it is important to qualify the view that growth performance was seriously constrained by the failure to devalue/deflate. There are three rather obvious reasons for suggesting this:

(a) Investment may well have fallen off in the late 1960s as a result of the relatively slack market conditions. Nevertheless it is wrong to assume that boom conditions are inevitably conducive to rapid structural change while depressed markets inhibit it. The fact is that boom conditions often provide an incentive to *delay* structural changes.

(b) These arguments rest on the assumption that governments are able to

Figure 4.7   Peak to peak growth rates

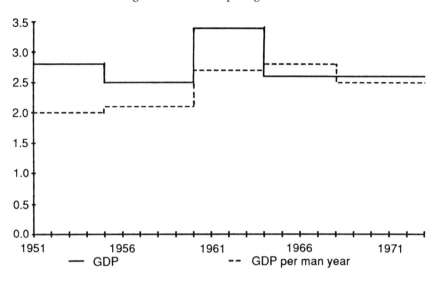

Source: R. Matthews et al. *British Economic Growth 1856–1973* (Oxford, 1982)

directly influence growth – even over relatively short periods. Viewed from the 1990s, however, this seems somewhat optimistic. A fair reading of post-war economic history would be that, although the direct contribution of governments to economic growth may have been positive, it has also been fairly small. It would not be difficult to argue, for example, that the French and Japanese economic miracles of the 1950s or 1960s owed something to government supply-side policies. But it would be much more difficult to maintain that they were the sole or even the most important factor.

(c)   The contention that the Wilson Government was frustrated from introducing its modernization strategy does not completely stand up factually. It is true that the National Plan withered with the July Measures and no doubt supply-side expenditure suffered from 1966 onwards. But most of the measures proposed in Opposition were subsequently implemented to a greater or lesser extent.

Thus we are left with the conclusion that a failure to devalue and deflate at an early stage very probably did impair performance in the late 1960s. But it would probably be wrong to argue that the deteriorating or disappointing performance was due predominantly to this.[31]

One of the electoral advantages which Labour enjoyed in 1964 was the prospect it seemed to offer for improving growth performance. Unfortunately it is difficult to make definitive statements about the subsequent record, because during the Wilson years there was only one cyclical peak (1968) and even then capacity utilization was below that in 1964. Nevertheless, there was no growth miracle. As Table 4.1 and Figure 4.7

show, output growth during the Wilson years was faster than during the second half of the 1950s, but less than during the first half of both the 1950s and the 1960s. This relatively low growth, of course, is partly explained by the deflationary stance of 1966–8.

More important, given their prominence in the National Plan, are the productivity figures. These show that growth increased from 2.3 per cent for 1960–64 to somewhere between 2.7 and 2.5 per cent for the Wilson years – well below the National Plan target of 3.2–3.4 per cent. However, it is possible to interpret this record in different ways. On the one hand it has been suggested that, in view of the deflationary policies of 1966–8, the increased productivity growth suggests that the Government's supply-side policies had a favourable, if small, impact on productivity.[32] Alternatively, it has been argued that productivity growth had been on an upward trend for much of the post-war period so that, even if we adjust for capacity utilization, the improvement was not much better than might have been expected, and may have been marginally worse.[33]

Even so, there is no reason to dispute the basic judgement that the productivity growth record was disappointing, and we need to raise the question why the Wilson Government was not more successful? As already mentioned, one of the factors was the deflationary measures which tended to inhibit investment and possibly structural change. There must, however, also be a suspicion about the potency of the specific growth-promoting policies.

At the heart of the original strategy was the National Plan of 1965. As the first chapter of the Plan indicates, its aims were twofold. First, to provide the Government with a programme of action, with which to correct market failures, not that a National Plan was strictly necessary to do this. Secondly, it was the intention to partially imitate French planning: by involving the private sector in the economic projections it was hoped that it would be possible to raise growth by improving consistency and raising expectations. However, there was an important difference between the French planning of the 1950s and 1960s and that of the Department of Economic Affairs in 1965/6 in that the latter never had much financial leverage over the private sector.

The Plan, with its emphasis on supply-side policies (e.g education and training) still reads quite well. In the event, given the gap between the Plan's targets and the subsequent outcome, the experiment must be regarded as a failure. The immediate cause of this was the July Measures, which inevitably undermined the credibility of the targets, while at the same time reducing Plan-related government expenditure. Nevertheless the demise of planning goes deeper. As Opie[34] has argued, planning never dominated the economic policy machine, as originally intended. To that extent the reaction to the 1966 sterling crisis was predictable.

In Labour Party circles the abandonment of (or lack of commitment to) planning has invariably been regarded as a serious mistake. But, could it have made a contribution to growth? Nowadays the conventional reply would probably be that the potential impact of planning is rather small. One reason is that there are serious practical and theoretical objections to planning. It is difficult, for example, to establish the credibility of a plan, while in mixed economies only a small proportion of decision-makers are directly influenced by official plans.[35] The possibility of successful domestic planning is also limited in a world in which countries are highly interdependent.

Nevertheless there may still have been a role for planning in the 1960s. Even then, however, it must be doubted whether it could have exerted a major role. This is largely borne out by the French experience. In their authoritative history of French growth Carré, Dubois and Malinvaud[36] argue that planning played a positive role in the early post-war period, but its impact was modest and its contribution should not be exaggerated, a view which is largely supported by Estrin and Holmes.[37] The conclusion would seem to be, therefore, that economic planning did possibly have a role to play in the 1960s, and that it is a pity that it was not given a greater opportunity to prove its value. But it must be doubted, even if it had received the necessary support from the Wilson Government, whether it would have transformed Britain's growth prospects.

Yet there was more to the Government's strategy than planning. As part of its supply-side strategy the Wilson Government, for example, introduced policies for promoting technology, for restructuring and redeployment and for encouraging investment. So we should also ask, why did these policies not have more effect on productivity growth? The general answer is that the strategy was a selective one, concentrated at the micro level. It was inevitable, therefore, that, whatever its long-run potential, its impact would be fairly limited over a five to six year period, although some of the measures were also less effective than anticipated. To reinforce these points it is worth reviewing briefly the four sets of measures listed above.

First, the technology policy, which came under the umbrella of the new Ministry of Technology (Mintech), was principally concentrated into three areas: a reorganization of the machinery for the support of research and development (R & D); provision of services for promoting R & D activity and encouraging the dissemination of best practice technologies; and the support of four high-tech industries – computers, machine tools, telecommunications and electronics.

It is as yet impossible to make any definitive judgements about the policy. Certainly the new department was expanded rapidly and Mintech could point to a number of successes.[38] Nevertheless, we can be fairly sure that its direct impact on productivity between 1964 and 1970, although no doubt positive, was fairly limited. For one thing the support for a limited number of high-tech industries could not, even under the best circumstances, have had more than a marginal impact upon aggregate productivity growth. For another, although the promotional work of Mintech may have had some impact in speeding up the diffusion process, it should not be forgotten that the spread of technology is dependent upon a range of factors. And it seems likely that any beneficial effects which Mintech may have had in this area were offset by the relatively slow output growth and uncertainty of the Wilson years. Finally, it is worth mentioning that Mintech did little to rectify some of the alleged weaknesses of Britain's R & D effort, such as the overcommitment to defence and aerospace. The available statistics also suggest that R & D spending in the late 1960s, although still fairly high in comparative terms, was declining in importance at a time when the international trend was upwards.[39]

Closely linked with the technology policy was that of industrial restructuring. This involved some selective attempts to reorganize the shipbuilding, aviation and textile industries,[40] but more important was the work of the Industrial Reorganization Corporation (IRC), which, of course, acted primarily as a merger broker on behalf of the government. Obviously its impact on productivity depended upon (a) whether the IRC-induced mergers had a favourable impact on the productivity of the organizations concerned, and (b) whether they were quantitatively important.

The first issue is not easy to resolve, because of the absence of quantitative 'before and after' productivity studies. Qualitative studies, however, suggest that it is difficult to generalize. The impact was mixed; sometimes the mergers were successful, but, on other occasions, less so.[41] With the benefit of hindsight, however, the implicit assumption that 'Big is Beautiful' seems somewhat naive.

On the second issue the evidence suggests that in aggregate terms the Corporation's role was rather limited. Over the period concerned it accounted for less than 2 per cent of the total number of mergers taking place amongst industrial and commercial companies, although by value the figure was probably slightly higher.[42] Furthermore, there must be a suspicion that some mergers would have taken place even without the IRC acting as a catalyst. It is unlikely, therefore, that the IRC had anything but a very modest impact on efficiency.

The third strand in the strategy was that of redeployment, at the heart of which was the Selective Employment Tax (SET). This was expected to raise productivity directly in the service sector by encouraging firms to shed labour. It was also claimed that it would improve performance in manufacturing, because the labour released from services would allow manufacturing to raise its output growth. This, in turn, was expected to raise productivity growth (Verdoorn's Law).

As with most policy measures the contribution of SET is controversial. In retrospect the safest conclusion is that it probably did raise productivity growth, but again its impact was fairly modest. One reason for suggesting this is that empirical evidence now suggests that the link between manufacturing output and productivity growth is not very robust, thus casting doubt on the strength of the indirect impact of the tax. Nevertheless it is quite likely that the tax had a direct effect on productivity levels in the service sector. Reddaway,[43] for example, has estimated that the combined effect of the abolition of Resale Price Maintenance (RPM) and SET was to raise the productivity level in retailing by roughly 5 per cent in 1968. As the trades concerned accounted for approximately 25 per cent of total employment in that year the impact was positive but small. However, even this should be qualified. For one thing it has not proved possible to identify the separate contributions of RPM and SET. Furthermore it has been argued that Reddaway's estimates are on the high side on the grounds that manufactur-

ing, which was not subject to SET, also experienced above average productivity growth between 1966 and 1968, thus raising the possibility that it was
the 1966 deflationary measures which were the main stimulus to productivity improvement in services.[44]

The other important element on the supply-side was the direct attempt
to stimulate investment. Two fiscal innovations were introduced with this
in mind: Profits Tax was replaced by Corporation Tax, one of the aims
of which was to encourage the retention of company profits; and
Investment Allowances were replaced by Investment Grants. As the latter
were more visible, it was expected that this would encourage company
investment.

Again there must be doubts whether the policy had very much impact. In
the first place there is not much evidence that the policies had a powerful
impact on investment. In fact, investment grew less quickly during the
Wilson years than hitherto, although this is to be explained principally by
the deflationary measures of 1966–8. On top of this, however, it would be
wrong to expect too much from higher investment. It was fashionable in the
1960s to argue that high investment was one of the foundations of high
growth. Yet this view now looks somewhat dated. For one thing, although
capital accumulation is a proximate cause of output and productivity
growth, it is plausible to argue that causation runs from growth to investment. Thus high growth countries tend to have high investment shares
because they need to expand their capacity more rapidly. But, in any case, it
is questionable whether Britain's problem was low investment. Evidence
from the 1960s and 1970s, for example, suggests that Britain's investment
share was not very different from that of West Germany. Differences in
growth were thus due to the efficiency of the investment.[45]

Thus we are left with the conclusion that the Wilson strategy probably
did have beneficial effects but its productivity impact was bound to be
limited over a five to six year period. The final point to make about the
strategy is that it was also a fairly narrow one. It was based on the
assumption that Britain's problem could be cured relatively easily through
industrial policies. However, this does not look so convincing now. As
already mentioned, Britain's growth problem has been the consequence of a
range of institutional weaknesses – weak management, low levels of education and so on. Such problems are not amenable to quick solutions. The
cause of Britain's malaise, therefore, was probably more deeply rooted and
difficult to rectify than Labour supposed in 1964.

Let us turn now to unemployment. The pattern is illustrated in Figure 4.1
(p.74). This shows that following the low level of unemployment in 1964
and 1965 the position started to deteriorate in 1966. By 1967 unemployment had reached 2.5 per cent and by 1970 2.7 per cent. Unemployment
thus remained low by historical standards. Nevertheless it would be wrong
to be complacent. When Labour left office unemployment was higher than
in the previous cyclical trough (2.1 per cent). And 1966 marks the beginning
of a rise in unemployment which occurred almost continuously until 1986.

This rise in unemployment obviously was not evenly distributed. For
example, there was a marked rise in the proportion of older workers

Figure 4.8 Working population and employment 1950–73

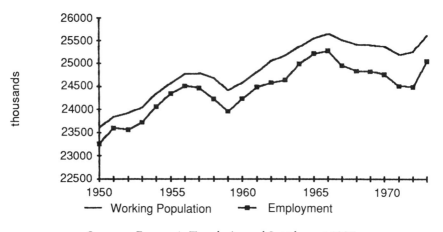

Source: Economic Trends Annual Supplement 1987

amongst the unemployed – more than would have been anticipated on the strength of previous patterns. The unweighted unemployment gap between the North and the South also widened between 1965 and 1970, although a decline in the inter-regional coefficient of variation points to the success of the Government's regional policy. The figures also suggest that male unemployment rose relative to that for females. Indeed the measured female unemployment rate was lower in the second half of the 1960s than it had been in the first. No doubt this was due to a structural shift towards industries which traditionally employed a high proportion of women.

Associated with the rise in unemployment there was also an increase in its average duration. Thus between January 1965 and January 1970 the average duration of the typical spell increased from 8 to 11 weeks for men and from 6 to 6.5 weeks for women.[46] Yet surprisingly the late 1960s was not a time when the incidence of long-term unemployment increased very much.[47]

One possible reason for the rise in unemployment is that it was due to a failure to adjust to an exceptional increase in the growth of the labour supply. However, this possibility can be discounted, because, as Figure 4.8 shows, from 1966 the labour supply actually declined. The reasons are partly demographic: by the second half of the 1960s the labour supply was influenced by the falling birth rates of the early 1950s. Probably more important was the declining labour force participation, which was itself a consequence of the increased opportunities for further education, training and retirement. In purely arithmetic terms, therefore, the rise in unemployment was due solely to a decline in employment which fell by 2.1 per cent between 1966 and 1971.

Perhaps the best-known feature of unemployment at this time is that it coincided with an outward shift in the Beveridge curve. The latter refers to

Figure 4.9   Beveridge curve

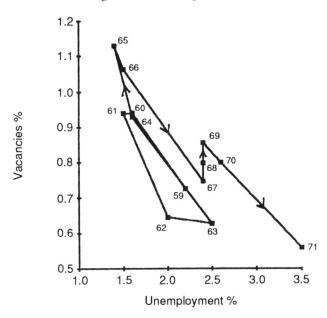

Source: Department of Employment *Employment Gazette*, various issues

the relationship between the vacancy and unemployment rates, and is shown in Figure 4.9. As we would predict the two variables are negatively related, implying that as demand contracts both employment and unfilled vacancies tend to fall, while unemployment rises. The figure confirms that, following the July Measures, the vacancy rate fell. However, it is also noticeable that from 1966 onwards the Beveridge Curve shifted outwards, implying that unemployment rose relative to vacancies.

How then can we explain these various facts? Obviously the rise in unemployment was triggered off by the deflationary measures. We argued earlier that the economy was overheating in 1964. It is likely, therefore, that the Government would have had to deflate sooner or later. Nevertheless, the necessary deflation was probably aggravated by the failure of the Government to take decisive action at an early stage. This explanation, however, only takes us part of the way. It explains why vacancies were lower in the late 1960s. But it does not explain why the Beveridge relationship shifted outwards.

There are two broad possibilities. The first is that it was due to structural or supply-side changes, which tended to increase the incidence of either frictional or structural unemployment. The most plausible structural developments of this type were the 1965 Redundancy Payments Act and the introduction of an Earnings Related Supplement in the 1966 National Insurance Act. These measures were introduced to encourage greater labour mobility. Yet, it has been claimed that they encouraged the unemployed to search longer for suitable employment, thus raising unemployment.[48] Subsequent research suggests, however, that, although the legislation did have some such effect, its impact was relatively small.[49]

The alternative explanation is that the Beveridge shift was the consequence of employment restructuring and a labour 'shake-out'. Such restructuring has been a feature of some, although certainly not all, economic downturns. At such times a combination of low profitability and slack demand will provide firms with both the incentive and the means to reorganize production. As a result, although some new jobs will be created, more will be destroyed, while some of those made redundant may have difficulty in securing rapid re-employment. Thus a restructuring downturn will not only tend to raise unemployment, it will also increase unemployment relative to vacancies, shifting the Beveridge curve outwards. Moreover, the empirical evidence is consistent with this 'shake-out' theory.[50] Not only does the shift in the Beveridge relationship post-date the July Measures but, in relation to previous trends, productivity improvements in the late 1960s were quite rapid given the sluggish rate of expansion.

But why should restructuring have taken place in the late 1960s? The answer can only be speculative, but three sets of factors spring to mind. First, it is quite likely that, in response to the severity of the deflationary packages and the unusual number of economic crises, business expectations were less buoyant than hitherto, and this may well have encouraged firms to de-hoard labour. Secondly, following the Fawley Agreements in 1961, manpower rationalization and productivity bargaining became fashionable in management circles. In all likelihood, however, this interest in manpower efficiency had a sound economic basis. With the liberalization of trade and the abolition of Resale Price Maintenance there was an intensification of competition. Thirdly, as we have seen, it was explicit government policy to promote efficiency growth through measures such as Redundancy Payments, Selective Employment Tax and the Earnings Related Supplement, It was also one of the aims of the incomes policy to promote productivity bargaining.

It is also worth mentioning that economic conditions before 1966 had probably encouraged a build-up of hoarded labour. Between 1945 and 1966 the economy had enjoyed an unprecedented period of expansion with extremely modest downturns. Whilst no doubt this uninterrupted expansion was conducive to productivity growth, the relatively soft market conditions also probably encouraged a build-up of x-inefficiency in large corporations. In other words, by the mid-1960s it is quite likely that there were some fairly large pockets of under-utilized labour, whose jobs would have been at risk in the more austere environment of the Wilson years.

The main conclusion to emerge so far is that the rise in unemployment was primarily a consequence of a weak demand for labour, associated with the deflationary measures. Yet it is also worth asking whether the weak demand had any obvious classical features; whether it was due to exceptional real wage growth? On the face of it this does not seem likely. The usual way to test for the impact of real wage growth is by measuring the so-called 'wage gap'. This is the difference between the growth of the (product) real wage and productivity. If real wage growth exceeds productivity then profitability will decline and there must be a presumption that this will have an adverse impact on employment. It is interesting to note, therefore, that between 1963 and 1969 the wage gap actually *declined* by 0.6 per cent p.a. in the economy as a whole, and by 1.0 per cent in manufacturing.[51]

It may be premature, however, to completely discount wage factors. It has been argued, for example, that by the mid-1960s employers, intent on restoring their declining profitability, pushed through rationalization policies with the aim of reducing their unit wage costs.[52] Thus the poor employment record and the shake-out might have been a lagged response to the earlier decline in profitability.

There is another way in which wage behaviour was important. It has been argued that the main foundation of the low unemployment of the 1950s was wage restraint.[53] However, in late 1969 such moderation broke down with the first of a series of wage explosions. Furthermore it was inevitable that this would force governments to raise unemployment in an attempt to choke off inflation. This was already evident in the last months of the Wilson Government. Specifically, in 1970 Roy Jenkins was reluctant to stimulate the economy for fear that this would aggravate the inflationary situation.

To summarize, it has been argued that the rise in unemployment was largely due to the Government's deflationary stance, which not only reduced the demand for labour but also encouraged a labour shake-out. The shake-out itself was the consequence of a number of factors: the earlier decline of profits, business fashion, unfavourable business expectations and government policy. Supply factors seemed to have played a relatively small part until 1969/70 when wage inflationary pressures started to emerge.

Finally, we need to account for the rise in inflation, illustrated in Figure 4.3 (see above). This shows that up until 1967 inflation remained fairly low, although the true picture is distorted by the 'hard' incomes policy of mid-1966 to mid-1967 which repressed inflation. Nevertheless there is no doubt that the trend was clearly upwards in the late 1960s. From a low of 2.4 per cent in 1967, inflation rose continuously for the next five years until by 1970 it had reached 6.3 per cent and by 1971, 9.4 per cent.

However, Britain's inflationary experience at this time was far from unique. As Table 4.3 shows, although Britain had an above average rate of inflation, most of the major Western countries experienced a rise in inflation during these years, implying that some common international factor was at work.

In proximate terms, one possible reason for this rise in inflation was an increase in import prices. Table 4.4, however, shows that the increase in import prices at this time, although higher than in the early 1960s, was still fairly modest. Not surprisingly, the exception was 1968 when, following devaluation, they increased by 11 per cent. The devaluation, moreover, can be expected to have had some knock-on effects for wage costs. However, this should not be exaggerated. It had only a relatively modest impact upon food prices, to which wage inflation would have been most sensitive.[54]

Nevertheless in the late 1960s and early 1970s wages – the other import-

Table 4.3 *Inflation rates: consumer prices* (Per cent)

Country	1960–68	1969–70
Canada	2.3	3.9
France	3.6	6.0
Germany	2.5	2.6
Italy	3.8	3.7
Japan	5.4	6.4
UK	3.2	5.8
USA	2.0	5.6
All Industrial	2.7	5.2

Source: IMF *Financial Statistics Yearbook* (1981)

Table 4.4 *Change in import prices* (Per cent)

1960	1.0	1966	0.9
1961	–1.0	1967	0.9
1962	–1.0	1968	11.0
1963	3.0	1969	3.3
1964	2.9	1970	4.4
1965	0.9		

Source: *Economic Trends Annual Supplement* (1990)

ant component of costs – increased very rapidly as Britain went through its first post-war wage explosion. Measuring the extent of the wage inflation depends upon the indicator used, but, using average weekly earnings, wages, which had been held at 4 and 5 per cent in 1966 and 1967, rose to 8 per cent in 1968 and 1969. Then from the third quarter of 1969 the position deteriorated markedly and in 1970 rose to 13 per cent. This increase, moreover, was associated with a *rise* in unemployment, which signalled a temporary breakdown of the Phillips relationship (Figure 4.10). Linked with this the late 1960s was also a period of labour militancy. Not only was there an increase in strike activity but trade union density, which had been remarkably stable from the late 1940s, rose quite rapidly. This increase was particularly evident amongst public sector workers.

How are we to account for these developments? This has been a controversial issue, and it has been argued elsewhere that the most promising approach is probably an eclectic one in which a monetarist explanation is combined with an analysis of the changing nature of wage bargaining.[55]

The monetarist explanation is to a large extent based on the belief in the importance of monetary and demand factors in the inflationary process. It partly rests on a criticism of domestic economic policy and, in particular, the Maudling Experiment and the Wilson Government's subsequent reluctance to deflate in the mid-1960s. The consequence of this was that domestic monetary conditions in the second half of the 1960s were fairly expansionary and thus potentially inflationary. Some confirmation for this comes from Figure 4.11 which shows the gap between the rate of growth of

Figure 4.10   Phillips relationship 1953–70

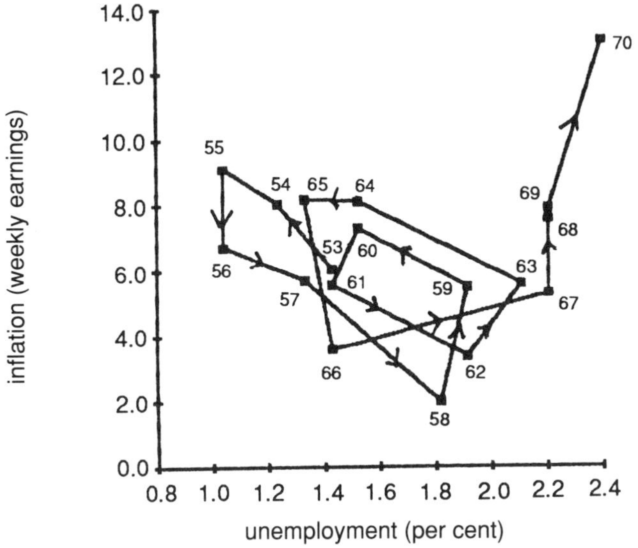

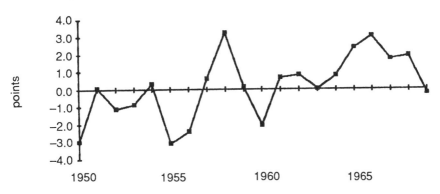

Source: *Employment Gazette*, various issues; *Economic Trends Annual Supplement* 1987

Figure 4.11   Excess money growth 1950–69 (M3 less real GDP)

Source: *Economist* (M3); *Economic Trends Annual Supplement* 1987 (GDP)

the (M3) money supply and real GDP. Monetarists, however, have tended to go further, arguing with some justification that for much of the 1950s and 1960s governments adopted over-ambitious employment targets with the result that by the mid-1960s there had been a loss of price competitiveness. As a result in the mid-1960s they faced the simple choice of a prolonged deflation or a devaluation, and in the last resort employment considerations forced them to adopt the latter. Inevitably, the devaluation, with its impact upon import costs, was bound to have a short-term effect on inflation. Thus a small part of the inflation should be viewed as a consequence of demand management policies.[56]

Occupying a more prominent place in the monetarist account is the role of international factors and, in particular, the change of policy in the USA. From the mid-1960s, under the influence of the Kennedy–Johnson social programmes and the intensification of the Vietnam War in 1965, both monetary and fiscal policy became expansionary, with the result that from around 1965 the US economy began to overheat.[57] Policy then became more restrictive in the first two years of the Nixon Administration, which brought about a mild recession in 1970. Yet for most of the period unemployment remained well below the equilibrium level. This produced a rise in US inflation and a deterioration in the balance of payments. As the latter led to a relaxation in the monetary stance amongst the other industrialized countries the consequence was an upward drift in inflation throughout the Western world (see Table 4.3 above). This was bound to influence UK inflation, because under the Bretton Woods system there was an automatic tendency for inflation rates to converge.

One might argue with some of the details of this account, but the basic story is a convincing one. It does not, however, have very much to say about the acceleration in wage inflation which also began at this time. The causes of this are open to a number of interpretations. But it can convincingly be argued that it was partly due to structural change within the labour market, which tended to undermine the wage restraint of the 1950s and early 1960s. For example, over the post-war period there was inevitably a shift in the age distribution of the labour force towards the post-war generation, whose expectations were conditioned less by the high unemployment of the inter-war years. For this age group, therefore, wage restraint appeared less attractive, although as time passed, and full employment seemed guaranteed, it was inevitable that anxieties concerning the possible impact of high wage demands on unemployment would weaken.

On the strength of this, it might have been anticipated that wage inflation would tend to drift upwards over time, and indeed a cursory examination of the Phillips relationship (see Figure 4.10 above) suggests that it was becoming somewhat less responsive to unemployment even before the late 1960s wage explosion.[58] However, the late 1960s was also marked by a number of disturbances which probably played a more direct role in triggering off the wage explosion. Some authors, for example, have drawn attention to the impact of the continental wage explosion, which originated in France in 1968 and then spread to certain other countries via a demonstration effect. However, it has also been argued that the emergence of labour militancy in both Britain and Europe was due to an accumulation of grievances in the second half of the 1960s.[59] These grievances were partly associated with the reorganization of work. In the second half of the 1960s, for example, Britain was in the midst of the first of two major post-war merger booms, while at the same time, and as already mentioned, the recession of the mid-

Figure 4.12 Growth of real disposable income

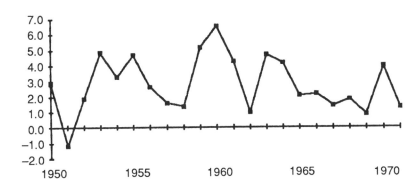

Source: Economic Trends Annual Supplement 1987

1960s was associated with an attempt to restore profitability and restructure employment. As this reorganization was largely imposed under less buoyant labour market conditions, a build-up of grievances was inevitable.

Another likely source of grievance was the incomes policy. Such policies, it is sometimes argued, have their own self-destruct mechanisms. Initially the policy commands widespread support, but as time progresses resentments against the policy accumulate, until a critical mass is reached, unleashing a wage explosion. Inevitably incomes policies also tend to upset the pattern of wage relativities, which then encourages those workers who have fallen behind to push for higher wages. Given the imitative nature of wage bargaining this will then tend to impart an upward shift to wage inflation. Judging from the public sector disputes in 1969/70 and the growth in trade union density, something like this probably happened in the latter stages of the Wilson incomes policy. Brittan,[60] however, has argued that the Wilson Government may also have fuelled the wage explosion by giving wage negotiators the wrong signals in 1969 (e.g. *In Place of Strife* and the decision to improve the position of the low paid under the incomes policy) and by pursuing a policy of appeasement in the run up to the 1970 election.

Yet another plausible explanation for the wage explosion is that it was the product of an 'aspirations gap', whereby frustration built up because of the gap between target and actual real wage growth. According to this argument, wage aspirations in the 1950s were fairly modest, conditioned as they were by wartime and reconstruction austerity. By the 1960s, however, fuelled by electioneering slogans, the spread of TV, motor car ownership, advertising and the like, and frustrated by the relatively low productivity growth, an aspirations gap started to emerge. This made it likely that the intensity of wage-push pressures would increase. However, the Wilson Government aggravated such grievances by its social programme which was largely financed out of taxation, and brought about, as Figure 4.12 shows, a slow-down in the growth of disposable income.

The picture that emerges, therefore, is a complicated one. It is evident that policy mistakes played a role in the process. The incomes policy, the refusal to initiate an early deflation and the taxation policy, for example, can all be paraded in support of the argument that the Wilson Government aggravated the position. However, as the monetarists have correctly reminded us, even with the best policies it is likely, given the world-wide acceleration in inflation, that the Wilson Government would have been faced with some rise in inflation in the late 1960s. Furthermore it is tempting to draw the conclusion that structural developments within the British labour market had increased the inflationary bias of the economy.

Why then was economic performance disappointing during the Wilson years? It has been a central argument in this chapter that to a large extent it was due to a deteriorating economic environment. In the first place, it has been argued that the economic situation that Labour inherited in 1964 was far from favourable. The gentle squeeze on profits from the mid-1950s implied a less optimistic future for employment growth and was to increase the likelihood of a labour 'shake-out'. At the same time high rates of growth throughout the Western world in the 1950s and 1960s had created a buyer's export market and, because of this and for a variety of other reasons, the balance of payments situation was fragile. Sterling was also viewed with a good deal of suspicion before Labour came to power. The most unfortunate legacy in 1964, however, was that the economy was overheating. This added to Britain's balance of payments and inflationary problems and needed to be corrected, but for a government facing an imminent election and committed to expansionary policies, it would be difficult to make the correct decisions.

It has also been argued that the economic environment deteriorated in the late 1960s. The inflationary financing of the Vietnam war and the wage explosion of late 1969/70, the causes of which can only be partly attributed to government policy, were important reasons for the rise in inflation. The wage explosion also influenced the direction of demand management in 1970 and contributed to the rise in unemployment, while the balance of payments difficulties were aggravated by increasing competition in world markets and a rising import propensity.

On the policy front, because of limitations of space and a concentration on the macro aspects of performance, too little emphasis has been given to the Government's positive achievements. But, for example, the Wilson years witnessed increasingly active regional and manpower policies; an improvement in the performance of the nationalized sector; and a controlled rundown of some of the industries concerned. Wilson was responsible for greater control of overseas military expenditure, and for a reassessment of Britain's role in the world economy which culminated in the Basle Agreement; and the Government's fiscal and welfare policies led to greater income equality.

Nevertheless the poor macro-performance owed something to government policy. Some authors have argued that the wage explosion was in part influenced by Labour's redistributive policies, and the introduction of Redundancy Payments and the Earnings Related Supplement may have played some small role in the outward shift of the Beveridge curve.

However, arguably the most serious mistake was the failure to deflate in 1964. It is a fair bet that if Labour had taken decisive action in 1964 it would have established its credibility in the foreign exchange markets, while placing the economy on a sound footing with which to mount a sustained expansion and a planning experiment later in the 1960s. It has also been argued that the failure to devalue earlier was a mistake, but there has been a tendency to unfairly criticize Wilson over this issue; the case for devaluation was never overwhelming until 1966 or 1967.

One of the reasons why the Wilson Governments failed to deflate and devalue was that they were too optimistic about the short-run potency of their supply-side measures. The greater emphasis on the supply side was a welcome development, but in macro terms Labour expected too much from its modernization strategy. Micro-structural policies inevitably take a long time to work through, although it has also been argued that the growth strategy was probably too narrow. The incomes policy also never held out much prospect of long-term success and was to be a destabilizing factor in 1969/70. Nevertheless, none of this should detract from the fact that in the late 1960s there was an underlying deterioration in the economic situation. Even with the best policy-making it was inevitable that there would be a deterioration in economic performance.

Notes

1 I am extremely grateful to Dr Jim Tomlinson for his comments on an earlier version of this chapter.
2 A. Maddison *Phases of Capitalist Development* (Oxford, 1982) pp. 44–5.
3 N.F.R. Crafts 'Economic Growth' in N.F.R. Crafts and N. Woodward (eds) *The British Economy Since 1945* (Oxford, 1991) pp. 261–90.
4 R. Layard, S. Nickell and R. Jackman *Unemployment: Macroeconomic Performance and the Labour Market* (Oxford, 1991).
5 S.A. Marglin and J. Schor *The Golden Age of Capitalism* (Oxford, 1990) pp. 1–38, 39–125.
6 M. Scott with R. Laslett *Can We Get Back To Full-Employment?* (1978) pp. 43–66.
7 R.J. Ball and T. Burns 'The Inflationary Mechanism in the UK Economy' *American Economic Review* Vol. 66 No. 4 (Sept. 1976) 467–84.
8 R. Matthews, C.H. Feinstein and J. Odling-Smee *British Economic Growth 1856–1973* (Oxford, 1982) pp. 445–94.
9 F. Blackaby 'Narrative: 1960–74' in F. Blackaby (ed.) *British Economic Policy 1960–74* (Cambridge, 1978) pp. 23–8.
10 R.N. Cooper in R.E. Caves (ed.) *Britain's Economic Prospects* (Washington, 1969) pp. 147–97.
11 S. Strange *Sterling and British Economic Policy* (1982) Chs 1–5.
12 *New Statesman* 25/9/64.
13 J.H. Wilson 'Labour's Economic Policy' in his *The New Britain: Labour's Plan* (1964).
14 C. Ponting *Breach of Promise – Labour in Power 1964–70* (1990) p. 65.
15 V. Bogdanor in V. Bogdanor and R. Skidelsky (eds) *The Age of Affluence 1951–64* (1970).

16 J. Callaghan *Time and Chance* (Glasgow, 1988) p. 152.
17 See, for example, Blackaby (ed.) op. cit. Chs 2 and 7; S. Brittan *Steering the British Economy* (1971) Chs 8 and 9; A. Cairncross and B. Eichengreen *Sterling in Decline* (1983) Ch 5; Ponting, op. cit. Chs 4, 6, 17 and 23; M. Stewart *Politics and Economic Policy in the UK Since 1964* (Oxford, 1977) Chs 3 and 4.
18 Cairncross and Eichengreen op. cit. 191–2.
19 R. Jenkins *A Life at the Centre* (1991) p. 291.
20 A.P. Thirlwall *Balance of Payments Theory and the United Kingdom Experience* (1980) pp. 148–53.
21 In J. Callaghan *Time and Chance* (p. 168) Callaghan records that deflation was briefly considered in 1964, but the argument of George Brown, that any rise in unemployment would have been politically intolerable, seems to have won the day. Similarly, in H. Wilson *The Labour Government, 1964–70: A Personal Record* (1971) Wilson recounts the story of how, during the 1964 sterling crisis, Lord Cromer, the Governor of the Bank of England, demanded a cut in public expenditure as a prelude to negotiating an international loan. This Wilson refused to do, threatening to call another election and float the pound.
22 Wilson *The Labour Government* op. cit. 6–7.
23 Callaghan op. cit. 159–60.
24 This, for example, is the position of Stewart in *The Jekyll and Hyde Years* (p. 27). Callaghan in *Time and Chance* (p. 223), however, takes a contrary position, arguing that when eventually the Government was obliged to devalue the political effects were damaging and 'were still being felt at the time of the 1970 election'.
25 Caircross and Eichengreen op. cit. 160–91.
26 J.H.B. Tew 'Policies Aimed at Improving the Balance of Payments' in Blackaby (ed.) op. cit. 304–59.
27 Ponting op. cit. 48–56.
28 W. Beckerman 'Objectives and Performance: An Overall View' in W. Beckerman (ed.) *The Labour Government's Economic Record, 1964–70* (1972) pp. 29–74.
29 M. Posner (ed.) *Demand Management* (1978) Chs 1–5.
30 Quoted in D. Walker 'The First Wilson Governments 1964–70' in A. Seldon and P. Hennessy *Ruling Performance* (Oxford, 1987).
31 This conclusion echoes that of David Walker (in Seldon and Hennessy op. cit. 186–215) where he writes: 'it is clear that the decision not to devalue has become a catch-all excuse, a fig-leaf for utopians'.
32 A. Graham 'Industrial Policy' in Beckerman (ed.) op. cit. 178–217.
33 M. Surrey 'The National Plan in Retrospect' *Oxford Bulletin of Economics and Statistics* Vol. 34 No. 3 (Aug. 1972) 249–68.
34 R. Opie 'Economic Planning and Growth' in Beckerman (ed.) op. cit. 157–77.
35 S. Estrin and P. Holmes 'Indicative Planning in Developed Countries' *Journal of Comparative Economics* Vol. 14 No 4 (Dec. 1990) 531–54.
36 J-J Carré, P. Dubois and E. Malinvaud *French Economic Growth* (Oxford, 1976).
37 S. Estrin and P. Holmes *French Planning in Theory and Practice* (1983).
38 R. Clarke 'Mintech in Retrospect – II' *Omega* Vol. 1 No. 2 (1973) 137–62; R. Coopey 'The White Heat of Scientific Revolution' *Contemporary Record* Vol. 5 No. 1 (1991) 115–27.
39 K. Pavitt and L. Soete 'Innovative Activities and Export Shares: Some Comparisons' in K. Pavitt (ed.) *Technical Innovation and British Export Performance* (1980) pp. 38–66.
40 P. Mottershead 'Industrial Policy' in Blackaby (ed.) op. cit. 38–66.

41 D. Hague and G. Wilkinson *The IRC – An Experiment in Industrial Intervention* (1983).
42 Ibid.
43 B. Reddaway *The Effects of Selective Employment Tax: The Distributive Trades* (1970).
44 J.D. Whitley and G.D.N Worswick 'The Productivity Effects of Selective Employment Tax' *National Institute Economic Review* No. 56 (May 1971) 36–40.
45 N.F.R. Crafts 'Economic Growth' in Crafts and Woodward (eds) op. cit. 276–8.
46 J. Bowers and D. Harkess 'Duration of Unemployment by Age and Sex' *Economica* Vol. 46 No. 18 (Feb. 1979) 239–60.
47 J.L. Baxter 'Long Term Unemployment in G.B, 1953–71' *Oxford Bulletin of Economics and Statistics* Vol. 34 No. 4 (Nov. 1972) 329–42.
48 D. Gujarati 'The Behaviour of Unemployment and Vacancies' *Economic Journal* Vol. 82 No. 1 (March 1972) 195–204; D. Maki and Z. Spindler 'The Effect of Unemployment Compensation on the Rate of Unemployment in Great Britain' *Oxford Economic Papers* Vol. 27 No. 2 (July 1975) 440–55.
49 Department of Employment 'The Changed Relationship between Unemployment and Vacancies' *Department of Employment Gazette* (Oct. 1976) 1093–9; S. Nickell 'The Effect of Unemployment and Related Benefits on the Duration of Unemployment' *Economic Journal* Vol. 89 No. 353 (March 1979) 24–49.
50 J. Taylor 'The Behaviour of Unemployment and Unfilled Vacancies: Great Britain, 1958–71. An Alternative View' *Economic Journal* Vol. 82 No. 328 (Dec. 1972) 1352–64; J. Bowers 'Some Notes on the Current Unemployment' in G.D.N. Worswick *The Concept and Measurement of Involuntary Unemployment* (1976) pp. 109–33.
51 R. Backhouse *Applied UK Macroeconomics* (Oxford, 1991) pp. 121–30.
52 D.W. Soskice 'Strike Waves and Wage Explosions, 1968–70: An Economic Interpretation' in C. Crouch and A. Pizzorno (eds) *The Resurgence of Class Conflict in Western Europe since 1968 – Vol 2 – Comparative Analysis* (1978) pp. 219–46 and R.J. Flanagan, D.W. Soskice and L. Ulman *Unionism, Economic Stabilisation and Incomes Policies – European Experience* (Washington, 1983) pp. 363–446.
53 S. Broadberry 'Unemployment' in Crafts and Woodward (eds) op. cit. 212–35.
54 Cairncross and Eichengreen op. cit. 197–213.
55 N. Woodward 'Inflation' in Crafts and Woodward (eds) op. cit. 180–211.
56 D. Laidler 'Inflation in Britain: A Monetarist Perspective' *American Economic Review* Vol. 66 No. 4 (Sept. 1976) 485–500.
57 R.J. Gordon in M. Feldstein (ed.) *The American Economy in Transition* (Chicago, 1980) pp. 101–62.
58 D. Laidler op. cit.; A. Budd and G. Dicks 'Inflation – A Monetarist Interpretation' in A. Boltho (ed.) *The European Economy: Growth and Crisis* (Oxford, 1981) pp. 104–31.
59 Flanagan et al. op. cit.
60 Brittan op. cit. 406–7.

5 Industrial policy in the white heat of the scientific revolution

Richard Coopey

In the 1964 election campaign Labour chose to highlight science and technology as a central issue. In the famous 'white heat' speech Harold Wilson called for the modernization of British industry through the rational use of the nation's scientific and technological resources. At Scarborough and elsewhere, Wilson stressed the need for redeployment and enhanced status for Britain's engineers and scientists, the fostering of new, technologically advanced industries, and a need to redirect the national scientific and technological emphasis away from military towards civil production. In addition to a run-down in military production Wilson also called for a shift away from related 'prestige' industries, notably aerospace and the nuclear sector, which had until the early 1960s dominated national research and development efforts.

To push through these changes Wilson called for the downgrading of Keynesian demand management, and the debilitating trend towards 'stop–go' in the economy. Instead he proposed a government policy based on 'purposive intervention':

What is needed are structural changes in British industry and we are not going to achieve those changes on the basis of pre-election spurts every four years in our industry . . . What we need are new industries and it will be the job of the next government to see that we get them. This means mobilising scientific research in this country in producing new technological breakthroughs.[1]

The record of the 1964–70 Labour Governments, as interpreted by most historians, has led to a dismissal of these pre-1964 modernization plans as empty rhetoric. In economic analysis most emphasis is placed on issues such as the balance of payments crisis and devaluation, the failure of the Department of Economic Affairs (DEA) and its National Plan, and the developing conflict with the trade union movement. Very little comment has been passed on the concrete initiatives, put in train after 1964, aimed at the fulfilment of Wilson's pledge to restructure British industry through a rationalized application of science and technology.

The principal institution set up to orchestrate Wilson's policy changes – the Ministry of Technology – lives on in popular memory, but has been largely ignored in historical accounts. This is surprising in view of the scale of activities in which Mintech, as the Ministry came to be called, was engaged. Perhaps this is more surprising when we consider that major problems which Mintech confronted remain unresolved and pressing in the 1990s – for example, the need to effectively exploit the very high levels of military R&D, deal with conversion and generally foster advanced technology industries in Britain.

Mintech was created in 1964 and underwent a series of phased expansions until it emerged in the late 1960s as one of the first 'superministries' with control over virtually the whole of the administration's industrial policy. It combined control of government scientific and industrial research in the defence and civil sectors by assuming control of the Ministry of Aviation and the Atomic Energy Authority (AEA) in addition to purely civil institutions such as the National Research Development Corporation (NRDC) and the Department of Scientific and Industrial Research (DSIR). As the Ministry grew it absorbed the functions of the Board of Trade and the Ministry of Fuel and Power in addition to the remains of the defunct DEA. It also oversaw the activities of the Industrial Reorganization Corporation (IRC), as well as exercising its own powers under the Industrial Expansion Act to buy into private industry using government funds. By the end of the 1960s the Ministry was in a position to co-ordinate a range of interlocking government industry functions including officially funded R&D, procurement, investment and regional policy.

Within this phased expansion to form what became informally a 'ministry of industry' were a series of 'technology' functions which remained throughout the life of Mintech. These represented the core of the 'white heat' strategy and comprised an attempt to combine and co-ordinate all scientific and technological activity over which the government had control. This included R&D and production in defence research establishments, the civil components of the AEA and ex-DSIR institutions, in addition to the administration of a large proportion of the defence procurement budget concentrated in the advanced technology fields involved in aircraft manufacture.

Following a survey of the existing accounts of the Wilson years, this chapter will examine the origins of the Prime Minister's strategy of modernization and the context in which this strategy was implemented in order to assess the relative success or failure of the Ministry's interventions. It will be argued that Mintech was the central industrial policy initiative of the period and also that, in order to understand the degrees of success and failure of the Ministry it is necessary to examine a wide range of technological, institutional and political influences.

Historians of the left, almost unanimously critical of the Wilson Governments, have a range of approaches, from individual indictments –

Wilson was 'very nearly the worst thing that has happened to the Labour party'[2] – to the more charitable accounts stressing the external and domestic constraints facing a socialist government without a radical set of policies.

Many such analyses are selective in order to illustrate a single theme. For example, Hinton is concerned to show Labour Party and working class interaction. He therefore takes the DEA's National Plan as the central focus of economic policy and highlights conflict around prices and incomes policy as it directly affected the trade union movement. He acknowledges the success of the unifying rhetoric of the early 1960s and notes that it placed 'the Labour party at the head of an offensive of professional managers, technicians, scientists and workers – all anxious to serve the nation – against the upper class deadwood in the boardrooms and the aristocratic amateurism that characterised the British elite'.[3] He is content, however, to characterize the actual policies undertaken as 'building on the Conservatives' initiatives' – chiefly the establishment by Macmillan in 1961 of the National Economic Development Council and the embracing of a role for planning. (The theme of continuity is one to which we shall return). George Brown and his National Plan, an over-ambitious blueprint for an annual growth rate of 4 per cent, were 'sabotaged' during the first of a series of deflationary packages designed to protect the pound and correct balance of payment deficits; the Treasury and finance capital apparently proved more than a match for the DEA. By 1965 it was 'already . . . becoming clear that a Labour Government which refused to tackle capitalist power would be forced instead to take on organised labour.'[4] The balance of Hinton's account is thus taken up with the continued difficulties between Labour and the unions epitomized by the conflict around Barbara Castle's *In Place of Strife*.

Howell also neglects the Ministry of Technology, concentrating instead on the DEA and the vacuous Plan – 'a permissive incantation, without the instruments of implementation'. Intervention in the form of the IRC is acknowledged, though this body is tainted with being staffed principally by leading industrialists. Taking a long-term view Howell identifies in Labour a 'deep-seated inhibition' against economic intervention and compulsion dating from 1945 onwards.[5]

Pursuing this long-term theme, a similar perspective can be found in Saville's account. Following the halcyon years of achievement and decline while in power after 1945, the 1950s are seen to be a barren period for socialist intellectuals. New Fabian essayists Crosland and Strachey are seen to be in the ascendency and full-employment Keynesian orthodoxy to the fore in an economy now experiencing the 'end of ideology'. This revisionist analysis saw the full employment and economic growth of the 1950s as proof that a radical socialist alternative, especially in terms of the social ownership of the means of production, was no longer necessary in a system where capital had become subject to the constraints of political power. This power was now available to a gradualist, and essentially parliamentary, Labour Party, thus justifying the strategies of 'Labourism'. For Saville these opposition years represent a period when Labour neglected to analyze the underlying weakness of the British economy in terms of productivity and modernization. Saville characterizes these as years when high levels of defence spending 'grossly distorted scientific and technological research'. However he is dismissive of Labour's policies in the 1960s. Following a brief discussion of the DEA and National Plan Saville castigates Labour for a continuous failure to recognize the crucial weaknesses in the manufacturing sector. All of these assertions are crammed into a single chapter of Saville's book, covering the whole period from 1951 to 1979.[6]

In none of the above narratives does the Ministry of Technology receive more than a passing mention. Coates gives a fuller account of the Wilson Government initiatives, recognizing the importance of the 'white heat' rhetoric in delineating a socialism with a unifying appeal to revisionists and traditionalists in the Party and portraying a popular image of efficiency and technocracy.[7] He acknowledges the Ministry of Technology's sponsorship role in the key industries of electronics, machine tools, computers and telecommunications and its expansion into sponsorship of the aircraft industry. What does not receive a mention, however, is the central initiative, which involved the control of military procurement and research and development, and which came with Mintech's takeover of the Ministry of Aviation in 1967. Nor, indeed, is there any mention of the general control of government research and development institutions which the Ministry took on. Instead, for Coates, the 'most important of all' Labour initiatives in industrial policy was the strategy pursued by the IRC.[8]

In this over-concentration on the role of the IRC Coates is not alone; indeed it is one of the key distortions within almost all histories of the period. As we turn to examine accounts of the Wilson years not written from a (primarily critical) left-wing position we find more mention of intervention in industrial policy beyond the DEA, though as with Coates above, in most cases the focus is not upon the role of the Ministry of Technology, but rather on the IRC. To be sure, the IRC was an interesting initiative. It was set up in 1966 as a body designed to promote the rationalization of British industry. A small directorate, predominantly comprising leading (and youthful) industrialists, was given a high level of autonomy and a budget of up to £150 million to intervene in key sectors, chiefly promoting mergers to eliminate wasteful competition and achieve economies of scale. The corporation sustained a high degree of notoriety, not surprising in view of its composition and operating methods. The seemingly odd mixture of an elite of industrialists working under a socialist government ensured continued scrutiny from the left. The IRC's operating methods and use of government funds ensured similar interest from the right, frequently tinged with accusations of 'back-door nationalization'.

Given the high media profile which the IRC sustained throughout its lifetime, it is not surprising perhaps that many accounts have chosen to concentrate upon its impact. Young and Lowe, for example, choose such a focus. They outline a useful matrix of government intervention ranging from neutral to discriminatory policies, and recognize the role of the Ministry of Technology as a discriminatory and interventionist body. This is seen as a contrast to previous official initiatives designed to 'hold the ring' between competing industries. Young and Lowe then choose, however, to exclusively highlight only the activities of the IRC.[9]

It must be noted that the IRC intervened in only 50 out of the 3,400 mergers which took place during its lifetime; the money under its control was fairly modest; and it was expected to earn significant returns on a commercial basis. In addition, following the Industrial Expansion Act of 1968, the Ministry of Technology itself, in addition to its wide range of other interventionary mechanisms, wielded similar powers of direct intervention. It masterminded the merger which created ICL, Britain's major computer firm, for example.

Many general surveys also over-emphasize the relatively marginal role played by the IRC. Jones and Keating, for example, follow Young and Lowe's pattern in seeing the IRC as 'the main strand of long term economic policy' following the collapse of the National Plan.[10] Similarly Leruez, in an earlier and very comprehensive account of intervention in Britain, when shifting his focus from the National Plan, emphasizes the role of the IRC, while the Ministry of Technology gets scant attention under the heading of 'other measures'.[11] Newton and Porter's more recent examination, while better than most general commentaries in identifying the 'structural intervention' inherent in policies pursued by the Ministry of Technology and the IRC, nevertheless continue to put undue emphasis on the latter, leading to the conclusion that such interventions were correspondingly small scale.[12]

By concentrating on the IRC in this way, critics of the 1960s Labour Governments have been led to assess policy as ineffective. From this critical perspective, Ingham, for example, asserts that the IRC's activities succeeded only in promoting 'paper mergers' with no apparent improvement in productivity or innovation.[13] Williams et al. similarly dismiss the IRC activities as merely pandering to the 'fashions of the moment'.[14]

Thus far we have seen how the role of the Ministry of Technology has been either ignored or misrepresented by over-concentration on other contemporaneous organizations, notably the DEA and the IRC. These institutions are portrayed as well meaning but inadequate attempts at planning and intervention given their relatively minor or short-lived impact. This approach leads us to another major theme in the historiography of 1964–70. By concentrating on these minor or unsuccessful strategies and by ignoring the scope and the power of the Ministry of Technology, the period is presented as part of a continuity of both Labour Party policy and general post-war consensus government.

One common theme of continuity in the historiography is that of incremental advance of state intervention or planning which predates the Wilson Government. Young and Lowe for example follow this trend in pinpointing the 1961 NEDC foundation and concomitant 'dash for planning' as the 'watershed' in industrial policy, quoting Samuel Brittan's assertion that 'Wilson's own "purposive physical intervention" had already been enacted before Labour came to office.'[15] Gamble too favours the continuity thesis, seeing Labour policy as 'built on the initiatives which conservatives had started'. Throughout the 1950s, in his account, the Tories are presented as having halted the drift of nationalization, promoted tripartite and dirigiste policies and fostered a shift towards 'Fordist' production methods in industry.[16]

This theme of continuity is also reflected in accounts which trace the contours of Labour's internal policy. Seen as embracing Keynesian orthodoxy and the primacy of the demand side, Labour policy was apparently fully formulated in the mid-1950s and epitomized by Crosland-style revisionism. As Holland, for example, asserts, Crosland represented a 'progressive Keynesian Social Democracy which was to dominate Labour thinking in the approach to the 1964 General Election and the Labour governments up to 1970'.[17] This view is usually presented in terms of a move away from social ownership concepts and nationalization, towards the general management of aggregate demand in a now mixed economy. Such interpretations are easily sustained given the resistance (with the exception of steel) to further nationalization after 1964. Yet it is a mistake to typify Wilson as an unreconstructed Keynesian. Wilson specifically pointed to the inherent weakness of such a strategy, with its accompanying 'stop–go' interruptions in economic activity and lack of precision in pinpointing key growth areas in the economy. A better policy lay in the thorough modernization of industry, particularly the identified leading sectors where Britain could develop a new technological comparative advantage. It was to this end that the Ministry of Technology was set up and expanded. That Wilson was later forced to fall back on short-term deflationary measures, which in some ways hampered the work of the Ministry, perhaps says more about the constraints facing Labour in power than the original intentions behind the setting up of the Ministry.

Where the role of the Ministry of Technology is acknowledged, for example in accounts specifically referring to government science and technology policy, a similar trend to the above is evident. In other words Wilson's initiatives are located in a consensual, evolutionary framework. Mottershead, for example, refers to the science policy aspect of the Ministry's powers as part of a linear progression from recommendations under the Trend Report of 1962, which called for greater co-ordination of research and development resources.[18]

In broader science and technology literature the Ministry of Technology is frequently located as part of a steady expansion of government intervention in the orchestration of scientific activity, promoted by wartime exigencies and the increasing needs for major interventions in 'big science'. Included in this linear progression are such events as the foundations of the National Physical Laboratory, the DSIR and the NRDC, the establishment in 1959 of a Minister for Science, the Trend proposals of 1962 and so on.[19]

Two essential features of the Ministry of Technology are absent from such accounts, however. First, they do not acknowledge that the size of the Ministry's responsibilities, with its overall co-ordination of institutes including the vestiges of the DSIR, the NRDC, the AEA and the military research establishments went well beyond previous recommendations, such as the advocacies of Trend, for example. Secondly, they ignore the fact that the fusion of military and civil research and development resources was attempted by the Ministry, and that this in itself was quite new in a peacetime environment.

There are numerous accounts which stress the debilitating effect of an over-concentration in Britain on advanced technology in the military sector. Kaldor, for example, outlines the ways in which military production generated a separate technology logic, insulated itself from the regulating effects of the market, drew in a disproportionate number of scientists and technologists and 'channelled technical innovation . . . along a dead end, towards the grotesque combination of complexity, sophistication and conservatism that characterises much of modern military technology'.[20] Few, by contrast, recognize Mintech's central role in attempting to redirect this imbalance or make better use of defence spending. Saville does note that high levels of defence expenditure 'grossly distorted scientific and technological research' in the years up to 1964, but makes no mention of the Ministry's role in attempting to remedy this situation.[21]

Given that most accounts of the period either omit to mention or fail to give sufficient emphasis to Mintech, it is necessary briefly to sketch the origins of the Ministry and its scope, before turning to an analysis of successes and failures. The decision to establish the Ministry of Technology can be seen to stem from a number of influences. The rhetoric employed at the time, the notion that only a socialist system, 'harnessing socialism to science' could fully exploit scientific and technological advance to its maximum social and economic utility, leant heavily on the ideas of J.D. Bernal and other socialist scientists whose ideas began to emerge in the 1930s. Bernal, for example, pointed to the wasteful duplication, secrecy and non-co-ordination of research and development inherent in competitive capitalism.[22] The natural community of science was frustrated under such a system.

As David Horner's chapter in this book has shown, Bernal himself had exerted some indirect influence over the formation of Labour's science policy during the leadership of Gaitskell, through his connections with members of various Labour advisory committees. Somewhat ironically Bernal found less favour with Wilson, however, even though the latter's socialism was ostensibly less revisionist than that of Gaitskell. Wilson, on his accession to the leadership of the Labour Party, took advice instead from a series of groups set up to discuss policy formation, variously headed by Richard Crossman and Patrick Blackett among others. Meetings such as those held in the Bonnington Hotel included an impressive array of scientists and industrialists sympathetic to the Labour Party.

Blackett is of particular interest in terms of the position he holds in the historiography of the Ministry of Technology, being one of the two individuals often credited with the original idea.[23] Blackett, a Nobel prize-winning scientist, wrote a series of memos and reports outlining the need to consolidate the national R&D effort, and advocating an expanded role for institutions like the NRDC and the use of government contracts to boost the numbers of scientists and technologists employed in industry. Indeed, Blackett has been credited with co-authorship of key sections of the 'white heat' speech.[24]

Blackett is also important in that he represents another influential strand of thought behind the marshalling of the national scientific and technological effort – the example of the Second World War. The war epitomized for many, including Bernal and Blackett, the successful mobilization of the scientific community for national ends. Many projects had received concentrations of staff and resources organized on rational principles unparalleled in peacetime and the impressive results in areas such as radar, electronics, atomic energy, etc. seemingly confirmed the advantages of such a strategy. The apparent effectiveness of controls and rationalizations in the wartime economy are currently the subject of some debate.[25] Nevertheless for many of Labour's policy planners in the late 1950s and early 1960s the experience was a formative one. Wilson himself was influenced by his experience in the supply ministries and by the structures of industrial control set up by Stafford Cripps during and after the war.

During the war and afterwards Blackett's name had become synonymous with the development of operational research, the ordering of fighting resources on rational scientific principles and statistical analysis – the scientific management of warfare – which had dramatically improved the effectiveness of the armed forces in some campaigns. Blackett's article 'Scientists at the Operational Level', written in 1941, was widely circulated and very influential. Blackett, among others, saw the transfer of these governing principles to the peacetime economy as relatively unproblematic. As he later asserted: 'There is not all that real difference between trying to cope in 1942–3 with submarine losses of 700,000 tons a month and trying to cope in 1965 with an adverse balance of payments of 700 million a year.'[26]

It was within this framework of an alternative, directly interventionist, technologically oriented strategy, rather than indirect macro-economic Keynesian controls, that the Ministry of Technology's ultimate form was debated. Revisionist analysis held that selective intervention by Labour could orchestrate a capitalist economy so that it ran more efficiently than when left to the laws of the market. Wilson took this one stage further by advocating much more direct intervention than demand management could offer. In this we can perhaps see a linear descendency from traditional Fabian ideas of marshalling available expertise.

In their precise form Blackett's proposals would have resulted in the enforced co-optation of scientists and engineers into the boardroom as a condition of governmental support.[27] Blackett also pointed to the increased prestige accruing to the R&D department if it was able to attract government funding. The irony of a Labour government presiding over a more efficient capitalist economy was not missed by such as Blackett who, echoing comments made by Stafford Cripps, saw it as 'obvious, even if paradoxical, that if the Labour Party is to be able to carry out a substantial part of its social programme, it must ensure that private industry functions better than it has done under recent Tory governments' – however 'emotionally distasteful' this might prove.[28]

One persistent factor in the shaping of Mintech was a pragmatic recognition that, despite Wilson's deriding of pump-priming Keynesian policy, electoral terms were of limited duration. Whatever measures were taken needed to produce tangible results in fairly short order. Thus, while Labour could support a Robbins style expansion of higher education to increase the output of qualified scientists and engineers, more immediate measures were also necessary. It was in this context that Wilson looked to the pool of resources and expertise in the military sector and other large but disaggregated government research institutions. The Ministry of Aviation in particular held great potential for transfer of work to civil industry, being the leading government sector involved in high technology fields of electronics and aerospace. This idea had the added advantage that it would respond to defence cuts which threatened to break up teams of researchers. Similar pressures were being exerted on the Atomic Energy Authority (AEA) (also later to be incorporated into the Ministry of Technology) as research programmes were nearing completion, necessitating major staff cuts.

A structure began to emerge centring on a new Ministry combining institutions like the AEA and the Ministry of Aviation's Royal Radar Establishment (RRE) and Royal Aircraft Establishment (RAE) with the industrial research expertise built up in the DSIR and NRDC.[29] Such a Ministry would provide an immediately available pool of administrative and technical expertise. Work in the institutions would be redirected to commercially viable projects and government contract systems could be applied to civil industry to foster the expansion of high technology sectors.

It was here that the ideas of Blackett and Wilson parted company. Blackett envisaged a 'new and small Ministry of Technology', staffed by technical experts along the lines of an expanded NRDC with strong 'intelligence' and information functions and a close relationship with industry.[30] He had earlier recognized the need to increase the amount of civil research and development and that ultimately 'a big migration of personnel (from defence firms) is likely to be essential to the renaissance of many branches of industry.'[31] Using the Ministry of Aviation directly, however, would take too long to establish, would prove unwieldy and would swamp civil with defence oriented work, complicated by the difficulty in 'unscrambling . . . the intricate texture of secret and non-secret work'. By 1964 he was describing such suggestions as 'overlordism gone mad' and decrying the inefficiency of the 'cost-plus tradition of the Ministry of Aviation'.[32]

In the event, Wilson rejected Blackett's model in favour of a Ministry which did include the Ministry of Aviation. This partly reflected time constraints, Blackett himself pointing out that his own limited, highly focused Ministry would need perhaps ten to fifteen years to make a significant impact. (He also castigated the Federation of British Industry suggestion that £50 million worth of R&D funding could be injected into British industry in as short a period as five years.) Wilson decided to continue plans for a larger Ministry incorporating the Ministry of Aviation in an attempt to orchestrate national R&D in the short term. That the formal amalgamation took until early 1967 only reflected the logistical difficulties in setting up the Ministry of Technology and organizing the takeover.

In addition to the constraints of time, there were other arguments and exemplars which influenced the shape of the Ministry. These included the widely held belief that there were clearly defined optimal levels of research and development largely dictated by the size of firms. This dovetailed with notions concerning size and scale to produce the general proposition that only very large firms could afford the necessary R&D budgets to innovate and compete successfully on an international scale. (The work of C.F. Carter and Bruce Williams was particularly influential in this respect, as was the work of Alan Cottrell who served as a member of staff in the Ministry of Technology.) This argument complemented the idea of keeping together the large-scale research facilities and teams within defence establishments and the AEA.

The policy of fostering large-scale R&D facilities dovetailed with merger policies pursued throughout the 1964–70 period. One of the major influences behind this policy, which was undertaken by both the IRC and Ministry of Technology, was American industry, with its large and multinational corporations which were deemed to be both a symbol of success and a threat to British manufacturing. Similarly the idea that the state should sponsor R&D through contract placement or work undertaken in its own institutions was influenced by practice in the USA. The US Defence Department when under the stewardship of Robert McNamara, a pioneer of systems analysis, was later held to be the model of professionalism applied to government. Tony Benn, the Minister of Technology from 1966 onwards, later described the activities of McNamara's department as the 'outstanding example of government industry get-together in the Western world'.[33]

The US examples are worth stressing given the over-concentration, in accounts of the Wilson economic strategy, on the supposed influence of the French indicative plan. This wrongful attribution partly reflects the aforementioned bias towards the history of the Wilson years as the history of the DEA and its own planning devices. In reality the example of the USA, its large corporations and governmental interventions, wielded a much greater influence, not least in terms of the difficulties of shaking off the notion that Britain should retain aspirations to resume its position as a great power in economic terms.

The new Ministry was thus the product of a combination of long- and short-term deliberation and shaped by examples of seemingly successful intervention and threats from abroad – most notably the USA. The policies, once formed, had added political attractions. Within the party the initiatives described had a unifying potential. Traditionalists and revisionists could be at least partially reconciled by what Crossman termed, 'a reaffirmation of (socialism's) traditional moral and political arguments in ultra-modern terms'.[34] For the left there was Bernalist rhetoric and a modified appeal to centrally guided science and technology, and for the right a progressive image and a jettisoning of the cloth-cappism of working-class politics.

Beyond the party the ideas had a wider appeal which Wilson had noted as early as 1959. Cultivating an image of youthful professionalism, in emulation of the successful Kennedy administration in the USA and in contrast to the moribund image which adhered to the Hume Government, Wilson aimed to appeal to a strata of white collar and technically oriented workers, newly identified as a key electoral sector by poll research. The appeal to modernity also came at a time when technological change had assumed a very high degree of visibility and when more positive and unproblematic connotations were placed on the notion of progress, certainly when compared to those pertaining in the 1980s and 1990s. Space and supersonic travel, nuclear power and computerization formed highly visible examples of achievement in the early 1960s, complemented by a proceeding revolution in consumer durables. These factors combined to induce a high level of receptivity to a political party placing itself in the vanguard of progress and modernity.

The multiple influences outlined so far shaped the form which Mintech was to take. Examination of the years after 1964 also demonstrates that policies designed in opposition became reshaped, modified and constrained by the context in which they were implemented.

Accounts of the early days of the Ministry usually emphasize the general characterization of chaos and improvisation surrounding Labour's first days in power. The new Ministry, in common with the DEA, had no formal institutional apparatus to inherit and was thus confronted with a plethora of mundane logistical problems involving provisions ranging from typewriters to offices, and appointments ranging from secretaries to senior administrative staff. Competition for resources soon developed between these two ministries. A shortage of trained economists remained a particular problem.

The Ministry was set up initially with Frank Cousins in charge, in October 1964. It took control of most of the DSIR research functions, had responsibility for the NRDC and AEA and exercised a 'sponsorship' function in relation to the four 'key' industries of computers, electronics, telecommunications and machine tools. The Ministry, with Tony Benn in charge from July 1966 onwards, then embarked on a series of expansions which took in the Ministry of Aviation in 1967, including the procurement functions and control of the RRE and RAE and civil aircraft projects including Concorde. The Ministry thus became 'the biggest state directed complex of scientific and industrial power in Europe' with a staff increased from around 8,000 to over 38,900.

A later phase of expansion in 1969 took in the Ministry of Power and its responsibilities for coal, electricity, gas, steel and oil. Also included in this phase was the responsibility for most of the remaining manufacturing industries including textiles and chemicals, the administration of investment grants and regional policy – taken over from the Board of Trade – control of the IRC and the takeover of the DEA's Central Industrial Group.

With the completion of this final phase of expansion the Ministry had either direct or indirect control, or responsibility for most manufacturing industries, including those in the public sector. It administered investment grant and regional policy and controlled the largest defence procurement budget in government, spending over £400 million annually on aircraft, electronics and related equipment. In addition the Ministry also ran 17 government research establishments with a combined staff of over 22,000 qualified scientists and engineers, including over 6,000 at the AEA alone.

Added to this, the Ministry had overall responsibility for the 43 joint government–industry research associations.

This extension of power made a range of potential policy instruments available to the Ministry, increasing incrementally as it expanded. The initial Ministry configuration conformed more closely to the Blackett model, Blackett himself becoming the major figure on the Ministry's Advisory Council on Technology. Initiatives undertaken included a range of advisory and service functions such as the establishment of pre-production order schemes in machine tools, whereby the government underwrote the initial risks and costs involved in introducing the latest manufacturing technologies. A series of information-related services were also set in train. The Technical Information Service was created, partly in recognition of the poverty of statistics available to British industry and government. Interlab was an attempt to establish a network of laboratory information exchanges. The National Computer Centre was set up to provide computer services and advice, particularly on software. A mobile Production Engineering Advisory Service provided demonstrations promoting the latest engineering techniques. A joint Ministry of Technology and AEA Programmes Analysis Unit aimed to provide feasibility and marketing studies on proposed projects.

These activities meshed with the role being played by the Ministry as a form of clearing house for technological information and promoter, in alliance with related bodies such as the British Calibration Service and the British Standards Institute, of quality and standardization methods to aid productivity.

In addition, grant and investment policies were initiated with the Ministry taking a stake in selected companies and making grants for development projects. Under one such scheme, for example, the Ministry funded the development of an automated warehouse project in return for the rights to freely publicize the methods developed. Work in the individual research associations was also continued. The beginnings of merger policy were undertaken. The computer industry was rationalized and funded as a precursor to the later amalgamation into ICL, for example.

The takeover of the Ministry of Aviation greatly enhanced two interventionary mechanisms which the Ministry of Technology was developing. First, defence procurement greatly expanded the civil procurement strategy which the Ministry had been pursuing up to that point and created the chance to directly intervene in the defence-related industries. Secondly, the takeover of responsibility for the major research establishments such as the RRE and RAE gave the Ministry control over the direction of projects in hand and power to redirect research into commercial channels, thus complementing the similar initiatives at the AEA.

AEA initiatives included a range of projects at Harwell including non-destructive testing, desalination research (in co-operation with AEA Risley and the Wier Westgarth Co.), carbon fibre development (in conjunction with the RAE and NRDC) and research into semiconductor and fuel cell manufacture and design. Harwell also offered an information service about latest developments on a subscription basis. Harwell began to establish a position as a model contractual laboratory. By 1968 approximately 18 per cent of the work undertaken there was commercially oriented, rising to 25 per cent in budgetary terms by 1969, when around 30 per cent of the staff were employed in this sphere. Similarly, the Atomic Weapons Research Establishment (AWRE) at Aldermaston undertook several important projects aimed at securing commercial returns and the diffusion of techniques to industry. One of the most widely publicized but least cost effective of these projects was an artificial limb using servo motors developed for guided missiles. Other more practical developments came in the form of technologies with applications in forensics, kidney dialysis and remote monitoring systems for hospital intensive care units. The AWRE also set up the important Aldermaston Project for the Application of Computers to Engineering (APACE) programme.[35]

The ex-Ministry of Aviation establishments followed similar patterns. The RRE, the largest electronics R&D organization in the country, set up an Industrial Applications Unit for research (but, importantly, not development) into computer languages, computer-aided design, air traffic control systems and thermal imaging. The RAE did significant commercial work on carbon fibre and set up an Advisory and Demonstration Unit running courses of training in the use of numerically controlled machine tools.[36]

The above initiatives contributed to the general shift in the balance of government expenditure on research and development away from the defence sector. Statistics on R&D are notoriously difficult to compile with any degree of accuracy, and in this case the problem is compounded by the fact that some reductions in defence R&D reflected substitution of British developed weapons systems for imported ones. Bearing this in mind the statistics issued on levels of R&D spending indicate a significant reversal of trends during the 1966–70 period, that is, following the amalgamation of the Ministries of Technology and Aviation. A reduction of around 10 per cent in defence R&D spending and an increase of around 20 per cent in civil R&D spending meant that by 1969 for the first time in the post-war period the government spent more on civil R&D than on defence R&D. There were a number of major problems with this attempt to shift towards commercially oriented R&D as we shall see below, but there is no doubt that significant progress was made.[37]

Returning to the Ministry's other general activities, we can see a significant change in their orientation after 1966. The public profile of the Ministry, always quite high, took on an added dimension when Tony Benn took over in 1966. Benn, more renowned in the 1960s for his tussle over the jettisoning of his hereditary peerage than for radical politics, was an energetic publicist ensuring a voluminous reporting of the Ministry's activity. With Benn in charge the Ministry began a phased expansion which was eventually to create its large 'industry' phase.

The final phase of expansion took place in 1969, when the Ministry took over the Ministry of Power and the vestigial institutions of the DEA and the Board of Trade. This represented the complete restructuring of the Ministry and its aims. This last phase of expansion reflected in part the demise of the DEA and the failure of its strategy of national plans and prices and incomes regulation. Thus the Ministry became one of the first 'superministries', in advance of the more usually attributed Heath ministries following 1971. The expanded Ministry now had the power to intervene in a fully integrated way in the management of industrial strategy. Programmed expansion could be directed via control of raw material and power through to the relocation and modernization of industry in general.

Within this expansion into industry-wide controlling structures the specific role of redirecting and managing research and development in the leading sectors – the high technology industries – was not forgotten. Despite some gains in the shift towards commercializing defence R&D and redirecting government institutions, a more effective organization of R&D was deemed to be necessary. Proposals were set in train for the establishment of an organization, the British Research and Development Corporation (BRDC) to achieve this.

These final proposals were not implemented, however, as Labour lost the 1970 election and Mintech was substantially restructured. The Heath administration used the Ministry to form the basis of the Department of Trade and Industry. Some initiatives were abandoned altogether, such as the IRC, while others went into a steady decline. The attempt to commercialize defence work was effectively halted as the Ministry of Defence subsumed Mintech's defence functions under a newly established Procurement Executive. Programmes were either abandoned immediately or allowed to slowly whither due to insufficient funds or staffing.[38]

An anatomy of the progress of the Mintech must chart a complex of political and institutional environments, some the subject of rapid changes, others resistant to change. We need to look at the interactions between Wilson's policy formation, the reaction to policy amongst the Ministry's permanent staff and staff in the other institutions affected, and the reactions of industry in terms of collective organizations and individual firms. Within the general context of policy formation we must examine pressures from within the Government and its bureaucracy for alternative strategies, for example, deflationary Keynesian policy, and increased defence spending. We must also be aware of external pressures which affected policy formation, including treaties and defence commitments, and contractual obligations such as the continuation of Concorde.

Because Mintech was tied into defence science and technology, strategic considerations impinged upon its activities. Wilson was unable or unwilling to totally shake off the notion of Britain as a great power, which had led to the consistent build-up of military R&D, for example. The retention of nuclear weapons programmes and the expansion in the later 1960s into the Chevaline development, aimed at uprating the Polaris missile system, is a case in point. From the perspective of the 1960s the Cold War was set to continue into the foreseeable future, uncertainty being fuelled by the Chinese development of nuclear weapons in the mid-1960s. Nuclear weapons continued to be seen as the cheap option to maintain Britain's defence in this environment. Unfortunately this policy took some of the urgency out of many commercialization programmes at the AEA.

The Cold War also affected the freedom of Mintech to forge links with Soviet technology and certainly curtailed the exploitation of potential markets in Eastern Europe. Exports of nuclear power technology and computers were cancelled under the COCOM restrictions which forbade the exports of what the USA deemed to be strategic technologies.[39] British security services also endeavoured to stop Mintech–Soviet technology agreements in order to restrict the number of Soviet personnel entering the country.[40]

Defence cuts were instigated during the Wilson Governments, including the scrapping of a number of aircraft projects, most notably the TSR2 fighter plane.[41] The first Minister of Technology, Frank Cousins, had argued against this cancellation on the basis that over 1,000 British companies were involved in the development of the plane.[42] Nevertheless it was decided that it was cheaper and safer to buy proven US technology 'off the shelf'. The TSR2 cancellation helped Mintech initially by releasing AWRE staff who had been working on the warhead which the plane was expected to carry, but these gains were later lost to the expansion of the Polaris programme.

In civil areas where Britain's prestige was seen to be at stake there was less success at cutting programmes and diverting resources. The Concorde was a case in point. A vigorous debate ensued between 1965 and 1968 over withdrawal from the joint Anglo-French project, but the penalty costs, estimated to be over £1,000 million, were deemed to be too great.[43] Similarly Britain continued to maintain an extensive and fragmented nuclear power programme. It was difficult from the perspective of the 1960s to shake off the belief that nuclear power was the energy source of the future especially in the light of inflated claims which were constantly made for its competitiveness.[44] Modern economics, incorporating environmental and decommissioning costs, make nonsense of these estimates, but during the 1960s it was difficult to gainsay the information provided by the nuclear lobby. Continuation of programmes meant a continuation of the legacy of mistaken policies initiated in the 1950s which had resulted in five different design and construction consortia and a total loss of economies of scale in the one area where they might have been appropriate.

Mintech drew back from cutting many programmes simply because it had no mechanisms to direct scientific and technological labour displaced in the process. Unlike in wartime when labour could be compulsorily moved around, the Mintech peacetime orchestration of science and technology relied on the compliance of workers. As Sir Richard Clarke, Mintech's permanent secretary, put it, 'the problem for Mintech was elusive, for neither Mintech nor anyone else had any levers to press'.[45] Many scientists and engineers were reluctant to leave the security of government employment, enhanced by generous pension rights, and if they did it was feared they were likely to go down the 'brain drain' to the USA, as highlighted by the Jones report in 1967.[46] A measure of the lack of effective policies to control the labour market in scientists and engineers was graphically revealed in 1967. The attempt by Westinghouse to recruit staff from Dounreay by placing advertisements in the local press could only be met with appeals to patriotism in an open letter from the minister.[47] Staff redeployment within government institutions also encountered significant degrees of resistance from professional organizations such as the Institute of Professional Civil Servants.[48]

Mintech's alternative strategy for the research institutions under its control was to keep the scientists and technologists together in existing teams where possible – in line with the belief in the logic of large-scale activities – but to diversify their work, out of defence and 'prestige' sectors, towards commercially viable projects or towards programmes aimed at the diffusion of information and skills. This strategy had its own set of inherent difficulties.

Staff at the major research establishments controlled by Mintech had some notable successes in commercializing their work and disseminating information about techniques in areas including computer hardware and software, machine tools, materials and production systems. The obvious problem about overcoming secrecy constraints did not, surprisingly, prove to be a major obstacle. There were other problems, however. Research workers in establishments such as the RRE and AWRE were not used to the cost constraints of commercial activity, which often dictated a trade off between quality and performance. This was in part due to the nature of defence work, characterized by the dominance of performance rather than expense criteria and short, often highly skill-intensive production runs. The distance between R&D and production was also a problem, frustrating feedback loops between the research, development and manufacturing stage of production. Perhaps the greatest problem, however, was the difficulty in identifying or creating markets for much of what the defence sector was producing. Infra-red technology is a good example of this. Developed at the RRE, infra-red sensors enhanced night-fighting capabilities to a remarkable degree. Yet few commercially viable civil applications could be identified in the 1960s. A similar picture emerges over attempts to commercialize radar technologies.[49]

Another problem facing the Mintech initiatives was the limited response from industry to many of its programmes. Workers at Aldermaston for example, where the Aldermaston Project for the Application of Computers to Engineering (APACE) was set up, were often frustrated with what they saw as the short-termism and lack of foresight in industry.[50] Industry was often reluctant to place contracted research outside its own laboratories, ironically due to a perception of a lack of security at government defence establishments. Also, firms already involved in government defence contracts were reluctant to participate in the wider diffusion of new products and methods. This is evidenced by the formation of the British Infra-Red Manufacturers Organization (BIRMO) in response to the RRE's attempts to publicize work on this technology. BIRMO attempted to build a monopoly of manufacturing within a group of six companies who had traditionally received contracts for production of infra-red related products.[51]

The disappointing response to Mintech initiatives by industry was highlighted in a confidential report commissioned by the Ministry into the progress of the pre-production order scheme, which was designed to promote the development and deployment of modernized machine tools.[52] The report found that machine tool manufacturers in Britain had limited design expertise in the crucial area of numerically controlled machine tools, poor production techniques, inferior management control and very limited market intelligence. Production control was a case in point. While Mintech experts were busy stressing the importance of critical path analysis and line of balance techniques they found manufacturers adhering to 'traditional Gantt charts with chasing from a shortage list, this resulting in large stocks of work in progress and little control over deliveries from outside suppliers.'[53] Machine tool manufacturers were also reluctant to take part in the programme because Mintech agreed to underwrite the costs of the development of new prototype machines, but not to provide them with a profit. Attempts to disguise profits within costing estimates were frequently uncovered by Mintech project officers, sometimes as many as six submissions being made before acceptance.[54]

Users of machine tools, who obtained the loan of new machines for a free trial period, with subsequent options to buy at a discounted price, presented another set of problems. Most companies were found not to have any forward looking machine tool procurement policy and few responded well to the overall precepts of Mintech's programme. Many were lax in providing contracted feedback information to the Ministry on reliability, output and maintenance accessibility, with only about 10 per cent having 'taken their responsibilities seriously in this area.'[55] There was resistance from unionized workers to the provision of data on production throughput, but the poor level of overall response reflected industry's overall lack of a sense of collective responsibility. Failure in this area perpetuated the poor state of existing practice. Alfred Herbert, for example, Britain's leading machine tool manufacturer was very keen to receive feedback data since up to that point it had no reliable statistics relating to the operational performance of its products.[56] Unfortunately the Mintech scheme was to fall short of overall expectations in this area. Staff at the RRE also found that industry was reluctant to put its own money into long-term investment in new technologies, even after these had been demonstrably proven to be efficient.[57]

At a more general level the response to Mintech from industry was cautious. The CBI frequently expressed its unease at government intervention in industry. Objections were particularly vociferous in connection with the Industrial Expansion Act powers assumed by the Ministry in 1968, as they had been over the activities of the IRC. The thought of government buying a stake in major private companies was hailed as 'back door nationalization' and by 1969 *The Times* concluded that 'relations between government and industry have reached an unusually low point'.[58]

One major change which it was initially hoped Mintech would bring about – the increased representation of science and technology at boardroom level – was not effected. There were never any realistic mechanisms proposed to promote this. Within the Ministry, however, this could be achieved and a significant proportion of Mintech staff were qualified scientists and engineers. By 1967 around 50 per cent of the top 100 staff were professional engineers or scientists, and of the top 11 appointments eight were graduates in science subjects.[59] This compared very favourably with the rest of the civil service, still held to favour generalists over specialists, yet may have engendered a serious shortcoming. Specialists recruited into the Ministry from organizations such as the AEA may have influenced Mintech policy in favour of maintaining their old establishments. Lord Penney for example, recruited from the AEA to become one of Mintech's controllers, retained very strong links with Aldermaston. Ieuan Maddock retained his job as Assistant Director of the AWRE while working as Deputy Controller at Mintech.

There was also the problem of the continued autonomy of organizations ostensibly under the control of Mintech. The AEA had, since its foundation, enjoyed a unique independence from the formal control of Whitehall. The Ministry of Aviation remained in the same offices with the same staff as before its amalgamation with Mintech. Members of the Defence Staff were often complacent about the need to restructure the relationship between defence and civil industry, as were some Mintech staff. As one departmental secretary informed the Select Committee on Science and Technology, 'contact with Defence remains much as before and discussions are on the same basis. The problem of reconciling defence needs with civil needs and having a sensible research programme which covers both aspects has already been solved'.[60]

There also remained the general problem of political control over Whitehall. This was often an unequal struggle given the information resources available to civil servants in contrast to politicians. Tony Benn's diaries frequently echo those of Richard Crossman in portraying a constant tension between the minister and his permanent secretary over key issues. Benn's description of Sir Richard Clarke as variously a 'slick operator' and 'arrogant' and acting on matters without reference to the minister[61] are instructive when set against Clarke's later published views on what he would have preferred Mintech policy to be, for he was in favour of much less intervention and abandonment of some initiatives, such as regional objectives, altogether.[62]

Clarke's Treasury background may have had a bearing on this tendency to eschew intervention. Certainly the Treasury's general preference for non-interventionary policy was a feature of the period. This stance had ramifications throughout the hierarchy of Mintech ranging from constraints on overall budgets[63] to onerous insistence that individual initiatives must be self-financing.[64] The strength of the Treasury in this respect was undoubtedly boosted by what the *Daily Mail* termed its 'knockout victory' over the DEA.[65]

Perhaps one of the most serious problems facing Mintech was the Ministry's adherence to the notion of the 'inexorable logic' of economies of scale.[66] This policy was informed by what were deemed to be simple rational calculations whereby the scale of R&D activity could be extrapolated through production activity to determine the optimum size of firms. Firms below a certain size could not undertake sufficient R&D and therefore could not hope to compete.[67] This meant that the large research and development resources at centres within the AEA and Ministry of Aviation needed to be kept intact, and hopefully act as surrogate R&D centres for smaller scale industry. A more radical policy would have seen the selective closure of certain sectors, but unfortunately, as we have seen, no mechanism was available to ensure the rational disposition of scientific and engineering staff displaced in the process.

In summary we can see that Mintech represented the major initiative on both science and technology and industrial policy of the Wilson years. Historians have been wrong to focus on more marginal organizations, notably the DEA and the IRC. Mintech enjoyed some success in redirecting national scientific and technological efforts. Its failures were in part due to the legacies with which it was forced to deal, ranging from the preponderance of military and prestige related R&D, tied to a continuing belief in Britain's world role and a mistaken conception that the USA was both a threat and a model. Mintech's attempts to deal pragmatically with the resources to hand met with a hierarchy of constraints. Technologies often proved unamenable to general industrial dispersion, and industry itself frequently reluctant to respond to initiatives on offer. Although, perhaps surprisingly, staff in the research establishments under Mintech's control were often enthusiastic about converting from military-related work,[68] inertia and resistance characterized other, higher strata of the permanent bureaucracy upon which Mintech had to rely in implementing policy. Given time beyond the restrictions of the electoral cycle, the more effective of Mintech's initiatives, based on the ideas formulated in the early 1960s, may have eventually had more success, arresting the downward trend of key industries such as computers, machine tools and electronics, and de-emphasizing the country's perceived need to be a leading defence industrial power.

Notes

Research for this chapter was undertaken at Manchester University under the ESRC Science Policy Support Group defence technology programme. I would like to thank Tony Benn for making available the manuscript of his diaries and extensive archive materials from the Mintech period. I would also like to thank David Edgerton, who originally identified Mintech as a neglected and important topic: see D. Edgerton 'Liberal Militarism and the British State' New Left Review No. 181 (1991).

1 H. Wilson Purpose in Politics (1964) p. 3.
2 M. Jaques and F. Mulhern (eds) The Forward March of Labour Halted (1981) p. 82.
3 J. Hinton Labour and Socialism: A History of the British Labour Movement 1867–1974 (Brighton, 1983) p. 186.
4 Hinton op. cit. 188–92; see also P. Seyd The Rise and Fall of the Labour Left (1987) pp. 18–21.
5 D. Howell British Social Democracy: A Study in Development and Decay (1980) pp. 253–4; for a similar focus on the DEA see G. Hodgson Labour at the Crossroads (Oxford, 1981) pp. 71–5.
6 J. Saville The Labour Movement in Britain (1988) pp. 122–142; for a similarly discursive treatment see K. Laybourne The Rise of Labour (1988) Ch. 8.
7 D. Coates The Labour Party and the Struggle for Socialism (1975) pp. 98–100.
8 Coates op. cit. 117–18.

9 S. Young and A.V. Lowe *Intervention in the Mixed Economy* (1974) pp. 11–14.
10 B. Jones and M. Keating *Labour and the British State* (1985) pp. 87–9.
11 J. Leruez *Economic Planning and Politics in Britain* (1975) pp. 214–16; see also A. Graham 'Industrial Policy' in W. Beckerman (ed.) *The Labour Government's Economic Record* (1972) pp. 189–95.
12 D. Porter and S. Newton *Modernisation Frustrated: The Politics of Industrial Decline in Britain* (1988) pp. 155–7.
13 G. Ingham *Capitalism Divided: The City and Industry in British Social Development* (1984) p. 216; see also C. Ponting *Breach of Promise: Labour in Power 1964–70* (1989) p. 272.
14 J. Williams, K. Williams and D. Thomas *Why Are the British Bad at Manufacturing?* (1983) p. 89.
15 Young and Lowe op. cit.. 13–14.
16 A.M. Gamble and S.A.Walkland *The British Party System and Economic Decline* (1984) pp. 64–8.
17 S. Holland 'Keynes and the Socialists' in R. Skidelsky (ed.) *The End of the Keynesian Era* (1977) p. 74.
18 P. Mottershead 'Industrial Policy' in F.T. Blackaby (ed.) *British Economic Policy 1960–74* (1978) pp. 441–2.
19 See for example H. Rose and S. Rose *Science and Society* (1969); N.J. Vig *Science and Technology in British Politics* (1968); P. Gummett *Scientist in Whitehall* (1980).
20 M. Kaldor 'Technical Change in the Defence Industry' in K. Pavitt (ed.) *Technical Innovation and British Economic Performance* (1981) p. 115.
21 Saville op. cit. 131.
22 J.D. Bernal *The Social Function of Science* (1967) passim; G. Werskey, *The Visible College* (1988) passim.
23 The other being Aubrey Jones, the Minister of Supply in 1957, who sent a memo to Macmillan suggesting that such a ministry be formed to consolidate and redirect defence research teams.
24 See for example Royal Society, Blackett Archive (hereafter *Blackett*) E.49 P.M.S. Blackett 'Government Participation in Industrial Research and Development' July 1959; P.M.S. Blackett 'The Case for a Ministry of Industry and Technology' Jan. 1964; P.M.S. Blackett 'The Case for a Ministry of Technology' Sept. 1964.
25 See for example C. Barnett *The Audit of War: The Illusion and Reality of Britain as a Great Nation* (1986) and criticism in D. Edgerton 'Liberal Militarism and the British State' *New Left Review* No. 185 (Jan. 1991).
26 *Blackett* E.49 P.M.S. Blackett 'Comments on Estimates Committee Report' 22/7/1965.
27 *Blackett* E.49 Blackett to R. Crossman 23/2/1964.
28 Ibid.
29 The NRDC had been set up by Wilson while at the Board of Trade in 1948, to promote the commercial exploitation of innovations made primarily in the government institutions.
30 *Blackett* 'The Case for a Ministry of Technology' op. cit.
31 *Blackett* E.49 P.M.S. Blackett 'Government Participation in Industrial Research and Development' July 1959, revised Sept. 1959.
32 *Blackett* 'The Case For a Ministry of Industry and Technology' op. cit.
33 *Financial Times* 15/1/1968.
34 R. Crossman *Planning for Freedom* (1964) p. 139.
35 For a general survey of Mintech initiatives see Ministry of Technology *The Ministry of Technology* (1970) passim.

36 R. Coopey 'Restructuring Civil and Military Science and Technology' in R. Coopey, G. Spinardi and M. Uttley *Defence Science and Technology: Adjusting to Change* (1992) passim.

37 Ministry of Technology *Ministry of Technology* op. cit.

38 Coopey op. cit.

39 Tony Benn Archives, London. Manuscript Diaries (hereafter *Benn Diaries*) entries for 18/9/1967; 2/7/1968; 1/8/1968; 22/8/1968; 5/9/1968.

40 *Benn Diaries* 17/1/1968.

41 H. Wilson *The Labour Government* (1971) pp. 41–2.

42 G. Goodman *The Awkward Warrior: Frank Cousins; His Life and Times* (1979) pp. 421–3.

43 J. Campbell *Roy Jenkins: A Biography* (1983); *Observer* 10/1/1965; *Benn Diaries* 4–5/1/1968.

44 *Atom* No. 133 (Nov. 1967) 274.

45 R. Clarke 'Mintech in Retrospect – II' *Omega* Vol. 1 No. 2 (1973) 148.

46 *Financial Times* 11/10/1967.

47 *Financial Times* 11/10/1967; *Engineering* (Nov. 1967); Benn Archive 'An Open Letter from the Minister of Technology to the Engineers and Scientists at Dounreay and Risley' 15/11/1967.

48 *Times* 10/2/1969; *Guardian* 7/5/1969.

49 Coopey op. cit.

50 B. O'Donnell, interview with author 12/3/1991; R. Latham, interview with author 27/3/1991.

51 Coopey op. cit.

52 Atomic Weapons Research Establishment (Aldermaston) Archive, K2984/001 Ministry of Technology 'The Pre-Production Order Scheme for Machine Tools, Parts 1 and 2' (March 1969).

53 Ibid. 12.

54 Ibid. 5–8.

55 Ibid. 8.

56 Ibid. 15.

57 Coopey op. cit.

58 *The Times* 7/5/1969; see also *Guardian* 21/9/1967; *The Times* 21/9/1967, 6/10/1969.

59 Ministry of Technology *Ministry of Technology* op. cit; Benn Archive 'Mintech's Year of Growth' speech by Tony Benn at Woolwich Polytechnic 15/2/1967.

60 Select Committee on Science and Technology 'Defence Research' (P.P. 1968–9 Vol. XXI) p. 77.

61 *Benn Diaries* 5/8/1966; 18/7/1966/; 8/3/1968.

62 R. Clarke 'Mintech in Retrospect I' *Omega* Vol. 1 No. 1 (1973); Clarke 'Mintech in Retrospect II' op. cit. passim.

63 *Benn Diaries* 12/1/1968.

64 This was a constant source of pressure on the APACE programme at Aldermaston for example. F. West, interview with author 27/3/1991.

65 *Daily Mail* 6/10/1969.

66 *Benn Diaries* 29/1/1967.

67 P.M.S. Blackett *Technology, Industry and Economic Growth* (1966); C. Hinton *Engineers and Engineering* (1970); *New Scientist* 8/9/1966.

68 Coopey op. cit.

6 Now you see it, now you don't: Harold Wilson and Labour's foreign policy 1964–70

Chris Wrigley

A major problem in assessing Labour's foreign policy between 1964 and 1970 is to disentangle style and substance. While its essential continuity with that of previous Labour and Conservative governments was often disguised by newsworthy sudden initiatives by Harold Wilson, so were its achievements, albeit achievements of a modest nature. Foreign affairs provided Harold Wilson with a prominent platform and a very large audience before whom he could display his considerable short-term political skills. In this he not only deflected attention away from other serious problems, both international and domestic, but also heightened expectations of Britain's influence in world affairs two decades after the end of the Second World War.

The 1964–70 Labour Governments' foreign policy set off along familiar tracks. The policy was firmly in the Bevinite tradition, with its main Anglo-American attitudes and assumptions largely frozen in 1941–51, the period of wartime co-operation, Marshall aid and the Korean War. The main Bevinite tenets had been reaffirmed during the later part of Hugh Gaitskell's leadership, especially in 1961. The greatest change in policy occurred in 1967. This came about not through a radical review made on the flood-tide of a massive general election victory but because of a seriously deteriorating economy and changed international political circumstances. In effect Labour was forced to face the facts that Britain had reached, or was nearing, the end of the line as far as major features of its old policies were concerned. Britain (or rather Britain within the Sterling Area) could no longer pose as a world power, even of second ranking and buttressed by the

US. As for 'the Atlantic partnership', notions of equality or even of independence had long been unrealistic. Britain needed new economic and international connections or she would continue to appear ever less the US's partner and more her European factotum. These realities speeded up the ending of Britain's major role East of Suez and pushed the Government to make a second application (the first being by Harold Macmillan) for Britain to join the European Economic Community.

The main constraint on Labour's foreign policy was the increasing lack of realism involved in expecting the British economy to sustain Britain's attempts to act as a world power. This role had been undermined by Britain's commitment to all-out war, regardless of the cost, in 1940 and 1941. By the time Nazi Germany and her allies had been defeated Britain had incurred 'the largest external debt in history' (as Sir Alec Cairncross has put it) – some £10,000 million.[1] Britain's relatively sluggish economic performance, compared with those of her industrialized rivals, in the 1950s and 1960s did not enable her to return to the ranks of major powers. Because of US willingness to subsidize British illusions of being a country of world political importance, Britain continued to try to play such an overcommitted role until 1967. As Michael Stewart, Foreign Secretary in 1965–6 and 1968–70, later sagely reflected:

The unwelcome truth was that, both in the Middle East and South East Asia, British influence was severely limited. Because in the past, Britain had administered Palestine and had become co-chairman of the Geneva Conference on the affairs of Indo-China, we had nominal responsibilities which we had not the power to fulfil.[2]

In essentials, the differences between Labour and the Conservatives were a matter of degree. Labour was more sensitive to Black Africa's views on Rhodesia and South Africa. The Conservatives, or at least those close to Edward Heath, were unambiguously keener on Europe. The Conservatives were more reluctant to accept the inevitable withdrawal from East of Suez; though after 1970 they made only the gesture of keeping a small force in Malaysia as a sign of having a different policy. Perhaps, most important of all, Wilson was determined not to be sucked into providing more tangible support for the United States' action in Vietnam, though it is open to doubt whether Edward Heath, had he been in office, would have sent the much-talked of token British force to join Australian and New Zealand soldiers alongside those of the US.[3] There is much to commend Robert Rhodes James's verdict, made soon after the 1970 general election, that 'Wilson's skill in the 1964–70 government was to give the appearance of great changes without in fact making any of substance'.[4]

While the broad lines of foreign policy showed continuity both with Labour's own past and with its Conservative predecessors, Wilson's actions were often remarkably volatile in the short term. This was partly due to Labour's parliamentary circumstances. Between 1964 and 1966 short-term considerations were often paramount as the Government had only a very small parliamentary majority and a further general election was only a matter of months away. But this volatility was also to do with Wilson's style of politics. As early as July 1966 Tony Benn was complaining in his diary that 'the short-term tactical dodging at which he is adept may have been perfect for the 1964–66 Parliament but has no place in the developing strategy for the next four years'.[5]

Harold Wilson's special initiatives in foreign policy often had a multi-faceted tactical aspect to them. He was like a master chess player engaged in several games at the same time. His moves need to be seen in the context of several interlinked political needs of the time, concerning other international issues and relationships with various allies; national opinion (which he often confused with the comments of the press); Labour Movement opinion, especially the powerful trade union leaders, the Labour and TUC annual conferences and, above all, the parliamentary Labour Party; often imaginary challenges, or future challenges, for his position from senior colleagues; and a desire to embarrass the Opposition. Two good early illustrations of this were the decision to allow the sale of 20 Buccaneer aircraft to South Africa to proceed and Wilson's June 1965 Commonwealth peace initiative to Vietnam.

Trading in arms with South Africa had been vigorously condemned by Labour in opposition. At the Labour Party Conference on 2 October 1963 Barbara Castle, on behalf of the National Executive Committee, had declared:

I am proud that we have taken an unequivocal stand on this question of an embargo on the export of arms. We accept the Security Council resolution; we intend to operate it . . . We know that Buccaneer aircraft are still being made in British factories for South Africa. The order has not been cancelled. We say that a Labour government would cancel that order and substitute a better one.[6]

Earlier in 1963, at a mass rally in Trafalgar Square, Wilson had also declared that a future Labour government would condemn 'the supply of arms to South Africa as long as apartheid continues'; though he had not mentioned cancellation of work underway.[7] However, faced with the loss of overseas earnings from the Buccaneer contracts at a time of international financial pressure, plus the legal problems of withdrawing from the contracts, Wilson and his Cabinet colleagues in November 1964 agreed to permit the existing orders to be met.[8] Wilson could feel that he had balanced a sop of 'economic realism' with the earlier principled risk of going ahead with the abolition of National Health prescription charges and an increase in pensions. In so doing he had provided some reassurance for those who lacked confidence in a Labour government's commitment to defend sterling and thereby pleased some of the Labour right as well as cheering those on the left by holding true to a major issue of his Bevanite past and prioritizing promises made to working-class electors. Permitting the sale of those aircraft can also be seen as part of his attempts to appeal to a wider public opinion by gaining favourable media coverage as a man who made tough decisions in the overall national interest.

Harold Wilson's Commonwealth peace initiative on Vietnam worked at several levels. In producing this scheme just before the Commonwealth Conference he ensured that it, not the serious developments in Rhodesia, would dominate that conference. It also provided him with 'proof' that his government was attempting something positive and pacific with regards to Vietnam, an increasingly desirable political asset when under strong criticism not least from Labour's left and many church people. Moreover that the 'something being done' was through the Commonwealth, as if a 'third force' (neither American nor communist), made it especially hard for such critics to condemn it outright. (In fact Wilson was careful to gain advance US government approval of his initiative, that government seeing such a development as a lesser evil than intervention by the non-aligned nations).[9] Moreover his peace initiative put the Opposition in a dilemma as to how to respond, to him an important consideration. Wilson in November 1964 had confided in Crossman:

Well, now I can sit back and study strategy and leave you chaps to do the tactics and detailed work in your Departments. My strategy is to put the Tories on the defensive and always give them awkward choices. . . . Whatever we do we must keep the initiative and always give them awkward choices.[10]

And yet with such initiatives by Harold Wilson it is easy to feel that for a brief period he himself believed each might achieve something. Alongside what Andrew Roth has dubbed his Walter Mitty-like fantasies,[11] he had an almost Gladstonian belief in his own righteousness. Indeed in making the 1965 Commonwealth peace proposal, however unlikely it was to achieve anything, Wilson and Michael Stewart could feel that they were taking seriously Britain's position as a co-chair (with the Soviet Union) of the Geneva Conference, which had been set up to watch over events in that part of South-East Asia. Indeed part of Wilson's problem was that he had too high an opinion of Britain's moral and other weight in world affairs – a delusion that he shared with many leading CND activists who equally believed that a moral lead by Britain would have a major impact on others. In Wilson, the would-be world statesman existed alongside the political master magician.

Early on in the Government Wilson's energy, exuberance and improvizations gained him great respect from many of his colleagues. Barbara Castle would not have been alone in her sentiments of mid-1965, when reflecting on his handling of Rhodesia and Vietnam:

But one can't help admiring his endless ingenuity. He is like a juggler with a dozen balls in the air at the same time. And it may pay off. After all, nerve is a political quality not to be despised . . . I don't care how Harold does it so long as the result is something I can approve.[12]

However, as time went on and in the absence of tangible foreign policy successes, colleagues such as Crossman expressed their 'disillusionment with his gimmickry' and his failure to settle down to 'a real job of work based on a real strategy'.[13] Benn, an initial acolyte, recorded in July 1969 Wilson still invoking 'his magic' – 'Isn't there always magic in my reshuffle, just as there's magic in my honours list . . .?' – and added, despairingly, 'You just can't communicate with him.'[14] With those who then felt they were the keepers of the Labour Party's conscience, or came to assume such a role, distrust of his style was articulated more readily than worries about major strands of government policy; for these, if seriously considered, would logically have been resignation matters. Though Crossman agonized over the statutory prices and incomes policy and Castle over Rhodesia, Wilson can hardly have feared their resignations from office. The diary writers would blame Wilson for lack of a true radical or socialist vision in external affairs while they themselves concentrated mostly on fighting for often very limited departmental objectives.

Wilson's means were often less defensible than his ends. In this he was somewhat like David Lloyd George. This is a comparison that was not distasteful to Wilson at the time, one which occurred to his contemporaries and which subsequently has been made by many historians.[15] In finding Lloyd George's energy and versatility attractive, Wilson was not alone in the parliamentary Labour Party: according to a 1961 survey of influences which had moulded 110 Labour MPs, the chief political ones were Keir Hardie and Lloyd George, the latter admired for his style.[16] Lloyd George had found that his stratagems became well remembered while his aims were obscured by his short-term expedients, so that even creditable achievements were soon forgotten. Similarly Wilson's delight in headline-catching foreign policy moves devalued prime ministerial interventions generally in foreign policy. Media commentators came to savage the hand which had once fed them so well. He earned judgements such as that of James Margach:

he became enraptured by the role of *being* premier, captivated by the thrilling interplay of today's performance and tomorrow's headlines. He typecast himself for the role of instant government.[17]

However, the substance of his policies was rarely other than orthodox. Indeed, his foreign policy was not a breach of promise with the Party's Bevinite/Gaitskellite line, reaffirmed in the 1961–4 period. Patrick Gordon Walker, in August 1964, when sketching in a notebook the key features of a future Labour government's foreign policy, commented on defence:

The basic fact is that we cannot afford a full nuclear armoury. . . . Whether we like it or not, we must rely on the US for nuclear protection . . . I think we must base our policy on the alliance with the US.

Overall he observed:

Almost every British policy will react in one way or another upon relations with the US. We must try to co-ordinate them and build a coherent whole out of them. If we are dependent upon the US for ultimate nuclear protection we must so arrange our relations with US [so] that our share in the pattern of this alliance is as indispensable as we can make it . . . In some matters we must adapt our views to theirs – in exchange for similar concessions by US in matters that greatly concern us.

He added: 'We must make the marginal help we can give indispensable: in [the] sense that if it were withdrawn the cost to US wd. be high'.[18] Gordon Walker's successors as Foreign Secretary, Michael Stewart and George Brown, shared these views; and so did Harold Wilson, for all his earlier speeches urging that British policy should be independent of the US.

This policy was made clear in the House of Commons on 3 November

1964 with the Queen's speech and the debate on it. After fine words about easing East–West tension, the speech stated:

My government reaffirm their support for the free world – the basic concept of the Atlantic Alliance; and they will continue to play their full part in the North Atlantic Treaty Organisation and in other organisations for collective defence.

Wilson made plain his government's dependence on the US not only for defence but also as regards support for sterling:

The fact is that after thirteen years of the easiest world economic conditions this country has known for half a century, we are reduced to an unacceptable degree of dependence on international borrowing, and this . . . from a party which tried to fight the election on the issue of an independent foreign policy. There is no independence without economic strength.[19]

However, Wilson, Stewart and the others were not reduced to supporting President Johnson in Vietnam simply because of Britain's precarious finances, as critics then and subsequently have suggested. In September 1965 William Warbey, the Labour MP who campaigned vigorously on behalf of North Vietnam and the Viet Cong, put this accusation bluntly:

They have done this one must suppose – because in the words of Dean Rusk, 'America supports the pound, and Britain supports America in Vietnam'.[20]

Vietnam was certainly always a case where Labour's Foreign Secretaries were willing to afford the US 'marginal help'. However, it can be doubted if there needed to be much adapting of views, for Wilson and the Labour right had as great an abhorrence of communist expansion as Lyndon Johnson and the Democrats.

They did not see the Vietnam conflict of the 1960s (as opposed to that against the French) as primarily a struggle for national liberation against the political divisions which had been imposed on the country by external powers. William Warbey, in telling Stewart during February 1965 that 'the West would eventually have to reconcile itself to the fact that in a number of Asian and African countries, just as in European countries like Poland and Yugoslavia, it was the communists and the revolutionary socialists who were the most patriotic and effective leaders of the movements for independence', would only have confirmed the latter in his Cold War Bevinite views.[21] Wilson and Stewart had their minds on possible repercussions in other areas, notably the British war against insurgency in Malaysia. Wilson told the Commons in July 1965 that American withdrawal from Vietnam would 'have incalculable results' not only in Vietnam but elsewhere, as 'it might carry the danger that friend and potential foe throughout the world would begin to wonder whether the United States might be induced also to abandon other allies when the going got rough'.[22]

Wilson, with a measure of success, kept his government's role linked to seeking to facilitate a peace settlement. In placing undue importance on the British Foreign Secretary's role as co-chair of the Geneva Conference he could avoid providing fighting forces in Vietnam yet still function as the US's faithful intermediary. Barbara Castle, in conversation with Wilson at the time of the proposed Commonwealth Peace Conference, discovered the true extent of the British role. She noted in her diary:

I asked him whether it wouldn't have been better to get one of the non-aligned PMs as chairman of the mission and he cracked back at once with, 'Washington would never have stood for it'. (Freudian slip?)[23]

Wilson also deployed his commitment to peace against those condemning the heavy American involvement in South Vietnam. Thus, in the Commons in July 1965 he stated:

That is the banner – the 'Peace in Vietnam' banner – that I hope we could all carry, although it is becoming clear that some of those who shout loudest for it, both here and in other countries, are concerned not with peace in Vietnam but with victory in Vietnam.

However, ironically, in the same speech he had earlier made clear that his own notion of peace in Vietnam was on American terms: 'when conditions have been created in which the people of South Vietnam can determine their own future, free from external interference, the United States will be ready and eager to withdraw her forces from South Vietnam'.[24]

If with Suez in 1956 Eden had been reliving the late 1930s, then Stewart and several other members of Wilson's Cabinet were back in the late 1940s and early 1950s with Bevinite responses to the spread of communist regimes in Eastern Europe and also the Korean War. Stewart was a very effective speaker on the US case in Vietnam. In his memoirs he emphasized that his commitment was not due to economic dependency on the US. There he wrote that he sometimes wondered if the Government's policy towards Vietnam should have been changed. However:

The only alternative would have been to express disapproval of US policy and urge them to withdraw. I should have saved myself much anxiety and distress by pacifying my critics in this manner; but I could not then, nor can I now, see that this line could be defended in the realm of morality and justice.[25]

Indeed in his firm belief in the rightness of the American involvement in Vietnam Stewart became a more convincing exponent of the US case than some of the American leaders. As for his innate hostility to the Soviet Union, it would have been deemed highly creditable by Ernest Bevin. His impact in the 1964–70 Governments deserves a measure of reassessment. He was a decent, straightforward, able man, with a mellow parliamentary wit; though he lacked the charisma and/or urge to self-advertise of the diarists or of other moderates such as Brown, Callaghan, Crosland, Healey and Jenkins. His views and his high promotion made him usually a reliable Harold Wilson man, but not simply a yes-man. In reserving the Foreign Office for such solid figures as Gordon Walker and Stewart, Wilson was not only avoiding promoting potential rivals. He was also indicating the likely direction of foreign policy and ensuring prime ministerial involvement in its formulation. With such unambiguous figures of Labour's right as Gordon Walker, Stewart and Brown in post, the British and American secret services should have been able to relax.

Yet with Wilson, on some major policy issues, it is often hard to judge to what extent he wished to go in any particular direction or to what extent he was pushed. For he was often very happy to disguise his choice of a change in direction by suggesting to those opposed to this that he had been forced by the exigencies of various new circumstances; and he was equally amenable to suggesting that where he had been pushed along an unchosen route, it had been in his mind all along to travel that way and that it had been a matter of 'right timing' when to reveal his intention.

Moreover he was a master at blurring the decisive point in a major change of policy. In this way he escorted his Cabinet colleagues, the parliamentary Labour Party or the wider labour movement step by step in a direction they were hesitant to take with no major issue of principle being confronted on the way. Eventually those accompanying him found it was hard to go into reverse, having gone so far. This was the case with the EEC and with the general, but not entirely unqualified, support for the United States in Vietnam. His colleagues found him a hard man to pin down. Barbara Castle, when very uneasy about government policy towards Rhodesia, noted: 'Opposing Harold is like playing blind man's buff'.[26]

Hence one can wonder whether his 1964 policy commitments to the US reflected short-term needs or longer term thinking. To what extent was Wilson in the thrall of the mighty dollar? The probability is that he gave President Johnson commitments in line with the policies he intended pursuing anyway – resisting devaluing the pound and maintaining a role East of Suez. This helped gain American financial support, and thereby bought time while he manoeuvred until Labour could win a second general election.

Wilson had a stronger commitment to sterling and to the East of Suez role than some of his senior colleagues. Wilson, like Callaghan, had entered office determined to avoid devaluation. They felt they had sufficient problems in securing the confidence of the money markets for Labour in office without a second post-war devaluation. Yet, faced with the alternative of deflation and thereby disenchanting Labour's supporters, several of Wilson's economic advisers, as well as Richard Crossman, aired devaluation from early on in the Government's life. Wilson however saw such a policy as a disaster before the second general election: 'Devaluation would sweep us away. We would have to go to the country defeated.'[27] As the price of not devaluing became more and more apparent in 1965 and 1966 there was growing anxiety among government ministers. Wilson's economic advisers repeatedly suggested floating the pound as an alternative to devaluation; but this was resisted for similar reasons. Wilson was only happy to discuss devaluation after the 1966 general election. Then he appears to have treated it as another pawn in his political chess game. Barbara Castle noted in her diaries him commenting:

When I do it, I want to do it for political not economic reasons. The Middle East might have given us the opportunity if the Arab nations had withdrawn all their reserves. I can just imagine how I should have gone on TV. These Arabs, Nasser and all that, trying to dictate our foreign policy. Or if Johnson had got tough. When I went to Washington I was expecting a blazing row. In Bonn, at Adenauer's funeral, Johnson had told me that if only I would put troops into Vietnam my worries over sterling would be over. Yes, I retorted, and I would be finished too. I went to

Washington . . . to say some tough things about escalation and found his mood had entirely changed . . . This must be a political issue when it comes: we devalue to defend our independence.[28]

Yet for all this bravado, Wilson realized that Britain could not be independent in the way she had been in the second half of the nineteenth century. The Atlantic link had serious limits; as George Brown put it, 'The only place for Britain in an Atlantic union would be as a 51st US state'.[29] Brown, an ardent European, bluntly urged Barbara Castle: 'We've got to break with America, devalue and go into Europe'. He went on to condemn Wilson's pledges to President Johnson on devaluation and support in the Far East:

both of those have got to go. We've got to turn down their money and pull out the troops: all of them. I don't want them out of Germany. I want them out of East of Suez. This is the decision we have got to make: break the commitment to America.[30]

In fact Wilson had long been eyeing Europe. For Britain to make moves in that direction did not entail breaking close ties with the US. Indeed Britain moving that way was something which successive American governments had favoured.[31]

The ending of Britain's major responsibilities East of Suez, when taken with devaluation, did mark another major stage in Britain at last coming to terms with her reduced post-Second World War status in the world. Again, Wilson long resisted efforts by a number of Cabinet colleagues and some members of the parliamentary Party to cut these British commitments. Powerful Cabinet figures such as Brown, Crossman and even Healey at times expressed doubts about this policy. However, in the early years of the Government the first two were locked in major clashes over economic policy (umpired by Wilson), Crossman was kept absorbed by the challenging problems of housing and local government and Healey's concerns in part were to do with the operational viability of forces in those areas if continuing financial cuts were made.[32] Yet there was a potential powerful coalition for major change, one which could muster those who wished to change policy to economize, those (like Brown) who wished to focus efforts on Europe, as well as left-wingers who were suspicious of a distant imperial role.

Wilson's change of policy can be seen as a clear example of his political right-timing. He was genuinely slow to change his mind. He may have been helped by further evidence in the Suez area of Britain's relative unimportance, with the six-day Arab–Israeli war of 1967, and by changed circumstances in Malaysia and Aden. More important were the changed circumstances following devaluation. Yet it is hard not to believe that domestic political considerations played their part.[33] An element of this was to do with the Opposition. On devaluation, there is the telling remark in Wilson's memoirs that in early 1967 he had been told that Heath 'was said to have asserted that the next election was safely in Conservative hands "unless Wilson devalues" '.[34] While his reporting of this could be an attempt to show himself cleverer over devaluation than he was, it could equally reflect his political gamesmanship. Similarly, over the East of Suez policy he had his eye on the Opposition. As early as October 1965 he was alert to new possibilities arising from the Shadow Defence Secretary, Enoch Powell, calling for withdrawal from beyond Suez. Crossman noted in his diary:

Harold and I agreed that pressure from our left wing and from Powell on the Right would have value since it would leave him free either to withdraw from East of Suez or to extract a higher price from the Americans for standing staunchly by them.[35]

In early 1968 Wilson was happy to change policy and thereby economize on defence, please the left and adopt a distinctive foreign policy (perhaps before the Conservatives did) which public opinion would readily accept on the back of devaluation.

Yet, if over several major issues Wilson was in part using US politicians and not simply being used, there are other lesser areas where Labour's principles were sacrificed hastily in the interests of good Anglo-American relations. One of the worst cases was Diego Garcia. Before taking office Gordon Walker had pin-pointed the desirability of helping the US in the Indian Ocean. He had urged shifting British resources there: 'This will increase our effective power and make us and [the] US interdependent in the area of the world where force can still be used.'[36] In line with this policy some 2,000 islanders were removed in order to provide the Americans with military bases,[37] an injustice which in 1992 was still being aired in Parliament by the Labour MP, Tam Dalyell. Another notably high-handed action was the use of paratroopers in Anguilla, an episode about which Michael Stewart later admitted his approach was mistaken.[38]

Similarly the Wilson Government was willing to take a tough line with Labour and nationalist figures where US, NATO or British interests would benefit. In opposition Labour had been highly sympathetic to Cheddi Jagan in British Guiana.[39] In office they actively co-operated with the US to ensure he was kept from power.[40] In the case of Malta, Michael Stewart tried to get the Cabinet to agree to provide extra funding with the aim of keeping Dom Mintoff, the Labour Party leader, out of office. This was narrowly rejected by the Cabinet.[41] Again, earlier there had been fraternal links between the British and the Maltese Labour Parties.[42] However, while the Foreign Office remained hostile to Mintoff, Crossman, when he visited Malta in May 1970, provided a less alarmist and more reasonable assessment of both Mintoff and his policies.[43]

The maintenance of the east of Suez role until early 1968 and the *realpolitik* exhibited in such cases as Diego Garcia and Cheddi Jagan show the Wilson Government following very traditional foreign policy. The hard-headed support for the federal government in Nigeria over the Biafran war and the limited support for the Americans in Vietnam, for a range of reasons including fears of US isolationism in Europe and wider communist incursions if she were defeated, are also illustrations that Labour in office did not make radical departures in policy.

Yet Labour then and later has been criticized both ways. Much of the Party was committed to a moral, socialist policy which could easily cause internal divisions, and might result in policy not consistent with Britain's national interests.[44] On the other hand the pursuit of traditional policy, however effectively done, could be condemned as a sell-out.[45]

Politically, the diminution of moral principles in the actual operation of foreign policy was damaging. A generation of Labour activists and potential activists were disillusioned over the Wilson Government's stance over Vietnam, Biafra and ending UDI in Rhodesia – though it is not so clear that these stances were unpopular with much of Labour's traditional electoral support. There, Ho Chi Minh was not so attractive, and the 1983 election manifesto's appeal to idealism did not mobilize sufficient of these electors to terminate Thatcherism after her first four years as premier. However, Wilson's political style was such that new directions were presented as inevitable and the least undesirable option, rather than as exciting new opportunities. This was so with the move towards Europe and with the ending of most of the old imperial role.

Of course such blurring of issues was Wilson's way of carrying nearly all his party and, indeed, most of the electorate along with him. He took the heat out of many issues, making the matter of contention how you handle something, not the issue of principle behind the matter. While Wilson avoided the turmoil of Algeria in handling the defiant white settlers of Rhodesia, there was ample hypocrisy involved in the actual application of sanctions. Similarly British limited support for the US in Vietnam descended steadily into expediency in the short term. Yet he did avoid greater direct intervention, a contrast to Britain's later readier support for US action under Thatcher and Major – such as the US bombing of Libya in 1986. For all this, too, Wilson did preside over major changes in foreign policy. Gordon Walker has even described the withdrawal from East of Suez as 'the most momentous shift in our foreign policy for a century and a half'.[46]

As for Wilson himself it is unfair to portray him as purely a pragmatist, drained of all principles.[47] Wilson had a genuine loathing for communism, especially of the Asian variety. He had much admiration for the US (though increasingly not for the person of Lyndon Baines Johnson). He was genuinely in favour of decolonization and more sympathetic than many of his colleagues to aid (though not enough to protect it from economic cuts). He loathed racism. His response to Gordon Walker's loss of his seat in Smethwick was heart-felt and not posturing.[48] Yet, sadly, his foreign policy rarely revealed much of his genuine radical concern. This was partly to do with his obsession with image. The reality was that Britain was led by a good-natured, Yorkshire boy-next-door type, who enjoyed playing the sophisticated worldly wise international diplomat. The starkness of Britain's diminished position soon revealed the absurdities of posturing as a major power or as a key intermediary between the US and USSR.

Notes

1 Sir A. Cairncross 'Reconversion 1945–51' in N.F.R. Crafts and N.W.C. Woodward (eds) *The British Economy Since 1945* (Oxford, 1991) pp. 26–7.

2 M. Stewart *Life and Labour: An Autobiography* (1980) p. 215.
3 A. Roth *Heath and the Heathmen* (1972) p. 202.
4 R. Rhodes James *Ambitions and Realities* (1972) p. 60.
5 Diary entry, 18 July 1966 in T. Benn *Out of the Wilderness: Diaries 1963–67* (1987) p. 456.
6 The Labour Party *Report of the 62nd Annual Conference, 1963* (1963) p. 223.
7 P. Foot *The Politics of Harold Wilson* (Harmondsworth, 1968) pp. 271–2.
8 This issue is invisible in H. Wilson *The Labour Government 1964–70* (1971) and in Benn's published diaries (though he was then not in the Cabinet). It is mentioned but not addressed in B. Castle's introduction to *The Castle Diaries 1964–70* (1984) p. xv. Crossman suggests he dozed off during a major Cabinet discussion on arms to South Africa: see entry for 12 November 1964 in R. Crossman *The Diaries of a Cabinet Minister, Vol. 1* (1975) p. 54.
9 C. Ponting *Breach of Promise: Labour In Power 1964–70* (1989) pp. 221–2.
10 Diary entry, 9 November 1964 in Crossman op. cit. 50.
11 A. Roth *Sir Harold Wilson: Yorkshire Walter Mitty* (1977), in particular pp. 51–4.
12 Diary entry, 21 June 1965 in Castle op. cit. 42–3.
13 Diary entry, 17 July 1966 in Crossman op. cit. 571–2.
14 Diary entry, 24 July 1969 in T. Benn *Office Without Power: Diaries 1968–72* (1988) p. 192.
15 Examples include: Wilson op. cit. 528; Crossman op. cit. 418; Benn *Wilderness* op. cit. 376; Rhodes James op. cit. 20–1 and 25; Roth op. cit. 6, 18; D. Walker 'The First Wilson Governments 1964–70' in P. Hennessy and A. Seldon (eds) *Ruling Performance: British Governments From Attlee To Thatcher* (1987) p. 188; and K.O. Morgan *The People's Peace: British History 1945–1989* (1990) pp. 247, 251, 310.
16 C.J. Bartlett *A History of Postwar Britain 1945–74* (1977) p. 212.
17 J. Margach *The Abuse Of Power* (1978) p. 141.
18 Patrick Gordon Walker Papers, Churchill College, Cambridge, GNWR 3/4. 'Thoughts on Foreign Policy', August 1964, pp. 5, 8, 12. Much of this document is printed in R. Pearce (ed.) *Patrick Gordon Walker: Political Diaries 1932–1971* (1991) pp. 298–302.
19 *Hansard* (30/11/1964) Vol. 701 cols. 37, 80–81.
20 W. Warbey *Vietnam: the truth* (1965) p. 10. For many more equally blunt US administration comments see Ponting op. cit. 49–58. For another contemporary account stressing financial dependency as the main explanation for the policy see P. Toynbee 'Dictators, Demagogues or Prigs?' *New Statesman* 5/1/1968 reprinted in K. Amis (ed.) *Harold's Years 1964–1976* (1977) p. 57.
21 Warbey op. cit. 127.
22 Speech of 19 July 1965 reprinteci in H. Wilson *Purpose In Power* (1966) pp. 91–2.
23 Diary entry, 18 June 1965 in Castle op. cit. 41.
24 Wilson *Purpose* op. cit. 101, 91.
25 Stewart op. cit. 157.
26 Diary entry, 25 November 1965 in Castle op. cit. 70.
27 Diary entry, 24 November 1964 in Crossman op. cit. 71.
28 Diary entry, 22 July 1967 in Castle op. cit. 282.
29 G. Brown *In My Way* (1972) p. 209.
30 Diary entry, 18 July 1966 in Castle op. cit. 148. Brown's hostility to strong US influence on British policy was a major part of why he resigned as Foreign Secretary on 15 March 1968, see Brown op. cit. 178–9.

31 A point which Heath had made in the US in his Godkin lectures at Harvard University in March 1967; see E. Heath *Old World, New Horizons: Britain, The Common Market, and the Atlantic Alliance* (1970).

32 T. Dalyell *Dick Crossman: A Portrait* (1989) pp. 112–13 and D. Healey *The Time of My Life* (1989) pp. 278–93.

33 Patrick Gordon Walker's assessment of a sage and statesmanlike decision made 'at the earliest moment when such a policy became practical' is to give it too much *gravitas*; see P. Gordon Walker *The Cabinet* (revised edn, 1972) p. 133.

34 Wilson *Labour Government* op. cit. 466.

35 Diary entry, 19 October 1965 in Crossman op. cit. 354.

36 Gordon Walker 'Thoughts on Foreign Policy' op. cit. 17.

37 On this, see Ponting op. cit. 234–7.

38 Ponting op. cit. 232–4 and Stewart op. cit. 245–7.

39 See, for example, Benn *Wilderness* op. cit. 75 (diary entry, 12 November 1963).

40 Ponting op. cit. 45.

41 Diary entry, 12 March 1970 in Benn *Office* op. cit. 251.

42 For example, the Maltese Labour Party had appealed to its British comrades for financial help for its election campaign in early 1964. Letter by A.J. Scerri in *New Statesman* 13/3/1964.

43 Crossman Papers, Modern Record Centre, Warwick, 154/3/DH/1/2–3. K.M. Critchley (Private Secretary to the Minister of Overseas Development) to Crossman's Private Secretary, with detailed briefing papers, 11 May 1970; 154/3/DH/1/112. M Stewart to Crossman, 16 June 1970; Diary entry, 16–25 May 1970, R.H. Crossman *The Diaries of a Cabinet Minister*, Vol. 3 (1977) pp. 922–4.

44 For a strong, but over-schematic, argument of this type see M.R. Gordon *Conflict and Consensus in Labour's Foreign Policy 1914–1965* (Stanford, California, 1969).

45 See Foot and to a certain extent Ponting op. cit.

46 Walker *Cabinet* op. cit. 122.

47 See, for example, Ponting op. cit. 402–5.

48 As revealed in his comments on the Queen's Speech, 3 November 1964, and in a private telegram to Gordon Walker, 16 October 1964; see Gordon Walker Papers, GNWR 1/16.

7 Labour's 'Gannex conscience'? Politics and popular attitudes in the 'permissive society'

Peter Thompson

For those on the radical right of contemporary British politics, the permissive values of the 1960s have underpinned the social difficulties of the 1980s.[1] In his Disraeli lecture of 1985, Norman Tebbit made this point with characteristic bluntness:

The permissive society scorned traditional standards . . . Family life was derided as an outdated bourgeois concept. Criminals deserved as much sympathy as their victims. Many homes and classrooms became disorderly – if there was neither right nor wrong there could be no basis for punishment or reward. Violence and soft pornography became accepted in the media. Thus was sown the wind; and we are now reaping the whirlwind.[2]

Margaret Thatcher was just as condemnatory. She also knew who to blame. For her, the responsibility for Britain's moral decline lay with the 'Gannex conscience' of the Wilson Governments.[3]

All this suggests two obvious questions. First, were the moral and social changes of the 1960s as widespread or as damaging as the radical right have assumed? And second, did the Labour Party play a leading role in encouraging the emergence of the 'permissive society'?

It is the first of these questions which has attracted the greatest interest. Both contemporaries and historians have had little difficulty in finding evidence which supports the claim that the 1960s were 'permissive'. In popular historiography[4] the 'permissive '60s' have been framed by the famous obscenity trials of *Lady Chatterley's Lover* in 1960 and *Oz* in 1971. Between, London was 'swinging', the Beatles were number one, and

Kenneth Tynan said 'fuck' on TV.[5] A 'new morality', particularly amongst the young, appeared to have undermined the Victorianism of much British life. Indeed in a recent overview of the post-war period, Kenneth Morgan has argued that the 1960s saw 'a tidal wave of permissive indulgence, homosexual as well as heterosexual. One-parent families, a huge boom in contraceptives, a crusade for sexual indulgence in whatever form, became accepted.'[6] Arthur Marwick has even suggested that this amounted to a 'cultural revolution'.[7] Other scholars have been more cautious, but all accept that the 1960s witnessed a liberalization of attitudes and behaviour amongst large sections of British society.[8]

The Labour Party's role in all this remains, however, more contentious. It is true that legislative changes between 1964–70 were both significant and numerous, as has already been well documented.[9] By the end of the decade, the laws relating to divorce and theatre censorship had been relaxed; abortion and family planning advice was available on the NHS; homosexuality had been decriminalized; and capital punishment abolished. But, as recent scholarship has demonstrated, such legislation should not be seen as an 'official endorsement of hedonism.'[10] On the contrary, the reforms were intended to alleviate distress, or to recast public morality in new and hopefully more durable forms.[11] The reforms, then, were not particularly radical.[12]

Secondly, it is commonly argued that party politics played little or no part in either encouraging or discouraging permissiveness. For example, historians point to the fact that MPs' support for the key reform Acts of the period – on abortion, censorship, divorce, homosexuality and so on – were matters of individual conscience rather than party loyalty.[13] Yet a detailed examination of the evidence reveals that the Wilson Governments provided considerable assistance to the reform Acts in question. And after all, it was Labour MPs who provided the bulk of the support for permissive issues in parliament. Indeed, the *Guardian*'s guide to the 1970 General Election concluded that 'There is no doubt that Labour is more identified in most people's minds with these changes than are the Conservatives.'[14] Following the radical right, it might even be reasonable to conclude that the Labour Party actively encouraged the emergence of the 'permissive society.'

In order to explore these issues we need to assess whether the permissive reforms between 1964–70 were the product of a distinct political strategy, or simply *ad hoc* responses to the perceived social changes outlined above. If a strategy can be discerned it is that created by the 'revisionist' arguments of Anthony Crosland and Roy Jenkins. The revisionist thesis has two central points of relevance which, although well known, bear brief recapitulation.[15] First, it was argued that the existence of the welfare state and the growth of managerial control in industry meant that the problems of society were no longer due to the structure of capitalism. Moreover, Crosland believed that as growth continued (he was writing in the mid-1950s) economic inequalities would become increasingly irrelevant. Thus the politics of nationalization and poverty (Labour's traditional agenda) could be replaced by other, 'and in the long run more important, spheres – of personal freedom, happiness and cultural endeavour'.[16] In practical terms this involved the reform of the unduly restrictive laws on abortion, censorship, divorce, homosexuality, licensing and women's equality.[17]

Crosland's second point was strategic. In 1959 Labour had suffered its third successive electoral defeat. Labour's traditional support – the 'cloth capped' manual working class – was in decline and with it the Party's political fortunes.[18] Electoral salvation lay, according to the revisionists, in a pan-class alliance between the workers and the increasingly numerous white collar technocrats and young professionals. Consequently, party strategists became increasingly preoccupied with the problem of attracting non-manual workers[19] and a Home Policy subcommittee addressed this very subject throughout 1961. It was the technocrats and young professionals who were thought to be most in tune with Crosland's new agenda of equality and personal freedom. Young professionals, in particular, appeared to have an intellectual rather than simply economic interest in politics. Indeed, such non-manual groups were often very active in politics, but, in the words of Geoffrey Drain, the deputy secretary of NALGO, they usually became involved in 'pressure-groups operating without any party political allegiance'.[20]

In a conscious attempt to address some of the concerns of these key sections in the electorate, revisionists criticized both Fabian puritanism and working-class moralism. For Crosland, the puritanical Webbs represented all that was out of place and out of date in Fabian thinking. He caustically remarked that: 'Total abstinence and a good filing-system are not now the right sign-posts to the socialist Utopia: or at least, if they are, some of us will fall by the wayside.'[21] The Labour philosopher Richard Wollheim expressed similar concerns when assessing Richard Hoggart's influential celebration of working-class life, *The Uses of Literacy*. Wollheim conceded that a sense of community, so beloved by many on the left at that time, was indeed admirable. But the working-class attitudes which underpinned it – 'a lack of curiosity about the unfamiliar and the unknown [and] a residual puritanism in sexual matters' – were 'by and large, unadmirable and ultimately undesirable'.[22] In an effort to distance themselves from both these Labour traditions, revisionists stressed the virtues of social mobility through educational reform, increased leisure, and the modernization of both the nation's industry *and* its morals. Labour, for so long the party of full employment, should now be also seen – to borrow a phrase from a member of the Research Department – as the party of 'full enjoyment'.[23]

It seems clear, then, that an influential wing of Labour thinking was advocating and encouraging 'permissive' – or to use Roy Jenkins preferred terminology – 'civilised' values, both as a matter of principle and as a basis of political strategy. And, as is well known, both Crosland and Jenkins (as Education Minister and Home Secretary respectively) were responsible for implementing the majority of the reforms during this period. Furthermore, many of the newly elected Labour MPs were advocates of the revisionist agenda.[24]

However, Jeffrey Weeks is surely right to suggest that this new agenda failed to dominate Labour thinking.[25] Permissive issues – with the exceptions of the abolition of capital punishment and the general principle of law reform[26] – were rarely highlighted in Party election material. The reform of the laws relating to abortion, divorce and homosexuality was indeed Party policy, but the process of reform would remain the Private Member's Bill. Labour's task was simply to ensure as smooth a parliamentary passage as possible.[27]

Nor is it at all clear how the Party came to adopt the particular social policy reforms associated with permissiveness. Roy Jenkins has recently given the impression that his own 1959 Penguin Special, *The Labour Case*, simply became party policy upon his appointment as Home Secretary in December 1965.[28] If the disagreements over the drafting of Labour's 1961 policy statement, *Signposts*, are any guide, then it is difficult to believe that the permissive agenda was adopted with much enthusiasm. Both Gaitskell and Wilson objected to the draft prepared by the secretary of the Research Department, Peter Shore. In particular, Wilson felt that the passage endorsing the findings of the Wolfenden Report on homosexuality would cost the party '6 million votes'. Gaitskell agreed, apparently adding: 'Can't we be sure this time not to say things which are going to lose us votes?' The offending passage was duly removed.[29]

Moreover, whilst it is true that Labour's electoral success in 1964 and 1966 was due to substantial support from white collar technocrats and young professionals, the current consensus suggests that this was largely achieved by appeals to modernize the nation's industry, rather than its morals.[30] If the new political agenda was only partially endorsed at the polls, it is also clear that it provoked disagreement within all levels of the Labour Party – not least when it touched upon the role of youth.

Few Labour MPs were as enthusiastic about permissiveness as the maverick left-winger Tom Driberg. In 1967 he even attempted to persuade Mick Jagger to become a Labour MP, in the belief that it would help the party secure the support of the young.[31] Had he succeeded, there is little evidence to suggest this would have helped Labour's cause much. Young people, particularly those involved in the many spectacular sub-cultures of the 1960s, tended to be apathetic or even antipathetic towards politics, to the dismay of many older activists. As one female Labour MP told a prominent Underground figure:

I can't understand your young people. The Labour Party has done everything for them. Without the Labour Party they wouldn't have had their education, and they wouldn't have their present spending power. Why are they so ungrateful? Why, for instance, don't they come out canvassing for Labour in the local London elections?[32]

The minority of young people who did support Labour showed little enthusiasm for the new permissive agenda. If 'Labour's paper for youth', *Focus*, is any guide then this group simply wanted the voting age lowered to 18 (which was achieved in 1969), so that they could participate in 'traditional' political debates about the economy, foreign affairs and so on.[33] Moreover, many in the politically active left-wing minority were – according to commentators throughout the 1960s – increasingly turning away from Labour.[34]

Yet even here, permissive issues were rarely seen as part of 'politics'. To an extent this simply reflected a long-standing puritanism which existed on the revolutionary left.[35] There were, of course, exceptions. Between November 1967 and March 1971, the Young Communist League (YCL) newspaper, *Challenge*, enthusiastically embraced a number of permissive issues. Pro-Dubček and pro-sex, by 1969 *Challenge* was attempting to win new subscribers with provocative photographs of young female comrades and the headline, 'Are you getting it regularly?'[36] Quite what the readers thought of all this is difficult to gauge, but the publication of photographs of 'semi-naked young ladies' in October 1969 provoked widespread criticism. Angry YCLers denounced *Challenge* as 'pornographic' and 'un-Marxist',[37] and by 1971 the paper had returned to the more conventional politics of the picket line.

It seems that this was where many on the far left thought 'politics' should remain.[38] In 1964, for instance, the Marxist historian, John Saville, could describe the campaign for the abolition of the death penalty and the reform of the law on homosexuality as 'important, but minor, and certainly politically innocuous'.[39] 'Real' politics clearly lay elsewhere. Although not a Labour Party member, Saville's opinions seem to typify a widespread assumption on the left. Even the 'New Left' with its generous definition of politics and interest in questions of culture was virtually silent on, say, the divorce laws or the relaxation of censorship. Raphael Samuel recalls how matters of personal morality 'were consigned, as it were, to some apolitical limbo'.[40]

But others in the Labour Party had very definite ideas on permissiveness. Indeed, divisions of opinion were many and various.[41] In general, younger Labour members were more sympathetic to reform than their elder colleagues; and those that supported one reform were more likely to support another. That said, it would be misleading to crudely divide MPs as pro- or anti-permissiveness. Leo Abse, for example, was a leading campaigner for changes in the law relating to homosexuality, but he opposed abortion reform. A significant minority of Labour MPs – particularly Nonconformists and Catholics – were actively hostile to permissiveness. Yet opposition was not simply voiced on religious grounds. It was held by many in the Party that the affluent society was directly responsible for the permissive society. Given the discomfort with which many Labour MPs felt about affluence,[42] it is not surprising that they were no more enthusiastic about permissiveness. Thus even Barbara Castle – who had voted for the abolition of capital punishment and the reform of the abortion law – could state in 1970 that:

We believe in human society, not the "permissive" society . . . This is the product of a commercialised society in which the questions people ask themselves are "Will it pay?" and "Can I get away with it?" . . . It is the Tories who are the permissive in society today for they subordinate moral imperatives to economic ones.[43]

Similar divisions can be found amongst the Party rank and file. Resolutions sent to Conference provide a somewhat crude index of constituency interest in permissive issues. (None of those cited in the following discussion, it should be noted, were actually debated.) However, of the many hundreds of resolutions submitted between 1962 and 1969, only nine called for the reform of the law on abortion; two for the abolition of capital punishment; two for stricter control of drugs; two for the implementation of the Wolfenden recommendations on homosexuality; and finally, one each for the abolition of corporal punishment in schools and the provision of free family planning clinics.[44] Of the 15 'liberal' resolutions, ten came from London and the South East. A similar geographical bias is evident in the discussion of divorce law reform in the pages of *Labour Woman*.[45] And an examination of the local Labour press seems to confirm that interest in permissive issues was largely confined to middle-class constituency parties in the South East of England. In Esher and Walton during the run-up to the 1966 General Election, for instance, Des Wilson welcomed the appointment of Roy Jenkins in terms which Crosland would have recognized and applauded: 'It is within the power of an imaginative Home Secretary to make Britain a freer, gayer, more tolerant place in which to live, and there is every reason for thinking that Roy Jenkins is such a man.' Indeed the reforms were so important that they made a 'good argument on . . . [their] . . . own for a return of the more humane and radical of the two major parties'.[46] In Richmond and Barnes, Mari Kuttna was no less enthusiastic. After Labour's poll victory, she argued that the government should now make permissive issues into Party issues.[47]

Working-class constituency activists in much of the Midlands, the North and Scotland might well have agreed. Only they would have argued that Labour should distance itself from permissiveness. Rank and file attitudes are notoriously difficult to uncover and we have to rely on evidence from occasional, and perhaps exceptional, incidents. One such event occurred in Burnley when homosexual activists tried to establish a gay club. Their attempt to rent premises from the Co-op was thwarted by pressure from the local labour movement and the Catholic Church. As one local Labour figure was supposed to have said, there would be no 'buggers club' in Burnley.[48]

All this suggests that the Labour Party was both disunited on the desirability of the permissive society, and the whole question of an expanded political agenda embracing, at least in part, issues of morality. The replacement of Roy Jenkins with Jim Callaghan at the Home Office in November 1967 tipped the balance firmly on the side of traditional working-class moralism. Callaghan opposed the death penalty, but had failed to vote in the final division on its abolition in 1965; claimed to be 'indifferent' to homosexual reform; and remarked that he could not 'bear the young men with hair hanging over their shoulders'.[49] In 1968 – whilst rejecting the liberal proposals of the Wootton Report on Drug Dependancy – he famously remarked that he was anxious to call 'a halt in the alarming tide of so called permissiveness'.[50] It would seem, then, that the analysis of those on the radical right is somewhat exaggerated. To argue that Labour encouraged the emergence of the permissive society is to ignore disputes within the Party over basic principles and strategies. But what of their other claim: that the moral and social changes of the 1960s were far reaching and clear cut?

For Christopher Booker, and many other contemporaries, the 1960s had seen an 'English "revolution" ' in 'almost every conceivable field'.[51] The evidence, however, is less straightforward than it at first sight appears. For example, *Time* magazine claimed that London was 'swinging' solely on the basis of evidence from Soho and the West End.[52] More knowledgeable guides to the metropolis presented a picture of greater complexity.[53] Soho may well have been swinging, but Streatham was most certainly not.

But such oft-quoted observations tell us comparatively little about popular attitudes. And, as O.R. McGregor pointed out in 1971, 'permissive legislation does not make a permissive society'.[54] The following paragraphs are an attempt – using opinion poll data and social surveys – to estimate how liberal public opinion had become in relation to a number of permissive issues.

To the dismay of many commentators the divorce rate rose relentlessly throughout the 1960s. A yearly average of 37,657 petitions for divorce were filed in England and Wales in the first half of the decade; in the second half this rose to 57,089.[55] Opinion polls suggest that the public was divided in its attitude to divorce reform, with the largest single group (30–40 per cent) in favour of making divorce easier.[56] But this did not mean that the institution of marriage became less popular. After all, a majority of all divorcees remarried. Gorer's 1969 survey of the under-45s found that an overwhelming number believed that faithfulness was still the key to a successful marriage.[57] Amongst young people – a group supposedly at the forefront of the 'new morality' – all but a tiny minority saw their adult life in terms of marriage. The views of schoolgirls (aged 14–16) in London in 1968 were just as 'traditional' as those who wrote to teenage magazines in the late 1950s.[58]

Evidence on sexual attitudes and activities is more problematic. Much of it comes from interviews and there are obvious social pressures which may have led some respondents to over- or under-exaggerate. An 18-year-old East Londoner expressed this dilemma succinctly: 'Some people with a big mouth say, "I do this and that with my girl". But they go home and masturbate, the same as everybody else.'[59] That said, the available surveys are consistent with one another, and are therefore probably accurate. Promiscuity seems to have been rare. Only 17 per cent of the 376 25-year-old men and women questioned by Michael Schofield in the early 1970s said they had had intercourse with more than one partner in the last year.[60] Attitudes towards pre-marital sex, particularly amongst the young, did, however, become more tolerant as the decade progressed.[61] In 1963, 66 per cent believed that pre-marital sex between young couples was wrong, even when they intended to marry. In contrast, surveys of young people in the later 1960s and early 1970s suggest that only a small percentage (10 per cent) strongly disapproved of pre-marital sex, although many (40 per cent) remained undecided.

The pill – one of the symbols of the permissive society – was rarely used outside marriage. In 1970, only 9 per cent of single women relied upon it.[62] None the less, the use of birth control by married couples was widely approved.[63] By 1966 there was even a slight majority in favour of providing contraceptive advice to young unmarried couples.[64] However, the decision of the Brook Advisory Centre to admit girls under 16 in 1967 caused public uproar.[65] Despite the increase in both the acceptance and availability of contraception, popular ignorance of sexual matters remained widespread. Many of those involved in the Family Planning Association were conscious of the narrow, largely middle-class, backgrounds of their clients.[66] Sex educationalists were often shocked by the ignorance of teenage boys and girls. This was perhaps not surprising, as a sample of over 500 schools in 1969 found that only 10 per cent 'gave direct information about methods of contraception, and the majority thought that such information should not be given at all'.[67] Sexual matters clearly aroused both fear and confusion in public institutions and private minds alike. In contrast, attitudes to abortion were – religious objections aside – more consistent and less contentious. Large majorities in favour of reform were a feature of every opinion poll between 1965 and 1967.[68]

But tolerance had its limits. The abolition of capital punishment provoked widespread hostility, regardless of age, gender or voting preference.[69] Between 61 and 82 per cent of the public were in favour of the death penalty across the decade.[70] Popular attitudes towards homosexuality were similarly illiberal. Only 12 per cent of those questioned by Gorer expressed a 'tolerant' attitude towards homosexuality; a further 24 per cent felt 'revulsion' and 22 per cent 'pity'.[71] Almost no one expressed tolerance or pity for drug dealers, or even users. In 1967, 88 per cent of the public thought that dealing in 'soft' drugs should be a criminal offence. Some 77 per cent thought that taking them should be as well.[72] The attitudes of young people were surprisingly similar to those of their elders. Only 25 per cent felt that Mick Jagger's sentence of three months imprisonment for the possession of four pep pills was 'too severe'.[73]

By the late 1960s drug taking was widely perceived as the most 'serious social problem' in contemporary Britain.[74] Some 38 per cent of those questioned in February 1970 considered the drug dealer to be the greatest single threat to law and order – more dangerous than professional criminals, teenage gangs, demonstrators and soccer hooligans.[75] 'Honesty' and 'standards of behaviour' were also thought to have declined, particularly since 1968.[76] Indeed opinion polls suggest that popular concern over law and order grew in the late 1960s, and that issues of morality became increasingly intertwined with those of criminality.

Thus a range of evidence suggests that popular attitudes were more complicated than has commonly been assumed. On the one hand, it is possible to trace a growth of liberal values in relation to divorce, abortion and some aspects of sexual practice. On the other, there is little sign of a relaxation in entrenched popular hostility to the abolition of capital punishment or the decriminalization of drugs. In 1969, the editor of New Society remarked: 'Shouldn't one talk of the Cautious Sixties, rather than the Swinging Sixties?'[77] Given the increasing concern with declining standards and law and order in the late 1960s, perhaps the 'Anxious Sixties' would be just as appropriate.

All of the above suggests that the analysis of the radical right is again mistaken. Not only was Labour divided on the desirability of the 'permissive society', but it is also clear that the moral and social changes of the period were far from clear cut. With this latter point in mind, perhaps Labour unease and increased popular anxiety were contributory factors in the Conservative success in the 1970 General Election? To answer this question it is necessary to look at how the Tories were dealing with 'permissiveness' in the late 1950s and 1960s.

Surprisingly, perhaps, the legislative beginnings of the permissive society can in fact be accurately traced to the Macmillan Governments during the years 1957–61. The Homicide Act of 1957 restricted the death penalty to specific types of murder. That same year saw the publication of the Wolfenden Committee Report on Homosexuality and Prostitution. This period also saw a relaxation of the laws relating to gambling with the introduction of Premium Bonds. Off-course betting, legalized gambling clubs and bingo were to follow.[78] Whether such Acts were significant or liberal is beside the point. What is important is that they clearly demonstrate that the permissive society (at least in its legalistic sense) predates the Wilson Governments of 1964–70. Indeed it is possible to identify an influential strand of Tory thinking which actively welcomed this widening of the political agenda. The Bow Group was central to this development and it is to their activities that we shall now turn.

The Bow Group was founded in 1951 as an attempt, at least in part, to provide a Conservative alternative to the Fabian Society. Its membership (largely young and intellectual) shared a belief that Conservatives must understand and respond to the modern world. In the early years their politics were intentionally vague, but by 1960 the *Economist* could accurately describe the Bow Group as a 'shorthand phrase for the Tory left'.[79] Despite the continuing electoral success of the Conservative Party throughout the 1950s, many members of the group became increasingly anxious that the Party's traditional class base was being eroded by affluence. Consequently, it was widely argued that the Conservative Party should attempt to address the upwardly mobile working class, who were at present 'politically homeless'.[80]

This approach was not simply a question of political strategy. It was also part of a wider analysis of post-war affluence which had distinct similarities with revisionist Labour thinking. It found its clearest expression in the pages of the Bow Group's journal, *Crossbow*. Between its inception in 1957 and the early 1960s, *Crossbow* provided a forum, to quote Stuart Hall, for 'the strategy of Conservative modernisation'.[81] Questions of public morality were held to be central to that strategy. Thus, an editorial of 1959 proclaimed 'that the moral fibre of this country *is* the concern of the politician'.[82] The 27 pages that followed addressed the problems of homosexuality, prostitution, divorce, obscene publications and crime. That three of these articles advanced a liberal argument is interesting, but somewhat irrelevant. What is important is the attempt to create a new political agenda based, at least in part, on questions of morality.

It is perhaps not surprising that *Crossbow*'s new agenda[83] failed to win widespread support within the Conservative Party. The Party sources are not abundant on this matter,[84] but it is clear that by the mid-1960s moral traditionalism was again in the ascendancy. In the years to come,

Crossbow's followers were to play their part in supporting some of the Private Members Bills associated with Labour's permissive reforms. Indeed, throughout the period 1964–70 *Crossbow* remained a distinctive and largely 'liberal' voice – on both economic and social matters – within the Conservative Party.[85] Consequently, its relationship with the more traditional wing of the Party was often tense – particularly over questions of morality. It was occasionally farcical too, as the furore which followed the October 1967 issue of *Crossbow* demonstrates. The cover, under the headline 'What are Young Conservatives really like?', showed a young woman, wearing little more than a man's shirt, kneeling before an empty wine glass. Objections came from many quarters. However, most of the adverse comment originated – as the editor of *Crossbow* explained – 'from disgruntled rank and file Tories'. The North West Area Group of the Monday Club, 'considered it in keeping with the simpering weakness of the majority of Bow Groupers' and, moreover, 'an affront to our Party's known feelings about woman and home'.[86] It is all too easy to exaggerate the significance of such outbursts. But the fact that rank and file Tories saw the need to respond is perhaps indicative of the genuine unease which many felt towards the permissive society.

This unease found its yearly release at the Party conference. As Andrew Gamble has noted, Tories debated some aspect of permissiveness in every year between 1965 and 1970.[87] Law and order was debated three times (in 1968 there was 26 motions on the subject); crime, drugs and student unrest were debated once each. Unsurprisingly, few liberal voices were heard. This is not the place for a detailed commentary on the particular debates. What is important for our purposes is the emergence of a redefinition of permissiveness. The 'civilizing' rhetoric of Crosland, Jenkins – or even the Bow Group – is entirely absent. Individual reforms – abortion, divorce, drugs, etc. – were often subsumed under the blanket heading of 'law and order'. In 1969, Conference succeeded in forcing (and winning) a vote on the restoration of capital punishment. The Party Leader, the comparatively moderate Edward Heath, refused to be bound by the decision, but 'it certainly influenced the leadership in making law and order an election issue'.[88]

The Tories, then, played a by no means unimportant role in the emergence of permissiveness. None the less, accepting this, it is clear that majority opinion within all levels of the party remained, at the very least, uneasy about the moral and social changes of the 1960s. Moreover, such unease became open hostility by the end of the decade. Indeed given the feelings of the Tory rank and file and, as we saw earlier, the survival of traditional moralism amongst much of the electorate, Conservative Party strategy in the 1970 election is somewhat puzzling.[89] Only 60 Conservative MPs mentioned law and order in their election addresses,[90] and the Party as a whole concentrated on the economy. Nuffield orthodoxy maintains that such 'bread and butter' issues are almost always more decisive in elections. Yet – as we have seen – opinion polls suggest that issues like crime, drugs and immigration were uppermost in electors' social concerns. How can we account for this lack of fit between popular anxieties and party electoral propaganda? A part explanation is that in the 1960s parties and electors alike had difficulty in embracing a wider definition of the 'political'. As long as permissiveness (or law and order, to use Tory phraseology) remained outside normal conceptions of what constituted politics, it was unlikely to be influential in elections.

After all, this was a problem which Labour revisionists had long struggled to overcome. All this suggests that the 1960s were perhaps an unpropitious time to attempt to construct a new political agenda based, at least in part, on the 'quality of life'. The revisionist analysis of Crosland and Jenkins assumed that economic growth would continue and with it, the decline of inequality. It also – like many other commentaries – seems to have exaggerated the liberalization of popular morality. As the decade progressed, the revisionist alliance became more problematic. By 1968, student unrest and worry about declining standards – particularly in education[91] – meant that the professional middle class was increasingly less convinced of the virtues of the permissive society.

Many in the Labour Party were clearly uneasy too, as this quote from the Labour MP Ted Bishop suggests. In 1970 he could rhetorically ask: 'is permissiveness a bad thing? If one speaks of the word with associations with sex, the Pill, sit-ins, hi-jacking, kidnapping and violence, then of course it is.'[92] The Party's electoral defeat in 1970 even led some revisionists to argue that:

social democracy should re-assert the primacy of its concern for the social and economic rights of its labour constituency and avoid being led down such enticing byways as fashionable libertarianism, the "new politics" of technological revolution, or "students' and workers' power".[93]

And by the early 1970s Crosland himself admitted that some of Labour's working-class supporters may well have felt that the Party no longer addressed their own priorities.[94]

As we have seen, by the end of the 1960s the popular definition of the 'permissive society' may well have had more in common with the version offered by Norman Tebbit than that of Anthony Crosland. Yet, like Labour, the Tories were divided on permissiveness. The Bow Group remained an influential and largely liberal minority voice within the party. In the short term, then, moral questions played little part in Conservative success. But in more recent years 'the assault on the sixties'[95] has stood Margaret Thatcher and the Tory faithful well.

Notes

1 I should like to thank Martin Durham, Joan Keating, Jon Lawrence, Jim Obelkevich and Miles Taylor for useful comments on earlier versions of this chapter. Ray Gosling and Allan Horsfall were generous with both their time and primary sources and for this I am grateful. But my greatest debt is to Nick Tiratsoo who provided criticism and encouragement throughout.
2 N. Tebbit *Britain's Future. A Conservative Vision* (1985) p. 15.
3 *Guardian* 20/3/1989. For an account of the contemporary radical right's attitude to issues of morality see M. Durham *Sex and Politics* (1991).

4 See e.g. B. Masters *The Swinging Sixties* (1985).
5 R. Hewison *Too Much* (1988) is a useful critical overview.
6 K.O. Morgan *The People's Peace* (Oxford, 1990) p. 259.
7 A. Marwick 'The 1960s. Was there a "Cultural Revolution"?' *Contemporary Record* Vol. 2 No. 3 (Autumn 1988) 18–20 and his *British Society Since 1945* (Harmondsworth, 1990 edn).
8 See e.g. C. Davies *Permissive Britain* (1975); T. Fisher 'The Sixties. A Cultural Revolution in Britain' *Contemporary Record* Vol. 3 No. 2 (Nov. 1989) 23.
9 See, in particular, P.G. Richards *Parliament and Conscience* (1970) and B. Pym *Pressure Groups and the Permissive Society* (1974). On the progress of individual reforms, see A. Grey 'Homosexual Law Reform' in B. Frost (ed.) *The Tactics of Pressure* (1975); K. Hindell and M. Simms *Abortion Law Reformed* (1971); S. Jeffrey-Poulter *Peers, Queers and Commons* (1991); A. Leathard *The Fight for Family Planning* (1980); G. Robinson *Obscenity* (1979); J. Weeks *Coming Out* (1977).
10 J. Weeks *Sex, Politics and Society* (2nd edn, 1989) p. 263.   .
11 On the 1969 Divorce Reform Act see J. Lewis 'Public Institution and Private Relationship. Marriage and Marriage Guidance, 1920–1968' *Twentieth Century British History* Vol. 1 No. 3 (1990) 234.
12 Abortion, for example, was not available on demand but by the decision of two doctors; whilst homosexuality was only decriminalized for two consenting adults, aged 21 or over, in private in England and Wales.
13 Richards op. cit. 28.
14 D. McKie and C. Cook (eds) *Election '70* (1970) p. 103.
15 The following paragraphs owe much to S. Hall 'Reformism and the legislation of consent' in National Deviancy Conference (ed.) *Permissiveness and Control* (1980) pp. 31–8 and Weeks *Sex, Politics* op. cit. 265–6.
16 C.A.R. Crosland *The Future of Socialism* (1956) p. 520.
17 Crosland appears to have formulated this aspect of his thesis as early as 1950. See Fabian Society Papers, Nuffield College Oxford, G 50/3 Item 1 [G.D.H. Cole] 'Summary of points: Second conference on "Problems Ahead" Oxford March 1950'. I am grateful to Martin Francis for this reference.
18 See the debate in *Encounter* on 'The Future of the Left' which raged throughout 1960; also M. Abrams et al. *Must Labour Lose?* (Harmondsworth, 1960).
19 See e.g. Labour Party *Labour in the Sixties* (1960) p. 14. The pamphlet was written by the Party's general secretary, Morgan Phillips.
20 Labour Party Archive, Manchester (hereafter *LPA*) Home Policy Sub-Committee minutes, RD. 250, April 1962, 'Non-manual workers and the Labour Party' observations from Geoffrey Drain.
21 Crosland op. cit. 524.
22 R. Wollheim 'Socialism and Culture' (Fabian Tract No. 331, May 1961) p. 12. See also Kingsley Amis (then on the left) reviewing Hoggart's *The Uses of Literacy* in *The Spectator* 1/3/1957 for similar comments.
23 P. Crane 'What's in a party image?' *The Political Quarterly* Vol. 30 No. 3 (1959) 239–40.
24 R. Butt 'Can the Centre be Held?' *Crossbow* Vol. 10 No. 38 (Jan.–March 1967) 21; D. McKie 'The Quality of Life' in D. McKie and C. Cook (eds) *The Decade of Disillusion* (1972) pp. 199–200.
25 Weeks *Sex, Politics* op. cit. 266.
26 See e.g. H. Wilson 'Law Reform and the Citizen' in his *The New Britain* (Harmondsworth, 1964) pp. 82, 84–6; Labour Party *Time for Decision* (1966) p. 19.

27 The most explicit statement appears to be the Labour Research Department's audit of Tory rule, *Twelve Wasted Years* (1963); see especially pp. 297–9.

28 R. Jenkins *A Life at the Centre* (1991) pp. 180–81. His policy blueprint is contained in Chapter 9 'Is Britain Civilized?' in R. Jenkins *The Labour Case* (Harmondsworth, 1959) pp. 135–46.

29 J. Morgan (ed.) *The Backbench Diaries of Richard Crossman* (1981) p. 944. I am grateful to Steve Fielding for this reference. Shore's earlier draft can be found in Modern Records Centre, University of Warwick, Crossman Papers MSS.154/3/LP/1/73.

30 D.E. Butler and A. King *The British General Election of 1964* (1964) and their *The British General Election of 1966* (1966).

31 F. Wheen *Tom Driberg. His Life and Indiscretions* (1990) pp. 359–60.

32 Quoted in P. Fryer 'A Map of the Underground' *Encounter* Vol. XXIV No. 4 (Oct. 1967) 8–9. The MP was very probably Jennie Lee, see J. Green *Days in the Life* (1988) pp. 125–6.

33 See e.g. a letter complaining about the lack of 'politics': 'I welcome the first issue of Focus as a paper, but if the paper is to be political I suggest we have more of it. The only article was on drugs, not very political.' *Focus* Vol. 1 No. 2 (July/Aug. 1966) 2.

34 See e.g. J. Daly 'Labour's lost students' *Socialist Commentary* (July 1963) 8; Editorial 'Youth and party' *Socialist Commentary* (March 1969) 3.

35 E.J. Hobsbawm 'Revolution and Sex' in his *Revolutionaries* (1973) pp. 216–19; Z. Curtis ' "Private" lives and Communism' in E. Phillips (ed.) *The Left and the Erotic* (1983) pp. 152–3.

36 *Challenge* No. 11 (May 1969); No. 14 (Oct. 1969).

37 *Challenge* No. 16 (Dec. 1969); No. 18 (Feb. 1970).

38 David Widgery has written of the 'pre-1968 Left's complete lack of interest' in, amongst other issues, women's and gay liberation. D. Widgery *The Left in Britain 1956–1968* (Harmondsworth, 1976) p. 14.

39 J. Saville 'The Politics of *Encounter*' in R. Miliband and J. Saville (eds) *The Socialist Register 1964* (1964) p. 197.

40 R. Samuel 'Born-again Socialism' in Oxford University Socialist Discussion Group (eds) *Out of Apathy* (1989) p. 51.

41 See Richards op. cit. 195 for an analysis of Labour members attitudes to each permissive reform.

42 N. Tiratsoo 'Popular politics, affluence and the Labour party in the 1950s' in A. Gorst et al. (eds) *Contemporary British History 1931–1961* (1991) especially pp. 53–5.

43 Quoted in *Richmond and Barnes Clarion* (April 1970) 4.

44 Labour Party *Resolutions for the Annual Conference of the Labour Party* various years 1962–9.

45 'Readers points of view. Should divorce be easier?' *Labour Woman* Vol. 57 No. 3 (March 1968) 50, 62; M. Marshall 'Putney sets up a working party' *Labour Woman* Vol. 59 No. 4 (April 1969) 67.

46 *Esher and Walton Clarion* (Feb. 1966) 5.

47 *Richmond and Barnes Clarion* (May 1966) 5.

48 R. Gosling *Personal Copy* (1980) p. 121 and further information supplied by the author. The club in Burnley was only one of a number of similar ventures. On that, and the difficulties of discussing homosexuality within the Labour Party in the late 1950s and 1960s see: *New Society* 29/8/1968; A. Horsfall 'Wolfenden in the Wilderness' *New Left Review* No. 12 (Nov./Dec. 1961) and his 'Battling for Wolfenden' in B. Cant and S. Hemmings (eds) *Radical Records* (1988) pp.

20–30.
49 Quoted in P. Kellner and C. Hitchens *Callaghan: The Road to Number Ten* (1976) pp. 77–8.
50 Quoted in Weeks *Sex, Politics* op. cit. 276.
51 C. Booker *The Neophiliacs* (1969) p. 12.
52 *Time* 15/4/1966.
53 H. Davies (ed.) *The New London Spy* (1966); L. Deighton (ed.) *Len Deighton's London Dossier* (Harmondsworth, 1967).
54 O.R. McGregor 'Equality, sexual values and permissive legislation: the English experience' *Journal of Social Policy* Vol. 1 No. 1 (1972) 57.
55 D. Coleman 'Population' in A. H. Halsey (ed.) *British Social Trends since 1900* (1988) p. 80.
56 *Gallup Political Index* (hereafter *GPI*) No. 42 (July 1963) 130; No. 80 (Dec. 1966) 161; Nos 93/94 (Jan. 1968) 214; No. 98 (June 1968) 70; No. 110 (June 1969)105.
57 G. Gorer *Sex and Marriage in England Today* (1973) pp. 189, 364–5.
58 *New Society* 30/5/1968; *LPA* Labour Party Youth Commission (1959) YC 13, 17, 24, 25.
59 P. Willmott *Adolescent Boys of East London* (Harmondsworth, 1969 edn) p. 54.
60 M. Schofield *The Sexual Behaviour of Young Adults* (1973) p. 179.
61 *GPI* No. 43 (Sept. 1963) 152; C. Farrell 'Sexual Attitudes and Behaviour of Young People' in W.H.G. Armytage et al. (eds) *Changing Patterns of Sexual Behaviour* (1980) pp. 60–61; M. Schofield *The Sexual Behaviour of Young People* (1965) pp. 130–31.
62 M. Bone *The Family Planning Services* (1978) p. 85.
63 *GPI* No. 52 (July 1964) 88; No. 100 (Aug. 1968) 107.
64 *GPI* No. 75 (July 1966) 90.
65 *Guardian* 3/1/1991.
66 L. Manning *A Life for Education* (1970) p. 252.
67 *New Statesman* 28/2/1969.
68 *NOP Political Bulletin* (hereafter *NOP*) (April 1965) appendix 1–2; (June 1966) special supplement 2; *GPI* No. 82 (Feb. 1967) 34.
69 I. Crewe et al. *The British Electorate 1963–1987* (Cambridge, 1991) pp. 408–9.
70 *GPI* No. 32 (Aug. 1962) 147; No. 58 (Feb. 1965) 13; No. 75 (July 1966) 90; No. 117 (Jan. 1970) 7.
71 Gorer op. cit. 255.
72 *GPI* No. 88 (Aug. 1967) 126.
73 Ibid. 130.
74 *GPI* No. 60 (May 1965) 53; No. 86 (June 1967) 90; No. 105 (Jan. 1969) 12; No. 129 (Apr. 1971) 75.
75 *NOP* (Feb. 1970) 15–16.
76 For example, 65 per cent were 'dissatisfied' with the honesty and standards of behaviour in Britain in 1971 compared with 51 per cent in 1964. *GPI* No. 51 (June 1964) 68; No. 98 (June 1968) 69; No. 107 (March 1969) 55; No. 126 (Jan. 1971) 7.
77 *New Society* 27/11/1969.
78 The passage of these Acts is described by the home secretary of the time, R.A. Butler, in his autobiography *The Art of the Possible* (1971) pp. 200–4.
79 Quoted in R. Rose 'The Bow Group's Role in British Politics' *The Western Political Quarterly* Vol. XIV No. 4 (Dec. 1961) 865.
80 See e.g. C. Curran 'The New Model Bourgeoisie' and R. Rose 'Going up and in between' *Crossbow* Vol. 6 No. 21 (Oct.–Dec. 1962).

81 Hall op. cit. 30.
82 'A New Conscience' *Crossbow* Vol. 2 No. 2 (New Year 1959) 7.
83 T. Raison *Why Conservative?* (Harmondsworth, 1964) remains the clearest statement of Bow Group thinking on moral and social questions, see in particular, pp. 82–96.
84 The Conservative Party archive allows only limited access to material dated 1965 and after.
85 The Bow Group maintained its interest in matters of social policy throughout the 1960s. For example, during the public debate on the Wootton Report it established a research team on drugs. See T. White 'Conservatives and Cannabis' *Crossbow* Vol. 12 No. 47 (April/June 1969).
86 *Crossbow* Vol. 11 No. 42 (Jan./March 1968) 6. The offending cover was even attacked during the conference debate on drugs! See Conservative Party *Conference Report 1967* (1967) p. 104.
87 The following is largely drawn from A. Gamble *The Conservative Nation* (1974) pp. 110–15.
88 Ibid. 114.
89 I. Crewe and B. Sarlvik 'Popular Attitudes and Electoral Strategy' in Z. Layton-Henry (ed.) *Conservative Party Politics* (1980) comes to similar conclusions in respect of the 1974 election pp. 260–72.
90 D. Butler and M. Pinto-Duschinsky *The British General Election of 1970* (1971) p. 438.
91 The first of the Black Papers on education was published in 1969. It is often forgotten that the editors claimed to have voted Labour in 1966. See C.B Cox and A.E. Dyson (eds) *The Black Papers on Education* (1971) p. 10.
92 T. Bishop 'Permissiveness – good or bad?' *Labour Woman* Vol. 60 No. 6 (July/Aug. 1970) 118.
93 J. Gyford and S. Haseler 'Social democracy: beyond revisionism' (Fabian Research Series No. 292, 1971) 1.
94 A. Crosland 'Labour and "Populism" ' in his *Socialism Now* (1974) pp. 98–102.
95 The phrase is David Edgar's; see his 'The Free and the Good' in R. Levitas (ed) *The Ideology of the New Right* (Cambridge, 1986) p. 55.

8 Wilson and the security services

Robin Ramsay

In Harold Wilson's book *The Governance of Britain*, there is a chapter titled 'The Prime Minister and National Security'. It is headed by this quotation from Harold Macmillan:

It is dangerous and bad for our general national interest to discuss these matters. It has been a very long tradition in the House to trust the relations between the two parties to discussions between the Leader of the Opposition and the Prime Minister of the day. I ask the House now to revert to the older tradition which I think is in our real interests. Otherwise we would risk destroying services which are of the utmost value to us.

Wilson added 18 bland lines on the formal relationship between the incumbent at Number 10 and the secret state and closed the chapter with these words:

The Prime Minister is occasionally questioned on matters arising out of his responsibility ['for national security authorities at home and abroad']. His answers may be regarded as uniformly uninformative. There is no further information that can usefully or properly be added before bringing this Chapter to an end.

The Governance of Britain was published in 1976, just after Wilson had resigned as Prime Minister. At the time Wilson was working with the journalists Barrie Penrose and Roger Courtiour in an attempt to mount a private investigation into the activities of MI5 against him and his Governments; in so doing he was breaking his Privy Council Oath and the Official Secrets Act.

The '13 wasted years' of Conservative rule from 1951 had also been years of uninterrupted growth and prosperity in the Anglo-American security services.[1] With the Cold War as the backdrop, they attempted to regulate the entire non-communist world.[2] Under the general rubric of 'the communist threat', and assisted by sections of the right-wing of the labour movement, the American and British security services tried to police the British

Labour Party and the trade unions.[3] Though much of the detail is still missing, it is now clear that in 1947 and 1948, a collection of loose alliances began to form in this country between some union and Labour Party officials, the Foreign Office/MI6 propaganda and psychological warfare organization, the Information Research Department, and some police special branches. The impetus was coming from US personnel in Britain, initially those attached to the implementation of the Marshall Plan. This network engaged in political and psychological warfare against people they described as the communists and their fellow travellers (but who now look more like the British left in general) and promoted the social democratic wings of socialist parties and trade union movements.[4] Known inside the CIA as the NCLs – the non-communist left – the social democrats were perceived by the more sophisticated, liberal wing of the CIA to be the most reliable anti-communist allies.[5]

Throughout the 1950s the British social democrats – now thought of mostly as the Gaitskellites – crossed the Atlantic on US government-sponsored visits to congenial locations with the anglophile WASPs of the east coast of America who were then running American foreign policy.[6] On such trips they acquired views of American society that were about as rational as those held by their equivalents 20 years before, who had seen in the Stalinist Soviet Union the embodiment of their yearnings for a socialist society.[7] Harold Wilson, on the other hand, travelled east as well as west. Exploiting the knowledge he had acquired of Anglo-Soviet trade while a minister in the Attlee Government, he had become a consultant to the timber importers Montagu Meyer, and was thus trading with the official enemy. Wilson, to use one of MI5's euphemisms, was suspected of digging with the wrong foot.

Regular visits behind the Iron Curtain during the Cold War's frostiest years was enough to put Wilson on the British security establishment's agenda. Worse, Wilson had led the Labour Party attack on the City of London during the Bank Rate affair in 1957, and then used the Profumo affair to question the competence of both MI5 and the Macmillan Government.[8] Attacking the City and the secret arms of Whitehall made Wilson the Labour politician hated most by the Conservative Party and the British establishment, then largely co-terminous.[9]

When Wilson took office in 1964 with a majority of four he suspected that the Tories would look for a Profumo-esque scandal to use against him. Centrally he saw his defence against this as avoiding the charge of not knowing what was going on, the weapon he had so successfully levelled against Macmillan. He changed the rules on telephone tapping, forbidding the British security services to tap an MP's telephone without permission from Wilson himself, and appointed George Wigg as Postmaster General to keep his eye on the intelligence services, especially MI5. His ally in the Profumo campaign, Wigg would warn Wilson of any Profumo-like embarrassments.

That was the theory, anyway. The success of the Wilson–Wigg team during the Profumo affair seems to have given them a false self-confidence about their ability to deal with the secret state. In fact, neither of them had experience of the security services. In Wilson's Cabinet only Richard Crossman could be said to have any knowledge of the secret corridors of Whitehall, and that had been in wartime psychological warfare, a long way out from the core intelligence and counter-espionage activities. To a degree which is now difficult to imagine, the 'secret services' were then still secret – at any rate from British tax-payers and their representatives in the House of Commons. For independent financial advice Wilson could turn to the banker Siegmund Warburg; but in this field he had no Warburg and followed the post-war custom that relations between the prime minister of the day and the security services be mediated through the Cabinet Secretary – in this case Burke Trend – and the Cabinet Office. The secret state would be left to regulate itself, as usual.[10]

In some accounts Wigg is portrayed as Wilson's 'spymaster' and some of the parliamentary Labour Party certainly disliked his enthusiastic application of security methods.[11] With Wigg dead the truth may never be known for certain, but Chapman Pincher, who knew him during this period, has provided a convincing portrait of Wigg the security *naif* being 'captured' by the agency he was supposed to oversee, and shunted off into the harmless backwaters of MI5's C Branch, to busy himself with the mundane, though not unimportant business of physical security and vetting in the Armed Forces.[12] Though Wilson is reported as being suspicious of the security services' activities within the Labour Party in the early 1960s, his behaviour in the security dramas during the early years of his terms in office is that of someone trying very hard to co-operate with a system he accepted as legitimate.

His first major encounter with the security system came during the seamen's strike in 1966. In pursuit of a pay claim, the National Union of Seamen struck for the first time since 1911. Although the employers were willing to settle, Wilson (and Cabinet) were trying to enforce a pay policy and the proposed settlement exceeded the figure they wanted to impose. MI5 and Special Branch comprehensively penetrated and covertly surveyed the strike leadership. To the disgust of the left-wing of his own party, Wilson eventually used this intelligence to denounce alleged communist influence on the strike.[13] For the left, Wilson's use of the anti-communist card against a trade union, in concert with the security services, was a tremendous blow. One of the things which had distinguished him from the Gaitskellites – and thus won him support from the left of the parliamentary Labour Party – was precisely his refusal to engage in this kind of anti-communism. But though the then young minister Anthony Wedgwood-Benn felt 'sick' at Wilson's naming of the alleged communists, he also added, two sentences later, that 'every trade union leader knew it [i.e. Communist Party involvement in industrial disputes]'.[14] For the practical politician in Wilson, however, the important thing about his naming of the Communists in the Commons was the fact that the strike crumbled almost immediately.

Was Wilson seduced by the potential political power of MI5's tapping and bugging facilities? This is unclear. He seems to have played the anti-communist card very reluctantly. Originally Wigg briefed the press with hints and nudges based on MI5/Special Branch penetration of the strike but most of the press refused to co-operate.[15] Only then, after a meeting with some of the officers from the operation, including the man in charge of it, the head of F-Branch, and after being shown transcripts of intercepts, did Wilson stand up in the Commons and read his list of the alleged Communists supposedly interfering with the strike.[16] Prime ministers rarely, if ever, meet operational security service personnel and it is hard not to see here Wilson needing to have his arm twisted to use the security material.[17] Despite the torrent of criticism from the left, Wilson was unrepentant, devoting nearly three pages of his memoir of the period to parts of the notorious speech.[18]

Equally unclear is the real status of the alleged Communist Party involvement in the strike. The Labour Government's attempt to impose a wages policy was being opposed by every left-winger worth his or her salt. Paul Foot called Wilson's use of MI5's information 'perhaps the worst example of the official use of MI5 disinformation for a short-term and reactionary political objective'.[19] But it is not clear that Wilson was given MI5 *dis*-information. We do not actually know what Wilson was told. He did not claim in the Commons that the Communist Party members were *controlling* the strike, merely that they sought to do so. The latter is axiomatic.[20] What is clear, however, is that Wilson was trying to co-operate with the secret state.[21]

For some the reality mattered not. By 1964 Wilson had visited the Soviet Union a dozen times and was viewed by the right-wing in MI5 and the CIA as a fellow traveller, or at best as someone who had been exposed too many times to the possibility of KGB entrapment, and who was therefore an actual or potential security risk.[22] Between 1964 and 1970 there were more or less continuous investigations by MI5 of Wilson and his friends in particular, and the parliamentary Labour Party in general. The impetus for some of this came from the CIA's counter-intelligence branch, the senior partners in the MI5–CIA relationship.[23] Useful pretexts for investigations were provided by a series of Soviet bloc defectors who alleged – or apparently alleged: media assets of the Anglo-American security services have reported that they alleged – Soviet bloc penetration of the Labour Party and the trade unions.[24] Nominally looking for 'threats to security', between 1964 and 1970 MI5 investigated Labour MPs Richard Crossman, Charles Loughlin, Raymond Fletcher, Barnett Stross, John Stonehouse, Tom Driberg, John Diamond, Niall McDermot, Harold Davies, Stephen Swingler and Bernard Floud that we know of, and unknown numbers of others.[25]

The promising career of junior minister Niall McDermot, for example, came to an end for no better reason than that 15 years previously his wife had (unwittingly, she said) worked for a Soviet film distribution company in Italy which turned out to have been a front for a KGB officer. Evidence that McDermot or his wife had done anything was not necessary. The cases of John Stonehouse and Charles Loughlin, also junior ministers, provide striking examples of MI5's hostility to Labour. Approached by Czech diplomats, both reported the contact to their departmental MI5 officers, as per regulations. Both were then used as bait, 'dangles', in intelligence terms.

Not informed that the Czech 'diplomats' in question were suspected intelligence officers, they were allowed to carry on meeting them. Loughlin eventually realized the danger he was in and complained.[26]

Stonehouse, unfortunately, apparently never did. MI5 believed – or found it useful to pretend to believe – that Stonehouse was a Czech agent. In late 1969 the Czech defector Joseph Frolik claimed that he had been told by his predecessor in London, Husak, that Stonehouse was an agent of theirs. But MI5 already knew about Husak and Stonehouse – from Stonehouse himself. Had Stonehouse really been an SIB (Czech intelligence) agent, as some in MI5 apparently believed, would the SIB send one of its officers to have lunch with him? Would that agent then report the contact to MI5? In 1969, armed with the Czech defector Frolik's account of what his predecessor Husak had claimed, MI5 went to Wilson about Stonehouse. Wilson had them question Stonehouse in his presence. With no evidence, merely the Frolik hearsay, MI5 did not convince Wilson that Stonehouse had a case to answer. In fact MI5 knew that Stonehouse was innocent. The MI5 officer at the Department of Technology boasted to his Minister, Tony Benn, that they had been surveying Stonehouse's meetings with Husak. Offering no evidence at the meeting with Wilson and Stonehouse, MI5 tacitly acknowledged that the surveillance had found nothing.[27] Rejected – correctly – by Wilson, MI5 promptly leaked the allegations about Stonehouse to their media contacts.[28]

These extensive investigations – and we must presume that those we know of are the tip of an iceberg – produced only one prosecution. Will Owen MP was identified by Frolik and eventually charged with breach of the Official Secrets Act. The prosecution turned to apparent farce when Owen's QC merely pointed out to the court that the material Owen had been passing to the Czechs was not, in fact, classified.[29] In his diary Richard Crossman commented at the time that he thought the Czechs were fools to pay for this sort of rubbish.[30] Did MI5 and the DPP's office really not notice that the material Owen was passing was not classified? Or was it simply that for political reasons they wanted the publicity a trial would generate?

When information on these various episodes leaked out after Labour's General Election defeat in 1970, many were inclined to dismiss them as simply part of Wilson's paranoia. Nevertheless, it is clear that what happened in the 1960s was part of a long-standing pattern, shaped by the belief, prevalent on the right and amongst those in sections of the security services, that Wilson was a dangerous leftist and possibly a Soviet agent.[31] Confirmation of the campaign against Wilson came in the 1970s, with a series of events that can be briefly summarized as follows.

In the early years of the new decade, the subversion hunters looked back on the 1960s – on CND, the rise of the new left, the emergence of the IRA, the anti-Vietnam war movement, and growing industrial unrest – and saw the Soviet 'hidden hand' at work. Confirmation of this 'insight' seemed to be provided by the 1973 abolition of Labour's 'proscription list' of organizations incompatible with Party membership – mostly inconsequential Communist Party fronts.[32]

But surely the Communist Party of Great Britain had been in decline since the end of the Second World War? Or was it the student membership of the International Socialists who would bring the system crashing down? It did not matter. Inside MI5, F-Branch, which monitored the domestic left, began rapid expansion in 1973.[33] As industrial conflict spread during the winter of 1973/4, the subversive-hunters regarded the prospect of another Labour Government with alarm. Against the background of the three-day week, power cuts and the revival of the British candle industry, Edward Heath campaigned in February 1974 on a straight anti-union ticket, asking the electorate, 'Who should rule Britain?'. Apparently unimpressed, half the voters said 'Not you, anyway', and, to Wilson's surprise, returned a minority Labour Government.[34] For Wilson it was like 1964 again; in March 1974 another general election could not be far away.

The period between the February and October general elections in 1974 is the most extraordinary in post-war British history. Onto the Labour Party in general, and Harold Wilson in particular, descended an unprecedented torrent of covert and psychological warfare operations, too complex to do more than merely highlight here. Wilson and all those around him were burgled repeatedly.[35] Private militias, notably Civil Assistance led by General Sir Walter Walker, recently retired from service with NATO, began to prepare to meet the 'communist threat'; the newspapers discussed the conditions for a British *coup d'état*; tanks and troops ringed Heathrow in 'anti-terrorism exercises'.[36] Packages of disinformation about Wilson and other Labour MPs were circulated to the media: some sent to *The Times* ending up at the magazine *Private Eye*.[37] Forgeries were circulated implicating Leader of the House of Commons Edward Short and Harold Wilson in financial corruption; and MI5 made a clumsy attempt to persuade Wilson that Cabinet member Judith Hart was a security risk.[38]

In Northern Ireland a general strike was organized by the Protestant wing of the labour movement against the so-called Power-Sharing Executive inherited by Wilson and Northern Ireland Secretary Merlyn Rees from the Heath Government. As only Robert Fisk seemed to notice at the time, the strike was condoned by the Army. More than a decade later, former British Army Information Officer Colin Wallace revealed that the MI5 personnel then in charge of the intelligence effort in Northern Ireland positively hoped the strike would succeed – and embarrass Harold Wilson in the process.[39] Information Officer Colin Wallace was also a member of the British Army's psychological warfare unit, the Information Policy Unit, in Lisburn Army HQ, Northern Ireland. Part of Wallace's work involved the creation of 'black' propaganda about the Northern Irish political scene. To do this he was supplied with briefing documents, some from MI5. After the February 1974 election the source material Wallace was given to work from changed. The names on the files began to change from the likes of Reverend Ian Paisley and Gerry Adams to Harold Wilson, Marcia Falkender and Jeremy Thorpe. In Wallace's notes made from these files in 1974 are the same allegations and disinformation about Wilson, Mrs Williams *et al* that emerged in this period through other sources.[40]

Yet this extraordinary onslaught between the elections failed to remove the Labour Government. Alas for MI5 and others, the indifference of the

British electorate to matters Northern Irish extended to the fall of the province's government. The disinformation campaigns came and went and the electorate refused to turn Labour out of office. In October 1974 the Labour Party was returned to power – though without the increased majority it had achieved in similar circumstances in 1966. At this stage no one in the parliamentary Labour Party knew for certain who was behind what they perceived as a 'dirty tricks' campaign. It was his publisher and friend George Weidenfeld who informed Wilson that his secret enemy was MI5. Wilson felt sufficiently angry to send a message to the CIA, using Weidenfeld and US Senator Hubert Humphrey as a 'back channel' to bypass the British security organizations; and then he called in Maurice Oldfield, Chief of MI6 and put it to him that MI5 were operating against him and his government. Seizing the opportunity to denigrate his bureaucratic rival, Oldfield confirmed the existence of a disaffected group of MI5 officers.[41]

'A section of MI5 is plotting against your government' was an extraordinary piece of information. But what could Wilson do with it? He had no evidence; and who would investigate MI5? Had this occurred at the beginning of his career, Wilson might have been forced to do something *qua* Prime Minister. As it was, he was close to retirement, and he did nothing.[42] Once he had resigned, however, he tried and failed to enlist the editors of the *Guardian* and *Observer* newspapers to investigate the operations against him, and ended up using two BBC journalists to run a secret investigation with himself acting as their clandestine source. News of this was promptly leaked from senior BBC management and instead of an investigation into MI5, Wilson found himself facing veiled threats from the British state about his apparent breach of the Official Secrets Act and his Privy Council Oath. With no political support from the parliamentary Labour Party or the media, Wilson abandoned his investigation, issued a completely false account of his activities with the two journalists, and gave the whole thing up.[43]

Since 1977 Wilson has said almost nothing on this subject. He had challenged the security services in a way no other prime minister has ever done – and got his fingers badly burned. Even though his memory has not been good in recent years, he must have felt at least a flicker of vindication as the combined testimony of Colin Wallace and Peter Wright forced the story of the security services' operations against him and his governments onto the political agenda in the late 1980s.

Notes

1 Rather than repeat the phrase 'security and intelligence services' over and over again, I have used the term 'security services' to stand for 'security and intelligence services'. That phrase, in any case, would be more accurate as 'security, intelligence, propaganda, covert operations and surveillance services'.
2 The best single volume survey on the CIA's post-war regulatory activities is W. Blum's *The CIA: a Forgotten History* (1986). Some idea of the ambition of the American effort is provided by declassified files from the 1950s which show that

the State Department was surveying the trade unions and left of tiny New Zealand. These files are described at some length in issue 65 of *Watchdog*, the newsletter of the Campaign Against Foreign Control of New Zealand, PO Box 2258, Wellington, New Zealand. The best account of the network of US-dominated intelligence and security treaties is J. Richelson and D. Ball's *The Ties That Bind* (1985).

3 Despite the millions of words on the Cold War, its revisionists and the post-revisionists, it is still unclear whether or not there actually was a 'communist threat' to post-war Western Europe, or simply communist-led opposition to the US Marshall Plan, amplified for propaganda purposes.

4 On IRD see, in particular, L. Smith 'Covert British Propaganda: The Information Research Department: 1947–77' *Millennium* Vol. 9 No. 1. On the role of US personnel see P. Weiler *British Labour and the Cold War* (Stanford, California, 1988), especially chapter 6, and A. Carew *Labour Under the Marshall Plan* (Manchester, 1987) in particular pp. 127–30. On two of this network's front groups, see R. Ramsay and S. Dorril 'In a Common Cause' in *Lobster* No. 19 (1989). An example of the Party-state collaboration is in the third published volume of Tony Benn's Diaries *Against the Tide* (1989) at p. 421 where Sir Harry Crane, of the GMWU, who had chaired the agenda-setting Conference Arrangements Committee of the Labour Party for years, tells Benn that he had acted as a conduit for information between MI5 and Sara Barker, the Party's National Agent.

The temptation to smear non-communist political opponents proved irresistible to some on the right of the labour movement. When the now retired trade union leader, Clive Jenkins, was seeking selection as a parliamentary candidate in the early 1960s, 'a foolscap duplicated document' was circulated among the members of the committee which selected the Parliament candidate. Depicting Jenkins as Britain's leading Trotskyist, the document was the work of Jim Mathews, a member of the Labour Party's National Executive. See C. Jenkins *All Against The Collar* (1990) pp. 49–51. More relevantly, 'Big Jim' Mathews was an active member of Common Cause, the anti-communist group which specialized in circulating lists of real or imaginary 'reds' and subversives. One such received wide publicity the year after the Jenkins document. Among its list of communists and fellow travellers were Bertrand Russell and Lord Boyd-Orr! See *The Sunday Times* 31/5/1964. On Mathews see *Private Eye* 17/9/1966.

5 It is too often forgotten that, especially in the early 1950s, the CIA had a distinctly liberal wing, centred round the International Organizations Division. The liberals had come from the CIA's predecessor, the OSS, whose wartime personnel had included one Herbert Marcuse. One of these operations was the Congress for Cultural Freedom network, through which the CIA promoted the social democratic wing of the Labour Party, providing money, access, contacts, travel and exposure through the columns of the Congress's world-wide stable of magazines, especially the British representative, *Encounter*. Another operation was headed by the US Labour Attaché at the London Embassy, Joseph Godson. Though he reported formally to the State Department, Godson's real superiors were probably the CIA. Some of the US Labour Attaché network in Europe at this time certainly was run by the Agency: their main agent in the international union movement was the late Irving Brown, whose case officer, the late Paul Sakwa, was in place under cover as the Assistant Labour Attaché at the US embassy in Brussels. (On Sakwa see J. Kwitney *Endless Enemies* (New York, 1984) p. 345). For a general account of the US union–CIA connection see W. Peck 'The AFL–CIA' in Howard Frazier (ed.) *Uncloaking the CIA* (1978) pp.

226–76. In the 1950s and early 1960s, however, the rivalry between the various US foreign policy and intelligence bureaucracies was not as pronounced as it became later, nor the CIA as powerful, and which arm of US foreign policy paid the bills was less significant than it seems now. CIA or not, Joe Godson became the confidant of many of the British social democrats, especially the leader of the Party, Hugh Gaitskell, and the Durham miners' leader, Sam Watson, Gaitskell's main ally on the Labour Party's National Executive Committee. (Watson's daughter married Godson's son.) It says something about the way British politics is taught and discussed in this country that Gaitskell's biographer, Philip Williams, could write in 1983 that 'Gaitskell came in time to feel that he [Joe Godson] was involving himself too deeply in Labour Party affairs', without anybody apparently being interested. (P. Williams *The Diaries of Hugh Gaitskell 1945–56* (1983) p. 384, fn 34.)

6 On this network see in particular L.H. Shoup and W. Minter *Imperial Brain Trust: the Council on Foreign Relations and United States Foreign Policy* (London and New York, 1977).

7 As we are still at the very preliminary stages in our understanding of the post-war operations in Britain by the Anglo-American security forces, it is impossible to even estimate how important all these clandestine influence operations actually were. Would the social democrats have carried the day without covert US support? I suspect so.

8 On the Bank rate affair, P. Ferris *The City* (Harmondsworth, 1962) Chapter 7 is the only account I am aware of.

9 There is also a particular congruence between MI6 and the City of London. In his *Inside Intelligence* (1990) former MI6 officer Anthony Cavendish describes (pp. 145–6) how, in the first year after joining the merchant bank Brandts, he hired 'three former MI6 operatives to help [him] track down international business for the bank'.

10 In practice this left Wilson at the mercy of the Cabinet Office and the Cabinet Secretary. It is unclear if Wilson knew that Trend was 'something of a shop steward for the secret servants of the state in lieu of the union they cannot join [and] made sure they got their fair share of honours and allowances and, naturally enough, became a great favourite with them' (P. Hennessy *Whitehall* (1989) p. 213).

11 See volume one of Tony Benn's diary *Out of the Wilderness* (1987) entries for 16 and 22 February and 1 March 1967: 'He is an evil man'.

12 See C. Pincher *Too Secret Too Long* (1984) p. 588 and his *The Truth About Dirty Tricks* (1991) p. 77.

13 Like so much of the Wilson period, the Seamen's strike awaits re-examination. A start is made in S. Dorril and R. Ramsay *Smear! Wilson and the Secret State* (1991) Chapter 18.

14 Benn *Out of the Wilderness* op. cit. 439.

15 This is a very curious episode. How often has the *Daily Mail*, for example, refused to print a story alleging communist influence in a union? In this instance it did.

16 In his memoir Wilson claimed that the state operation produced intelligence so good that 'we could predict the exact line the group would take at the next meeting'. (*The Labour Government* (1974) p. 308).

17 See D. Leigh *The Wilson Plot* (1988) pp. 105–6.

18 In a letter to the author Tony Benn suggested that Wilson's later inability to really go for MI5 when he discovered they were plotting against him was the result of his earlier use of the same service. This is plausible, but unsubstantiated.

19 *Spectator* 16/11/1991.

20 In the *Independent* 14/11/1991, a senior CPGB member from the period admitted that there was covert CPGB funding from Moscow at this time. This raises the possibility – no more yet – that MI5's thesis that 'Moscow gold' was influencing the strike may yet turn out to be true.

21 He was still trying to co-operate with the secret state during the D-Notice Affair the following year; and, once again, his co-operation got him into trouble. The Affair is too complex to describe adequately here but it is now clear that much of Wilson's apparently inexplicable behaviour during 'the Affair' could have been explained had he been willing to reveal the subtext which involved GCHQ at Cheltenham and the US National Security Agency. Unwilling to divulge the secret subtext, Wilson had to ride out a torrent of incomprehension and scorn. The D-Notice Affair is discussed at some length in chapter 19 of Dorril and Ramsay op. cit.

22 It is unclear to me if there actually is any operational difference between a potential security risk and an actual security risk. Neither are employed by Whitehall; both are investigated by MI5.

23 See E.J. Epstein *Deception* (1989) pp. 80–82 for one example.

24 I write 'apparently' because accounts of what each of these defectors actually did or did not say have emerged through a variety of Anglo-American intelligence 'assets' in the media whose credibility is intrinsically low. My impression is that between them the defectors had almost no concrete information, and that either their allegations were simply useful pegs on which to hang various security service prejudices, or the defectors involved systematically exaggerated the nature of their contacts with the Labour Party and union movement. A defector exaggerating his exploits would hardly be news. For a more than usually balanced assessment of the significance of some of the post-war Soviet defectors, see G. Brook-Shepherd *The Storm Birds: Soviet Post-war Defectors* (1988).

25 The potential list is much longer than this. In 1974 Colin Wallace received derogatory information from MI5 on a great many other Labour MPs. On this see below.

26 *New Socialist* (May 1985).

27 Tony Benn diaries vol 2, *Office Without Power* (1988) entry for 12 March 1970.

28 On media leaks, see C. Pincher *Inside Story* (1978) pp. 112–12 and Leigh op. cit. 193. Loughlin described his experiences in *New Socialist* (May 1985). The best account of Frolik is in Leigh op. cit. 163–80.

29 The best account of the Owen case is in Leigh op. cit. 174–6.

30 *The Diaries of Richard Crossman* vol 3 (1977) p. 913.

31 The rationality of this view may be measured against the single fact of Wilson's support for Barbara Castle's union-regulating legislation in the 1969 *In Place of Strife* proposals.

32 Best single volume from the anti-subversion lobby is B. Crozier (ed.) *We Will Bury You* (1970). The significance of the proscription list abolition is to be found in virtually all the commentators on the political right with contacts in the security services. Chapman Pincher, for example, announced in his 1978 *Inside Story* (pp. 326–7) that after its abolition 'members of the Labour Party, including MPs, were free to join organizations such as the British–Soviet Friendship Society, the International Union of Students, the British Peace Committee and the World Peace Council'. To Pincher these are clearly the names of organizations worthy of being called 'subversive'. The truth is, however, that in 1973 they had no influence whatsoever on the British left, let alone wider British society. Nor is it obvious that they ever had any influence in Britain.

33 P. Wright *Spycatcher* (New York, 1987) p. 359. A cynic might argue that, having expelled over 100 alleged KGB officers from Britain in 1971, there was not much of a 'Soviet threat' left for MI5 to combat. What there was, however, was the British domestic left.

34 Heath tried and failed to do a deal with the Liberals. It would not have succeeded anyway, if Joe Haines, then Wilson's press officer, is to be believed. According to Haines there were at least two Labour ministers who would have used the Norman Scott allegations of homosexuality against Liberal leader Jeremy Thorpe to stymie any Lib–Con deal.

35 Perhaps 30 such burglaries in all – and how many undetected? Many were described in Wilson's submission to the Royal Commission on the Press, published in *The Times* 14/5/1977. A fuller list is in Dorril and Ramsay op. cit. 292–4, 373 n.6.

36 Civil Assistance began as the Civil Assistance wing of George Kennedy Young's Unison Committee for Action. Young had retired in 1961 as Vice Chief of MI6.

37 Examples of one of them are reproduced in P. Marnham *Trail of Havoc* (1987). According to Peter Wright, the distribution of such packs, based on MI5 files, was planned by some MI5 personnel. See Wright op. cit. 369.

38 The best account of the Judith Hart episode is Leigh op. cit. 228–30. The Short forgery episode was re-opened in 1987 by Labour MP Dale Campbell-Savours without any great illumination. Tory MP Rupert Allason ('Nigel West'), with access to security service personnel, claimed in his *Molehunt* (1987) p. 102 that the Short forgery was the work of MI5.

39 See R. Fisk *The Point of No Return* (1975). Wallace first made his allegation in a 24-page document written in 1984, while he was still in prison. The claims of Fisk, Wallace and corroboration from a former UDA 'intelligence officer', James Miller, are discussed in P. Foot *Who Framed Colin Wallace?* (1989) pp. 68–74.

40 Over 70 Westminster Members of Parliament are named in Wallace's notes, almost all of them in derogatory or 'enemy' contexts. The notes have been reproduced as an appendix to P. Foot op. cit. Wallace's notes are thus that rarest of rare creatures in this field – primary evidence. As well as some of his handwritten notes, a range of forged documents have survived – leaflets, minutes of meetings, false memoirs and bank statements, manufactured by MI5 and Information Policy itself. They show that the anti-subversion lobby had persuaded itself that the Labour Party, the Liberals (Labour's allies), and what we would now call the 'wet' Tories – the Heathites – were part of the 'subversive threat'. This derogatory material was kept under lock and key by another Information Policy Unit member, security clerk Michael Taylor. Taylor was eventually guardedly forthcoming about his role, confirming key sections of Wallace's allegations. The author discussed this with him in 1987 while working for ITN. See also Foot op. cit. 29. Wallace's handwritten notes were examined in 1987 by the late Dr Julius Grant, then this country's leading forensic expert on paper and ink. Grant concluded that the documents were genuine. See Foot op. cit 29–30.

41 The content of Wilson's message to the CIA is on p. 139 of Chapman Pincher's *The Truth About Dirty Tricks* (1991). There is some ambiguity about what Wilson actually said to Oldfield. In one version, reported by two of Oldfield's closest friends, the late George Kennedy Young and Anthony Cavendish, Wilson actually invited Oldfield to use MI6 to investigate MI5. See Cavendish op. cit. ix for Young and 163 for Cavendish.

42 The fact that Wilson resigned after talking with Maurice Oldfield, and after sections of the security services had tried to get rid of him, has led some on the

political right and on the fringe of the security services to conclude that Wilson's resignation was somehow the result of the covert operations against him. See Cavendish op. cit. 163–4, for example. In fact in 1970 he had told his inner circle that, if re-elected, he would serve only two more years; and he repeated this to his intimates on taking office again in 1974. See, for example, B. Donoghue *Prime Minister* (1987) p. 86.

43 On this episode see B. Penrose and R. Courtiour *The Pencourt File* (1978). Penrose and Courtiour secretly taped their conversations with Wilson using a 'bugged' briefcase and the quotes attributed to Wilson in their book are (edited) verbatim.

9 Labour and its critics: the case of the May Day Manifesto Group

Nick Tiratsoo

On 19 June 1970, Labour supporters woke up to find that their party had been decisively beaten in the previous day's General Election.[1] Many contemplated the fact with some surprise. Labour had been tipped to win, despite the problems of the past few years. Yet the Tories were now back in power with an overall majority of 30, as a result of a 4.5 per cent swing in their favour. In all, some 88 constituencies had changed hands, with the Conservatives making a net gain of 66 seats, both post-war records.[2] Little wonder that some commentators were to be heard talking of a possible sea change in the outlook of the British electorate.

In subsequent discussions about the Wilson administrations of the 1960s, left-wing critics of Labour have tended to see the 1970 result as somehow fitting – a disastrous end for a disastrous government. Wilson, it is argued, was originally elected on a radical ticket but soon dropped all pretence of socialism and opted for already discredited traditional policies. This led to technical failure (the policies did not work) and, more seriously, political bankruptcy, in that the Government's opportunism alienated party and electorate alike. Wilson stands accused, therefore, of not solving Britain's problems. But his bigger crime, from a left perspective, is that he made Labour weaker and more unpopular, thoroughly undermined socialism, and thus opened the door perhaps, in the longer run, to Thatcherism.

The aim of this chapter is to reassess this latter charge against Wilson, the allegation that his leadership diminished Labour as an institution and an electoral force. In practice, this means giving considerable attention, throughout the various stages of the argument, to one particular contemporary critique, the *May Day Manifesto* (MDM), since this turns out to have introduced many of the themes that have been repeated in the later left demonology.

The origins of the *MDM* lie in Cambridge during the second half of 1966.[3] Raymond Williams – don, novelist and literary critic – was disgusted with the way Wilson had handled the seamen's strike and the sterling crisis earlier in the year, and felt he was now 'at the end of the road' with Labour. As a consequence, he decided to 'put aside one of . . . [his] own books' and begin work on an analysis of what had gone wrong. The end product was the *Manifesto*, a volume of nearly two hundred pages, drafted by a group under Williams's editorship, and published as a Penguin special in 1968.[4]

The *MDM*'s immediate impact was considerable.[5] For one thing, it had attracted support from an unprecedented array of 'new left' figures, ranging from the playwright Arnold Wesker to the radical psychiatrist R.D. Laing, by way of historians like Angus Calder, Royden Harrison, John Saville as well as Dorothy and Edward Thompson.[6] More importantly, the book appeared to offer a clear and reasoned exposition of Labour's current malaise, and a warning of the likely crisis that lay ahead.

The *MDM* recognized that Labour had once been involved in an 'historic mission, to end poverty and unemployment by transforming the existing society'.[7] Yet, it argued, things were now very different. There had been, to start with, a fundamental change in capitalism, as laissez-faire competition became superseded by a more planned system of exploitation revolving around giant corporations.[8] The latter needed, and had created, the passive consumer, and were now moving to further bolster their position by re-shaping the character of politics so as to maximize consensus and minimize dissent.[9] The 'new capitalism' was using several tools to achieve these ends, relying to a great extent, for example, on the mass media to inculcate suitable values.[10] Nevertheless, its central instrument of control, the *MDM* argued, was the very political grouping that had once sworn to oppose everything that capitalism stood for – the Labour Party.

To capital, Labour had always seemed vital, because of the hold it exerted on working-class voters and trade unionists. Consequently, much time and effort had been spent trying to co-opt or assimilate Labour leaders and this was finally achieving substantial results, with 'the central political develop-ment of the sixties', as the *MDM* explained, being 'the internal transform-ation of the Labour party'.[11] The socialism of the past had been 'quietly written out, allowed to lapse'.[12] Now the party appeared to its traditional supporters as an 'alien form': Labour's leadership had 'redefined . . . [it] to fit in with new capitalism and managed politics'. The erstwhile harbinger of change was, in effect, reduced to 'a voting machine; an effective bureauc-racy; [and] an administration claiming no more than to run the existing system more efficiently'.[13]

All of this made the future situation in Britain, the *MDM* concluded, extremely perilous. The new bourgeoisie might have grand plans to mono-polize political power and might even have been able to put some of them into effect, yet it could not solve the economic contradictions that were inherent in capitalism, so that the whole system was headed towards crisis.[14] However, the likelihood of socialist advance did not seem very great either. For if Labour's transformation was welcomed in the boardroom, it hardly appealed on the factory floor. Consequently, many were simply deserting the party, to join single issue campaigns or other, more radical political organizations. In this situation, it was necessary to say clearly that attachments to Labour should be ditched for ever. The need was for a fundamental realignment on the left and the authors of the *MDM* hoped that they had provided the catalyst for just such an event.[15]

This was certainly a forceful analysis, and for many it became ever more convincing as Labour first lost the 1970 election and then floundered through the various contests of the 1970s. In fact, the *MDM*'s central theses have rapidly gained the status of common sense on the left, to be repeated in academic dissections and polemical tracts alike.[16] The basic message is that the Wilson administrations of the 1960s were marked by, in Clive Ponting's recent phrase, 'a breach of promise', and that this has continued to act as a millstone around Labour's neck ever since.[17] What needs to be asked, in these circumstances, is whether the eloquence and frequency of the denunciations are justified in terms of the historical evidence.

The first point to establish in this enquiry must be about Labour's actual predicament in the late 1960s. Was the Party collapsing as an institution and an electoral force at this time, as the *MDM* alleged, or was the situation less clear-cut?

Certainly, evidence to support the critics' case is apparently not hard to find. Individual membership of the Party fell between 1966 and 1970 by 12 per cent on official figures, though unofficial estimates suggest a very much sharper decline.[18] Secondly, activity levels in certain areas were clearly very low. Glasgow had 15 constituency and 37 ward organizations on paper in 1968, but 8 of the former and 9 of the latter were totally inert. Moreover, even in the city's functioning units, as an official report noted, it was often only 'the devoted work of two or three persons' that had prevented complete collapse.[19] More generally, what activism there was in the Party seemed sometimes to be less about politics and more about socializing. Indeed, Dennis Potter could have his character Nigel Barton, a prospective Labour MP, describe the typical local organization as consisting of 'a harmless bunch of broken-down old women who prefer to raffle jam sponges rather than discuss the bank rate'.[20]

In addition, the Party's standing with the public was undeniably shaky. Gallup polls frequently emphasized Labour's unpopularity, with, for example, only 19 per cent approving of the Government's record in May 1968.[21] Actual electoral performance, too, was unimpressive. Local contests were lost with alarming frequency, allowing the Conservatives to take control of numerous towns and cities (see Table 9.1); and, of course, there was the Party's indisputably poor showing at the 1970 general election, when Labour's share of the vote fell to 43 per cent, from 47.9 per cent in 1966.[22]

All of this tends to substantiate the *MDM* position. However, examining the evidence more closely suggests that matters were not quite so straightforward. Firstly, declining membership figures and low activity rates long predated the Wilson premiership. Individual membership had been falling almost continuously from its 1952 peak, with rises only in the four years 1956, 1957, 1962 and 1963.[23] Moreover, even in what many take to be the

Table 9.1 *Labour's control of various local government units*

	1966	1969
County Boroughs		
Labour controlled	47	10
All	82	83
Urban District Councils		
Labour controlled	158	102
All	538	522
Rural District Councils		
Labour controlled	29	21
All	473	468

Source: Labour Party Archive. Labour Party NEC 21/5/1969 *Report on Local Government Election Results*, Appendix C.

'golden years' of Labour rule, between 1945 and 1951, it was by no means unusual to find local sections of the party either weak or dependent on one or two very active individuals.[24]

More significantly, there is no doubt that the *MDM*'s characterization of Labour as a dead institution was more than a little one-sided. Party life, for example, could sometimes be quite vibrant, whilst events and activities were certainly not only about socializing. Thus, a typical Young Socialist programme, put on by the Sittingbourne branch in September 1969, included a meeting with a local councillor over the Maud Report and a discussion on equal rights for women, alongside 'putting and tennis', 'table tennis and darts' and a hike.[25] Similarly, a search through one random copy of *Labour Woman* (for April 1969) reveals that the Gloucester and District Women's Supper Club had enjoyed a demonstration by a 'Beauty Councillor', the Filton Women's Section was planning a continental tour, the Glasgow Women's Advisory Committee had met on prices and incomes, and the Wavertree Women's Section was continuing its campaign on safety in launderettes.[26]

Moreover, concerns at Labour's centre encompassed more than mere vote catching. Thus, policy discussion, for example, continued to be a significant part of headquarters' life. The key organizations here were the study groups, 13 in all by 1969, which covered both traditional subjects (like 'finance and economic affairs') and emerging problem areas (like 'immigration' and 'discrimination against women'). Further, it is important to note that the output of this apparatus was often of high quality, so that, for example, no less a person than Len Murray could admit that the TUC's thinking on industrial democracy had been shaped by minds in Smith Square.[27]

Indeed, contrary to the *MDM* view, it can be argued that the intellectual vigour of the Party during these years remained considerable. This can be illustrated by looking briefly at debates that went on about a fundamental question – how the Party should relate to the electorate. Labour had traditionally believed that its best course of action was simply to present the public with a policy statement, in the belief that structural factors were making the population 'ripe' for socialism, and that, anyway, socialism was so morally superior that exposure to its message would guarantee mass conversion.[28] In the 1960s, however, there was growing recognition of this model's deep flaws. In particular, more and more in the Party realized that popular conservatism and apathy could not just be dismissed as superficial – easily brushed away once subject to the socialist broom – but needed to be understood in terms of deep social and cultural formations. This, in turn, it was acknowledged, meant reviewing Labour's style of politics. There would have to be much less emphasis on 'giving the word' and much more openness to genuine two-way communication.

Theoretical or abstract summations of this new thinking were not abundant, with George Brown's speech on 'Britain: Progress and Change' at the 1968 Conference standing out as one of the few examples of an attempt at systematic exposition.[29] Yet the lessons that were being learnt did clearly flavour a number of headquarters' initiatives, ranging from the decision to launch a non-sectarian youth paper (*Focus*)[30] to the inauguration of an imaginative new scheme for consulting with the membership over policy ('Participation '69').[31] Moreover, the new political perspectives were clearly having an influence on the ground, as developments in the women's sections illustrate.

Labour women's involvement remained quite impressive during this period – supporting around 1600 functioning units and a monthly magazine capable of selling 10,500 copies per issue[32] – but there was a feeling that this position would not last unless some changes were made in both structure and politics. The problem, it was argued, stemmed from the fact that more and more women (especially younger women) no longer found Labour politics, as currently practised, at all appealing. The solution was not to keep trying to 'jam' the women into the politics, but rather change the politics so as to better reflect ordinary lives. Betty Lockwood, the Women's Organizer, put this as follows:

> It is all too easy for those of us who have come into the Party by conviction and have been prepared to do hard slogging all the time to be self-righteous and say that other women should do the same. It would be nice to think they would. The whole point is . . . there is not the same economic compulsion to come into a political organisation. Yet as an organised political force we need the contact and the point of view of these younger women. Therefore let us meet them half-way.[33]

One consequence of such thinking was experimentation with 'fringe' or 'informal' political forums – tea-groups, discussion circles, young mothers' groups and supper clubs – which eventually led to a whole new organizational set-up for the women's part of the Party, ratified by Conference.[34] At the same time, there was also quite a change in the substance of Labour women's politics, the subjects which were thought worthy of concern. One initiative was an enquiry on 'Discrimination against Women', finished in 1968, and based on detailed questionnaires from 170 Women's Sections and 148 local authority Labour groups.[35] In a similar vein, new topics appeared on the Labour Women's Conference agenda papers – 'Pollution and our Environment', 'The Under Fives', 'Planned and Unplanned Pregnancies' and so on. These were not, it was recognized, traditional 'party political subjects'; yet they would have to be tackled if Labour was to maintain its influence in the future.[36]

In the light of this, it seems reasonable to conclude that the Labour Party of the late 1960s was considerably less moribund than the *MDM* indicated. What of the situation with the electorate? Were the *MDM*'s authors at least right in seeing voter disillusionment increasing during these years?

Re-examining the data on electoral attitudes and voting behaviour suggests that exaggeration about Labour's predicament may be in evidence here, too. An important point to note is that although Labour certainly remained very unpopular during 1967 and 1968, in 1969 and early 1970 it was beginning to stage a recovery. Thus, an April 1970 Gallup poll found 42.5 per cent of their sample intending to vote Labour, 40 per cent approving of the Government's record to date, and 45 per cent satisfied with Harold Wilson as Prime Minister.[37] In this situation, it is hardly surprising to find Labour making a much better showing in the following month's local government elections, ending up with 891 net gains (as opposed to 919 net losses in 1969).[38] Nor is it surprising, perhaps, to find that the result of the 1970 general election was much closer than some pundits have implied.

First, it should be noted that in the run-up to polling day, Labour was actually widely tipped to triumph. As one contemporary journalist put it, 'Wilson said he was going to win . . . Wilson looked like he was going to win, the Tories thought Wilson was going to win . . . and the pollsters agreed with them all'.[39] In the event, of course, Labour lost, but by a much smaller margin than the blunt, overall figures on votes or seats suggests. The Nuffield Study's comment on the final result makes this point very clearly:

Although the 1970 election gave power to the Conservatives with a workable majority, it was scarcely a resounding victory. The party won only 14 seats more than the minimum needed to form a government – and there were 14 constituencies where less than 750 votes separated their candidates from defeat. Success at this level is almost like scraping through to a football title on goal average: the title is there . . . but it is gained so fortuitously that what demands explanation is why the two teams were so equal.[40]

Given this situation, the Conservatives, at any rate, were not inclined to write off their opponents, so that in November 1970, Douglas Hurd could confidentially advise his party's Tactical Committee: 'as we have seen again in the last two years the Labour Party has a resilience which will always make it a formidable political force'.[41]

All in all, then, there is quite evidently something of a gap between the *MDM*'s characterization of how Labour was doing at the end of the 1960s and the reality. The party was unarguably experiencing difficulties, but these had by no means reached crisis proportions. Having readjusted the focus, as it were, to put things in proper perspective, some attention can now be given to the second part of the *MDM* thesis, which relates to the explanation for Labour's problems. If the *MDM* was wrong on the question of scale, was it at least right on the question of causation? The *MDM* hypothesis, it will be remembered, was that Labour's predicament stemmed from leadership revisionism. Wilson and his allies, the argument ran, had moved to the right after 1964, thereby alienating working-class support. What the *MDM*'s authors thought they detected, therefore, was a discredited leadership and a myriad of rank and file ex-members, who were real socialists, deserting Labour to create something new. Can this be substantiated?

It is undeniable, to begin with, that Wilson was to some extent responsible for Labour's electoral problems. The Prime Minister believed he had the golden touch when it came to understanding the electorate, and this made him ignore well-founded advice from the party machine, and thus sometimes miscalculate over political decision-making, perhaps even over questions as serious as the timing of the 1970 general election.[42] Moreover, some of the Labour Government's policies were certainly unpopular with working-class voters, and did lead to disaffection. An example here was the chosen strategy for controlling inflation, which never seemed to match up to the electorate's perception that rising prices were a major, perhaps the major, cause for worry during much of the period.[43] In this sense, it is quite possible to talk of Labour contributing to its own downfall.

However, accepting these points does not, of course, mean accepting the *MDM* case, since what the latter was proposing involved a much more profound rupture between leaders and led, as revisionists attempted to undermine a long-standing socialist tradition. To find out whether this kind of polarization was also taking place, it is obviously necessary to investigate what the *MDM* implied were the particularly revealing manifestations of a popular, left-wing revulsion against Wilsonism – notably, the radicalization of sections of the electorate, the growth of rank and file opposition within Labour's ranks and the rebirth of a strong non-Labour Marxist or anti-authoritarian left. Was the reality, and thus significance, of these changes as the *MDM* described?

The perception that part of the electorate was becoming radicalized rested on a number of observations. There was, for example, an increase in the frequency of strikes during this period, with the number of stoppages and days lost rising from 1,937 and 2.4 million in 1966 to 3,116 and 6.8 million in 1969 and some saw this as evidence of a new, shop-steward led militancy. Moreover, many felt they detected a new sense of rebelliousness amongst the young, symbolized by the confrontations at Essex University and the London School of Economics, and the huge pop concerts in Hyde Park and on the Isle of Wight. Finally, it could also be argued that the late 1960s were witness to a more general flowering of social conscience, as indicated by, amongst other things, the widespread support for single issue campaigns like those organized by Oxfam and Shelter. Added together, all of these might indeed seem to indicate a growing wave of 'revolt'.

Yet looking at the evidence in greater detail produces a rather less dramatic picture. Radicalism in specific groups purportedly at the cutting edge of change, firstly, was considerably less prevalent than might be supposed. Strikes occurred for a number of reasons and very rarely demon-

strated any great class consciousness, being most often marked by sectional-
ism. Certainly, as W.E.J. McCarthy's authoritative research for the
Donovan Commission spelt out, shop stewards were hardly as ideologues of
the left, and the right frequently imagined:

> For the most part the steward is viewed by others, and views himself, as an accepted,
> conciliatory and moderating influence; more of a lubricant than an irritant.
> Certainly he does not emerge as an embattled opponent of management, working on
> the grievance of workers to develop dissatisfaction.[44]

Students, too, were nowhere near as 'alienated' as was sometimes imagined.
Some were certainly highly critical of aspects of higher education. On the
other hand, a poll in 1969 found that four out of every five were glad to be
at the universities that had selected them, while three out of four reported
themselves generally content with student life.[45] In this situation, militants
were left complaining about the difficulty of attracting support: disputes
might flare up and temporarily gain some attention in the student body but
it was very difficult to get a real mass campaign going. A participant in the
'Warwick University events' of 1969–70 was very much struck by the
fragility of campus commitment:

> The bourgeois university is dead. Long live the bourgeois university! This week an
> open university was declared at a poorly attended teach-in . . . Irrelevant speeches
> were delivered to an apathetic audience. Already many students had left on vacation
> and all that was left behind was the small band of militant organisers, and some
> hundred or so students who were waiting for the trendy music from London . . .
> From what Edward Thompson is arguing, a few inexperienced and militant students
> will attempt, next term, to dismiss the Vice-Chancellor and restructure the whole
> university. The only possible outcome is further disillusion.[46]

Finally, the situation with youth in general could easily be exaggerated.
Small numbers of young hippies did, it is true, take part in actions like the
occupation of 144 Piccadilly, but other groups of style conscious teenagers,
like the skinheads, were as likely to be drawn to the ultra-right.[47] For the
most part though, young people remained famously apolitical. Michael
Wood's review of a Beatles album in 1969, stressing the group's frivolity
about politics, said much, necessarily, about the attitudes of their fans:

> the Beatles . . . have never been political. They were against politics when politics
> meant Macmillan and Profumo, and they are against politics now, when some kind
> of attempt at radical social change seems the place to start. They haven't changed,
> but the world has. So they sing about revolution. It's going to be all right they tell us.
> We don't need a revolution . . . They're not being ironic, they're simply being
> irreverent: no time for pieties of the right or the left.[48]

In the wider population, too, radicalism was most notable by its absence.
Investigations by journalists into 'the condition of Britain' frequently
touched upon the strength of popular conservatism and the extent of white
racism. Jeremy Seabrook, visiting Blackburn during 1969, was most struck
by how far traditional communal values and affiliations had degenerated, to
be replaced by, what were for him, an altogether less attractive set of
prejudices:

> The ideology of the Left is in retreat. Most people I met who said they were Socialists

offered a ritual and mechanistic account of their convictions, which would not compete with the drama and appeal of the Right, which talks of the guts of the nation having been sapped by the Welfare State, and of a coddled and feather-bedded generation of shirkers and spongers and loafers – words with an emotive power which the lexicon of the Left has lost.[49]

Moreover, quantitative data from the numerous opinion polls of the period mostly pointed in a similar direction. If the *MDM* thesis had been right, then the polls should have been identifying a combination of quite distinctive trends – dissatisfaction with Wilson, especially amongst Labour supporters, a growing popular interest in politics, and a yearning for more radical solutions to the country's problems. Yet such trends were, in fact, hardly evident.

Wilson's popularity amongst the whole population, as can be seen from Table 9.2, waned quite significantly during 1968 and 1969, to recover somewhat in 1970. However, the Prime Minister remained for all but a few months very much better liked than the Leader of the Opposition. Furthermore, it is clear that Labour sympathizers continued to see Wilson in a very much more favourable light than those with other political predilec-tions. Thus, 71 per cent of Labour voters in June 1969 felt that he had made good decisions rather than poor ones; while 87 per cent were generally 'satisfied' with him in February 1970.[50] In fact, Wilson's popularity with the Labour electorate was such that only a very few could even toy with the idea of another leader: as NOP found at the time of the election in 1970, 'Mr. Wilson . . . [was] the undisputed favourite amongst Labour voters'.[51]

Table 9.2 *Satisfaction with Prime Minister and Leader of the Opposition, quar-terly average percentages, 1966–70*

	Quarter	Those satisfied with	
		Prime Minister	Leader of the Opposition
1966	4	47	38
1967	1	54	26
	2	44	35
	3	44	30
	4	38	40
1968	1	35	31
	2	29	29
	3	31	27
	4	32	31
1969	1	33	32
	2	31	29
	3	35	33
	4	41	33
1970	1	42	39
	2	48	30

Source: Calculated from material in N. Webb and R. Wybrow *The Gallup Report* (1981) pp. 173–5

What of more general attitudes to the issues of the day? The first point to make is that indifference to politics continued to be very pervasive. NOP polls in November 1969, February 1970 and May 1970, the period of the run-up to the election, found that only between 8 and 11 per cent of respondents described themselves as 'very interested' in politics and that this category was least in evidence in socio-economic groups D and E.[52] Secondly, it seems clear that, though many disagreed with Labour's actual policies, relatively few did so because the measures were not socialist enough. Thus, a big majority believed that the Government was right to attempt the reform of the unions, and a good number would have actually introduced even more stringent legislation than Labour intended. NOP found that punitive attitudes were even prevalent amongst union members themselves, concluding from a poll in the summer of 1968 that:

1 60 per cent of trade unionists believe that unofficial strikes should be made illegal and 58 per cent think that agreements between management and unions should be legally binding . . .
2 There is overwhelming support for having a secret ballot of union members before an official strike can take place.
3 Most trade unionists are in agreement with the Conservative policy that there should be a compulsory cooling-off period before a strike begins . . .
5 Most trade unionists think that Communists should be banned from becoming officials.[53]

A similar situation was evident over immigration. Here, a large majority was also in favour of the government's legislation (the Immigration Bill), while, again, a substantial portion of the electorate would have gone much further along an illiberal road, with two out of three, for example, believing that immigrants who were already resident should be given financial inducements to return home.[54]

Nor does looking at 'deeper' questions about hypothetical or fundamental values contradict this general picture. Gallup found that only 9 per cent of an October 1968 poll wanted more nationalization, while NOP at around the same time discovered significant minorities who wanted denationalization – 41 per cent in relation to steel, 38 per cent in relation to the railways and 32 per cent in relation to coal.[55] A survey of December 1969 which asked 'If you could pass one law, what would it be?' is also revealing, since the four most popular selections were for legislation to bring back hanging (26 per cent); impose stricter discipline or bring back the birch (25 per cent); tighten up welfare benefits (5 per cent); and stop immigration (5 per cent).[56] All in all, therefore, it is hardly surprising that when Gallup asked in late 1969 whether the Labour Government's policies were 'too socialist', 'about right', or 'not socialist enough', 32 per cent said they were too socialist, a similar proportion said 'about right' but only 18 per cent replied 'not socialist enough'.[57]

It would appear, to sum up, that the *MDM*'s characterization of the electorate's general mood was simply wrong. Individuals and groups were involved in protest (as they had always been); but there is little evidence to support the idea of mass radicalization. Was the *Manifesto* any nearer the truth about the situation in the Labour Party itself? Were the rank and file moving to the left in disgust at Wilson's leadership?

It is quite apparent, to start with, that some activists did feel deeply disillusioned with the way their Government was behaving. George Hodgkinson, veteran stalwart of the Coventry party, detected ' "MacDonaldism in new clothing" '.[58] Lena Jaegar, an MP who prided herself on being in touch with grass roots left opinion, was equally scathing:

The special failure of this government is that it has widened the ranks of the offended beyond all precedent. It antagonises both Alf Garnett and Professor Titmuss; and that is an achievement in alienation which must set new standards of offence.[59]

Given such opinions, it was always likely that there would be trouble at Conference, and in fact rebellions occurred on a number of well publicized occasions.[60]

However, the scale and coherence of left-wing revolt can easily be overstated. Certainly, organized opposition in the party never gained much momentum. In Parliament, the Tribune Group could call on only about 40 MPs, perhaps 10 per cent of the parliamentary Labour Party.[61] More surprisingly, perhaps, campaigns aimed at mobilizing the rank and file against Wilson also tended to be weak. Agitation from the far left, the Trotskyist fringe, had long been concentrated on Labour's youth movement, the Young Socialists, but in the late 1960s does not seem to have achieved any greater measure of success than in previous years.[62] Indeed, Young Socialist events were often most notable only for their endless sectarian wrangling and could easily descend into pure farce. One disenchanted participant reported that the 'saddest spectacle' of the 1967 Young Socialist Conference was 'the succession of young innocents' who appeared on the rostrum to read out 'interminable sectarian tracts prepared for them by the sloganisers the night before'. He added:

They clearly did not know what they were talking about. Any of them daring enough to depart from their tract were lost for words, and delegates endured an embarrassing silence while they found their place again.

The comic element on this occasion soon followed, with delegates passing not one but two sets of contradictory motions.[63]

Elsewhere in the Party, the major hope for left-wingers was the *Tribune*-backed Socialist Charter movement, launched in 1968. This campaigned around eight 'socialist principles' – such as 'the redistribution of wealth' and 'full accountability of all institutions' – and at first seemed to be doing quite well, quickly claiming a membership through affiliated organizations of 400,000 (or around 7 per cent of the Labour Party total). Again, however, the initial surge did not last, and the movement threatened to disintegrate because of squabbling. Typically, a convention held in late 1969, attended by notable left MPs like Norman Atkinson, Stan Newens and Ian Mikardo, as well as representatives from *Tribune*, *Voice*, *Militant* and *Left*, reportedly made some progress determining policy but was badly disrupted by 'a lengthy organisational and procedural wrangle which took up several hours of . . . [the] proceedings'.[64]

Outside of these formal organizations and campaigns, the mood of the membership was more diffuse than might be imagined. Left-wingers, as has been suggested, often attacked Wilson, but they did not necessarily believe that he alone was to blame for Labour's predicament. Thus, Hodgkinson's denunciation of 'MacDonaldism' was accompanied by withering criticism of 'the Big Bust of Booze, Betting and Bingo' which had, he believed, 'seduced the community, young and old, from . . . matters of high principle . . . and social obligation'.[65] Indeed, this feeling, that it was the public which had let Labour down and not vice versa, seems to have been fairly widespread in these years, as a correspondent of the *Houndslow Clarion* (a local Labour broadsheet) noted:

The action of so many people over the colour question, the self-seeking greed that acts upon the country like a running sore has made many Socialists wonder whether it was all worth it.
   If we haven't said it ourselves, we must have heard Socialist friends say: "People aren't worth the trouble".[66]

Furthermore, being radical on one issue did not necessarily mean being radical on another. Dick Taverne met an activist in Lincoln who was incensed that the House of Commons 'spent all its time debating Bills for homosexuals when they should be discussing unemployment every night'.[67] Bedford CLP was centre-left on many issues, yet when it discussed race, struggled to contain a xenophobia that had one member declaring:

We might just as well give the whole dam country to the Blacks as they would get it in the end anyway. Before long we should have a Black King on the throne and then it would be God help us! The poor old white man might just as well emigrate and leave the place to them.[68]

Thirdly, it is important to recall that some ordinary members of the Party did not espouse any kind of leftism, anyway. The Dehrers, rapidly emerging as 'hard left' luminaries, candidly admitted that militants often found themselves isolated in ordinary constituencies because of their particular style and orientation:

The Left-wingers . . . are frequently prima donnas: reluctant to do any donkey work, and regarding their membership of the party as a great favour . . . Can it be wondered that their "radical" posturing . . . commands little respect among hard working, if more naive, party members.[69]

Indeed, many older members believed that loyalty to the organization should be paramount, which made public criticism unforgivable. Typical here were the middle-aged East Anglian party supporters who told Christopher Mayhew how proud they were of what Labour had achieved over the years:

Living conditions had been transformed in the villages, and this was attributed to full employment and better wages, for which the Party and the farm workers' union were given the credit.

If there was cause for worry amongst this group, it was because of 'scrim-shankers' who abused the social security system and young people who wore 'the same dirty old jeans seven days a week'.[70]

Finally, it is worth noting that if criticism of Wilson had flared in some quarters in the middle years of the Government's term, as the general election approached, all sections of the Party tended to pull back together. Dick Taverne found that this was true of his Lincoln constituency and it was also noted in many other parts of the country. Practical proof of the new mood was the fact that most of the regional campaigns in the run up to polling day were judged successful. The London Organizers' verdict was representative:

It was a good campaign, fought with enthusiasm and with many coming in to help. The display of window-bills, too, was most encouraging and reminiscent of earlier campaigns. The will was there – the work was done . . .'[1]

Once again, the *MDM* seems to have misrepresented the situation. What of the third allegedly significant development, the growth of a strong 'outside Left', composed of those who had seen through Labourism as a result of Wilson's policies? Was the *MDM* perhaps more in touch here?

For some, certainly, these were 'Street Fighting Years'[72] – years of big demonstrations against US involvement in Vietnam, Institute of Workers' Control conferences capable of drawing 1,000 delegates, a reborn women's liberation movement, and a vibrant counter-culture, formed around papers like *International Times* which could readily sell 30,000 copies per fortnight.[73] Yet reviewing the evidence reveals, once again, that the position can be easily exaggerated. Some Trotskyist and Maoist factions did grow during this period, and a few large demonstrations were held, but this should not obscure the fact that the organised far left as a whole nevertheless remained very small, divided, and to some extent locked in long-standing traditions. Moreover, the counter-culture was simply irrelevant in terms of mass politics. The blithe epithet 'Street Fighting Years' can only be regarded, in the light of what actually happened, as a wild romanticism.

Looking at the organized non-Labour left, first, it is immediately obvious that none of the constituent organizations had come anywhere near building even a moderately sized following. The Communist Party's membership at this time stood stable at a mere 30,000, while the two leading Trotskyist factions, the Socialist Labour League (SLL) and the International Socialists (IS) were growing slightly, but still had only about 2,000 and 1,000 members respectively. Nor were circulation figures for the left press very imposing: the International Socialists' broadsheet was selling at about 10,000 copies per week in 1969, and though the *Daily Worker* claimed a circulation of 50,000–60,000 copies per day during these years, this included an unspecified but large number of copies which were sent to Moscow.[74]

Yet the left was, in fact, even weaker than these figures imply. Support tended to be very unevenly distributed in one way or another – witness the SLL's strength in Liverpool or the IS's base in some parts of higher education[75] – so that most people were completely untouched by any of the various parties' activities. Moreover, there was little common ground between, or even sometimes within, the left groups, with division taking a number of forms. The Communist Party had been recently traumatized by the Soviet invasion of Czechoslovakia and was becoming increasingly split into 'tanky' (i.e. pro-Soviet) and liberal factions. The Trotskyist and Maoist organizations, on the other hand, were bitterly hostile both to each other and to any Moscow influence, and continued to insist on the sanctity of their various theoretical heritages.

In this environment, co-operative activity was almost impossible. All the left groups were highly critical of Labour, and many agreed that the main task was, as Tariq Ali put it, 'to completely destroy and discredit social democracy'.[76] Yet trying to decide what this meant in practice proved much more controversial, with each of the parties holding to a slightly different 'principled' position – 'Vote Labour without Illusions!', 'Vote Labour – and Go On Fighting!', 'Keep the Tories Out!' and 'Critical Non-Opposition'.[77] Indeed, much of the far left's political activity was in fact essentially directed inwards and aimed at protecting particular versions of the holy writ or praising true believers. Debate could, therefore, often be sharp and very sectarian, with particular derision aimed at those who lacked 'revolutionary commitment'. A review by the IS's Raymond Challinor of the apparently innocuously academic *Socialist Register* illustrates the tone:

Anybody who suffers from insomnia and does not want to resort to drugs should take *The Social Register*. It is definitely sleep inducing but non-addictive. The book creates its soporific effect by combining the bad features of the "old" . . . New Left: academic sterility, detachment from the class struggle and a concern about expressing the simplest concepts in the most convoluted way.[78]

The upshot of this was that much of the practical activity amongst the groups tended to take on the features of a long-standing game, where the object was always to 'build the organization'. Discipline and ideological purity were at a premium here, prized before any other consideration. A small but revealing example of the general approach occurred at the first ever Women's Conference in 1970, when a man was heard to remark, after leaving a room where the International Socialist women were meeting, 'I've just been telling our girls what to say'.[79]

Outside of the left groups, in the so-called counter-culture, the situation was even less impressive. Many of those involved here professed radical feelings, but this radicalism was usually lightly worn and highly selective, so that, for example, male predatory sexual behaviour went wholly unchallenged. Moreover, much of the social activity, and many of the ambitions, were to do with drugs, which hardly encouraged serious political intervention.[80] In these circumstances, communal events inevitably tended towards the chaotic. At the 1967 Roundhouse festival, participants learned 'how to get high on oxygen . . . [and] stoned on human communication', and then took part in a finale which even Tony Hancock would have been proud of. This featured local children, who had been wandering in and out of the event for some time:

One afternoon, when a large audience was sitting waiting for Herbert Marcuse to arrive for a lecture,the kids settled themselves on the platform; one urchin took the microphone and announced that he would now recite some of his own verses. He did so, to enthusiastic applause.[81]

A 'revolutionary festival' at Essex University two years later fell prey to the same spirit. On this occasion, as *New Society* reported, 'a car was set on fire and a student and a mathematics professor struggled over possession of a hosepipe'; John Arden, David Mercer and Michael Kustow discussed art and revolution, only to be 'interrupted by a smoke bomb'; and painted wall slogans proclaimed 'Revolt or fester', 'The shit heap is smouldering' and 'Don't just stand there – wank'.[82]

All of this hardly gives the impression of a strong and newly vibrant 'outside left'. But what clinches the argument is what happened to the *MDM* itself. Those who had put the document together hoped, it will be remembered, that their initiative would provoke a major realignment on the left and perhaps, even, the birth of a new grouping to challenge Labour. However, as will be seen, little of what was planned actually transpired, precisely because, once again, of the fragility of the desired constituency.

The basic facts about the political developments that occurred as a result of the *MDM*'s appearance can be easily summarized. The *Manifesto* was published in April 1968 and early the following month, at the invitation of the drafting committee, interested parties gathered together to explore what the text meant in terms of precise political perspectives. This meeting agreed that there was indeed need for radical change: the Labour Party had 'become the agent of the new capitalist system' and so all progressives should commit themselves 'to the formation of a political movement, radical and socialist, primarily extra Parliamentary, but accepting the significance of a national presence, though rejecting the notion of Parliamentary Socialism which the Labour Party represents'. In practical terms, this meant holding discussions with as many of the left groups as was possible and then organizing a 'National Convention', where a new 'unified socialist movement' could be launched. This 'Convention' was duly held in April 1969 and attracted some 600 participants. The outcome was a draft statement on common perspectives (drawn up under seven headings, from education to imperialism) and an agreement to form a continuing commission, with representatives from all the far left groups, in order to develop points of policy. Discussion about the latter forum made some progress but was effectively ended by the 1970 election, which was held to usher in a new political era.[83]

How should this whole episode be assessed? Raymond Williams claimed that the *MDM* story was essentially a heroic one. He argued that producing the *MDM* was itself an achievement ('the fact of a self-organising, self-financed socialist intellectual organisation is important'); suggested that the document had been widely influential in encouraging new thinking; and praised the progress that had been made in developing a fresh approach to politics.[84] In his view, things had only begun to go wrong in 1970, when principled division surfaced about exactly what should be done in the forthcoming election. As he later explained:

A movement which had managed to sustain a significant amount of left unity disintegrated over the electoral process – over whether it was permissible to make electoral interventions to the left of the Labour Party.[85]

This interpretation has certainly impressed some subsequent historians of the period, yet close investigation reveals its beneficent conclusions to be more than a little misleading. In fact, a sober assessment of the *MDM* movement suggests that it struggled right from its inception. Members of the original drafting committee generally agreed on grand theory (such as the idea of 'new capitalism') but divided as soon as practical political questions were raised, which left the Penguin volume rather deficient in this area.[86] The launch meeting, too, was fraught with difficulties. Little had been done in terms of organization, so that there was, for example, no secretariat on hand to record resolutions.[87] Moreover, many leading figures seem to have treated the whole event in an extremely cavalier manner. Ken Coates, a luminary of the Institute of Workers' Control, arrived late but still wanted to play a leading role, instructing the meeting with some fervour that it should discuss topics which had in fact been dealt with the previous day.[88] More surprisingly, the central triumvirate on the drafting committee – Williams, Stuart Hall and Edward Thompson – were all apparently conspicuous by their absence, leading one participant to complain about the 'second eleven' having been turned out for what had, he assumed, been a major fixture.[89] Given these handicaps, it is hardly surprising to find that the meeting itself was less than satisfactory. According to David Widgery, 'the first speaker from the floor came to bury not to praise, denouncing the platform vigorously for "having no representative of the working class" on it'.[90] What followed, in the words of *New Society*'s reporter, was 'an explosive affair, studded with clashes'.[91] Many certainly saw the meeting simply as a recruiting ground: at its finish, according to Widgery again, 'at least a third of the audience streaked to the door to sell their various periodicals with much muttered greeting and cursing'.[92]

Nor is there any reason to believe that things improved after this somewhat inauspicious beginning. Many of the original drafting committee were disillusioned by events at the launch meeting and quietly withdrew from any further involvement.[93] Meanwhile, the rump that remained continued to bicker over politics and botch practical initiatives. Typically, therefore, an action designed to build up interest in the *MDM* amongst the trade unions, which involved a lobby of Parliament over the government's incomes policy, ended in fiasco, with forty assorted intellectuals and shop stewards staring at each other in a hall which could hold 300.[94] In this situation, support and enthusiasm quickly waned, to be given only a brief boost by the April 1969 Convention. Thus, while the *MDM* movement probably had some 250 to 300 supporters in 20 to 25 groups at the end of 1968, by the late summer of the following year it could be described by a key activist as, quite bluntly, 'quasi-moribund'.[95] If Raymond Williams's 'principled disagreements' about electoral strategy did in fact occur in 1970, they can only have involved a very few participants.

What conclusions can be drawn from the preceding discussion? This chapter has been concerned with the allegation that Wilson ruined Labour as a party and as an electoral force in the period 1966–70. Such a view was first argued systematically in the *MDM* and has subsequently been repeated in many left-wing texts. Nevertheless, as the evidence presented here has shown, it is almost entirely misleading. Labour was not in crisis during the late 1960s and remained a strong political force. Some were disillusioned by the Government's record, but the idea that large numbers deserted because Labour was not socialist enough is misplaced. There was no mass radicalization in these years. Ordinary voters who switched away from Labour did so for a number of reasons, with more than a few feeling that the party was too far, not to the right, but to the left. Socialists who felt betrayed by Wilson enough to leave Labour's ranks were in a small minority, and demonstrated their impotence by ending up in a long-established cul-de-sac. Almost every part, in short, of the *MDM*'s evaluation of politics turns out to have been wrong.

How could a misreading on this scale have come about? Part of the problem, without doubt, stemmed from the mode of analysis used. The *MDM*'s authors were steeped in the traditional Marxist view of historical development, even if this had sometimes been given a decidedly 'new left' gloss. Their approach was coloured, in other words, by the idea that a maturing capitalist economy, such as Britain's, was moving inexorably towards a final crisis, delivering, at the same time, a proto-socialist proletariat as its inheritor. In this scenario, politics had necessarily to be about unmasking sources of disinformation (the media, the Labour Party), and, most of all, about creating an adequate programme of socialist demands to match the unfolding revolutionary mood. It did not have to be about any sustained analysis of or engagement with, say, popular apathy or working-class conservatism, since such phenomena could be a priori discounted as manifestations of false consciousness, which would disappear under the twin hammers of economic crisis and socialist propaganda. In a real sense, therefore, the methodology adopted had an inbuilt and self-reinforcing tendency to mislead, encouraging predetermined conclusions regardless of how empirically valid they were.

At the same time, other, less tangible factors clearly reinforced the thrust of this erroneous reasoning. One important point to recall is the fact that all of those involved in putting the *MDM* together lived and worked in the same rather insular world of university leftism. This meant that their contact with the working class was normally shaped in quite specific ways. Many of those encountered tended to be of a particular type: the trade union activist, the dedicated adult student met at extramural classes, or their predecessors recreated in research time. Conversely, there was little exposure to or curiosity about any of those who were (or had been) simply indifferent to the whole idea of Williams's 'educated and participating democracy'.[96] In this way, again, 'the long and tenacious revolutionary tradition of the British commoner' – as Edward Thompson described it – could dominate the mind-set regardless of reality.[97]

Similarly, several of the *MDM*'s authors were quite clearly moved by emotion more than reason when it came to the question of the Labour Party itself. Williams and Thompson, in particular, were men of some standing in their professions and on the left at this time, and undoubtedly felt that they should be listened to by any reforming governing party.[98] Yet Labour was not an organization that valued intellectuals very highly. There was, for example, no equivalent of the Communist Party's History Group, nor any attempt to involve university figures in decision-making. Moreover, many rank and file members remained deeply suspicious of all middle-class radicals.[99] Given this situation, it was, perhaps, inevitable that Labour would seem unattractive to a university don. Williams had already had an unhappy involvement with a local branch of the Party prior to 1966,[100] and it may well be that his and others' emotional distaste for what Labour represented had more than a little to do with the way that the *MDM* analysis developed.

Hopefully this chapter has shown that the verdict on the *MDM* (and on those who have uncritically repeated its assertions) must necessarily be a harsh one. Much of the left's case against Wilson is simply built on sand. It seems tragic that in 1992 such a conclusion should still be in any way controversial, and this is testament indeed to the left's reverence for its 'great figures'. The Labour mainstream have always been suspicious of the progressive intelligentsia in Britain, as has just been noted, and there are those who would explain this simply in terms of the former's trade union inspired philistinism. What the *MDM* story illustrates is that blame for the rift cannot be so easily apportioned. Intellectuals, even when they have put down their own work to look about them, can sometimes be much more illiterate about politics than the lesser mortal whose only guide is the *Daily Mirror*.

Notes

1 I would like to thank staff at the Modern Records Centre (the University of Warwick), the Coventry City Records Office, the Conservative Party Archive (at the Bodleian Library, Oxford) and the Labour Party Archive (at the National Museum of Labour History, Manchester) for help and advice whilst researching this chapter. I am also grateful to Colin Barker for permission to use MSS 152 at the Modern Records Centre; to Dr Sarah Street and the Conservative Party for permission to use the Conservative Archive; and to Stephen Bird, Steve Fielding, Tom Jeffery and Peter Thompson for various stimulating observations on the argument advanced.

2 D. Butler and M. Pinto-Duschinsky *The British General Election of 1970* (1971) p. 338.

3 This account is based upon R. Williams *Politics and Letters* (1979) p. 373 and *The Listener* 25/4/1968.

4 R. Williams (ed.) *May Day Manifesto 1968* (Penguin edn, Harmondsworth, 1968) [hereafter *MDM*]. A preview version of the Manifesto had been privately published as *1967 New Left May Day Manifesto* (1967). The connection between the two texts is explained in *MDM* pp. 9–10.

5 The original version of the Manifesto was reviewed in *The Sunday Times* and in *Le Monde*: *MDM* p. 10.

6 *1967 New Left May Day Manifesto* op. cit. 45.

7 *MDM* p. 44.

8 *MDM* pp. 144–5.

9 As the Manifesto put it, 'corporate government' needed 'the assimilation and control of all popular and representative institutions' (*MDM* p. 153).

10 *MDM* pp. 145–6.

11 *MDM* p. 44.

12 *MDM* p. 156.

13 *MDM* p. 155.

14 *MDM* p . 189.

15 *MDM* pp. 161–8, 187–90.

16 See e.g. R. Miliband *Parliamentary Socialism* (2nd edn, 1973) pp. 360–61; D. Coates *The Labour Party and the Struggle for Socialism* (Cambridge, 1975) p. 128; G. Hodgson *Labour at the Crossroads* (1981) p. 78; P. Seyd *The Rise and Fall of the Labour Left* (1987) pp. 16, 43; and F. Cripps et al. *Manifesto* (1981) pp. 110–12.

17 C. Ponting *Breach of Promise* (1989).

18 The Labour Party *Report of the Seventieth Annual Conference* (1971) p. 62; and Butler and Pinto-Duschinsky op. cit. 264–7.

19 Labour Party Archive Manchester [hereafter LPA] Labour Party NEC 26/2/1967. Report on 'Enquiry into Party Organization in Glasgow'.

20 D. Potter *The Nigel Barton Plays* (Harmondsworth, 1967) p. 14.

21 N. Webb and R. Wybrow *The Gallup Report* (1981) p. 174.

22 Butler and Pinto-Duschinsky op. cit. 353.

23 The Labour Party *Report of the Seventieth Annual Conference* (1971) p. 62.

24 N. Tiratsoo *Reconstruction, Affluence and Labour Politics: Coventry 1945–60* (1990) p .48.

25 *Labour Organiser* No. 561 (Sept. 1969) 172.

26 *Labour Woman* Vol. 59 No. 4 (April 1969) 76–80.

27 Labour Party *Report of the Sixty-Eighth Annual Conference* (1969) pp. 31–2; LPA Labour Party Home Policy Committee Re. 290/April 1968. Sub-Committee report on 'Industrial Democracy', enc. Letter L. Murray–T. Pitt 3/4/1968.

28 N. Tiratsoo 'Popular politics, affluence and the Labour party in the 1950s' in A. Gorst, L. Johnman and W. Scott Lucas (eds) *Contemporary British History 1931–61* (1991) pp. 56–8; S. Fielding ' "Don't know and don't care": popular political attitudes in Labour's Britain, 1945–51' in N. Tiratsoo (ed.) *The Attlee Years* (1991) pp. 106–25.

29 Labour Party *Report of the Sixty-seventh Annual Conference* (1968) pp. 191–6.

30 *Focus* ran from 1966 to 1967 and covered such topics as drugs, 'The Other Leamington', pirate radio, votes at 18, housing, hunger, cookery, football and abortion. It sold between 3,000 and 5,000 copies per issue, but was eventually wound up for financial reasons (LPA Labour Party NEC 28/6/1967 Minutes of Sixth Meeting of Youth Sub-Committee 19/6/1967).

31 The 'Participation '69' exercise was based on a scheme used in the Swedish Social-Democratic Party, and involved circulating the membership with details and background on a specific policy, in order that there could be a dialogue about future legislation. The first topic proposed by headquarters ('Women and Social Security') was discussed by 3,000 people in 250 groups over a five week period (LPA NEC Minutes Vol. 146 Labour Party Research Department. Information Paper No. 43 Jan. 1970 'Participation '69 . . .').

32 LPA National Labour Women's Advisory Committee Minutes 18/9/1969 53(a); *Report of the Forty-Fifth National Conference of Labour Women* (1968) p. 4.

33 *Labour Woman* Vol. 59 No. 8 (Aug.–Sept. 1969) 143.

34 Ibid, and *Labour Woman* Vol. 59 No. 4 (April 1969) 63.

35 *Labour Woman* Vol. 57 No. 5 (May 1968) 90, 99.

36 *Labour Woman* Vol. 60 No. 5 (May 1970) 83.
37 Webb and Wybrow op. cit. 173.
38 *Labour Organiser* Vol. 50 No. 572–3 (July/Aug. 1970) 123.
39 P. Jenkins 'Electoral Post-Mortem' in *Encounter* Vol. XXXV No. 2 (Aug. 1970) 12.
40 Butler and Pinto-Duschinsky op. cit. 347–8.
41 Conservative Party Archive, Bodleian Library, Oxford CCO 500/10/5 D. Hurd 'Harassing the Labour Party' 23/11/1970.
42 Butler and Pinto-Duschinsky op. cit. 47–8; and Jenkins op. cit. 17.
43 Jenkins op. cit. 17; *NOP Bulletin* (July 1969) 4 and (June–July 1970) Special Survey, 1–6.
44 *New Society* 25/4/1968.
45 *Encounter* Vol. XXXII No. 5 (May 1969) 68.
46 *Black Dwarf* 23/3/1970.
47 *New Society* 9/10/1969 and 26/6/1980.
48 *New Society* 2/1/1969.
49 J. Seabrook *City Close-Up* (Penguin edn, Harmondsworth, 1973) p. 198.
50 *NOP Bulletin* (June 1969) 5 and (Feb. 1970) 4.
51 *NOP Bulletin* (June–July 1970) 6.
52 *NOP Bulletin* (Nov. 1969) 4–5, (Feb. 1970) 6, (May 1970) 9.
53 *NOP Bulletin* (Aug. 1968) Supplement, 1.
54 *NOP Bulletin* (April 1968) Supplement, 1.
55 *Gallup Political Index* No. 102 (Oct. 1968) 147 and *NOP Bulletin* (Sept. 1968) 8.
56 *NOP Bulletin* (Dec. 1969) Special Supplement, 3.
57 *Gallup Political Index* No. 114 (Oct. 1969) 187.
58 Coventry Record Office, Hodgkinson Correspondence 14/7/1, Letter Hodgkinson–T. Benn 20/4/1969.
59 *New Statesman* 5/4/1968.
60 These rebellions are documented in several places; see e.g. P. Jenkins *The Battle of Downing Street* (1970).
61 This estimate comes from Seyd op. cit. 78. Alan Watkins' contemporary estimate was that 'left MPs' numbered only around 30. See *New Statesman* 28/11/1969.
62 Z. Layton Henry 'Labour's Lost Youth' *Journal of Contemporary History* Vol. II Nos. 2–3 (July 1976) 299–304.
63 *Focus* Vol. 1 Nos. 7–8 (April–May 1967) 2 and LPA Labour Party NEC 26/4/1967 Chief Officer's Report on Y.S. National Conference 1967.
64 *Tribune* 13/9/1968, 5/12/1969.
65 Coventry Record Office, Hodgkinson Correspondence 15/1/8, Letter Hodgkinson–P. Noel Baker 1/5/1968.
66 *Houndslow Clarion* (June 1968) 2.
67 D. Taverne *The Future of the Left* (1974) p. 38.
68 London School of Economics, Bedford Constituency Labour Party Archive, Minute Book FM2, GMC Meeting 12/10/1967.
69 *Tribune* 28/2/1969.
70 C. Mayhew *Party Games* (1969) pp. 67–9.
71 Taverne op. cit. 48; *Labour Organiser* Vol. 50 No. 572–3 (July–Aug. 1970)139.
72 See T. Ali *Street Fighting Years* (1987) passim for this view.
73 The numerical estimates presented here come from *Tribune* 4/4/1969 and *New Society* 3/10/1968.

74 For the left at this time see P. Shipley *Revolutionaries in Modern Britain* (1976) and *New Society* 3/10/1968.
75 M. Crick *Militant* (1984) and Modern Records Centre, University of Warwick MSS 152 Box 3 File 21 Document headed 'The Organisation of the I.S. Group' (which shows that 300 of IS's 880 members – i.e. 34 per cent – were studying or working in higher education at the time of the organization's 1969 Conference).
76 *Black Dwarf* 14/2/1969.
77 *Black Dwarf* 12/6/1970.
78 *International Socialism* No. 35 (Winter 1968/9) 42.
79 *New Statesman* 6/3/1970.
80 As is amply demonstrated in J. Green *Days In The Life* (1988).
81 J. Nuttall *Bomb Culture* (Paladin edn, 1970) p. 57.
82 *New Society* 20/2/1969.
83 *May Day Manifesto Bulletin* [hereafter *MDMB*] No. 5 (May 1968), No. 14–15 (June 1969); *New Society* 2/5/1968 and 1/5/1969; and *Tribune* 28/3/1969 and 2/5/1969.
84 *MDM* p. 10 and Williams op. cit. 374–5.
85 Williams op. cit. 375.
86 *MDMB* No. 2 (Feb. 1968) 1 and No. 3 (March 1968) 6.
87 *MDMB* No. 5 (May 1968) 1–2.
88 Ibid 14.
89 Ibid 18.
90 D. Widgery *The Left in Britain 1956–1968* (Harmondsworth, 1976) p. 207.
91 *New Society* 2/5/1968.
92 Widgery op. cit. 207.
93 *MDMB* No. 14–15 (June 1969) 4.
94 *MDMB* No. 7 (July 1968) 23–4.
95 *MDMB* No. 10–11 (Jan.–Feb. 1969) 30 and No. 16–17 (Sept.–Oct. 1969) 1.
96 R. Williams 'Culture and revolution: a comment' in T. Eagleton and B. Wicker (eds) *From Culture To Revolution* (1968) p. 32.
97 E.P. Thompson 'Revolution' in E.P. Thompson (ed.) *Out Of Apathy* (1960) p. 308.
98 See e.g. Williams's later rather hurt comment that 'throughout the entire six years of Labour government . . . I never had one enquiry, formal or informal, private or public, one invitation to a committee or a conference, from anybody in the Labour government or Labour machine. Not one line'. (Williams *Politics and Letters* op. cit. 371).
99 For which see, *inter alia*, D. Marquand *The Progressive Dilemma* (1991).
100 Williams's relationship with the Labour Party is outlined in A. O'Connor *Raymond Williams* (1989) pp. 17–22.

10 The Conservative Party in Opposition, 1964–70

Lewis Johnman

When the Conservative Party lost the general election of 1964 it meant that the political agenda was being set by Labour for the first time since 1951.[1] Labour's theme in 1964 was the modernization of the British economy in particular and of British society in general. On this issue the Conservative Party was quick to recognize its vulnerability. Between 1960 and 1963 elements within the Research Department had formed a Psephology Group which in its final report during 1963 concluded that the Party had lost the label of 'competence' which had proved its mainstay throughout the 1950s.[2] On the economic front there were a series of poor balance of payments figures in 1962, a post-war unemployment record and a series of damaging industrial disputes in engineering, shipbuilding and nursing. There were also problems over Skybolt, a series of spy scandals and De Gaulle's veto of application for EEC membership. These were compounded by Macmillan's responses, for example, in the 'night of the long knives', and in the manner of his resignation and succession, all of which served to contribute to the image of a government which had lost its way and a party which was out of touch with the public mood.[3]

The loss of the mantle of 'competence' and exposure on the issue of modernization coalesced for the Party around the theme of 'the establishment'. Sir Gerald Nabarro observed that the Party in the country resented the number of Old Etonians in the Government,[4] Sir Michael Fraser – head of the Research Department – told R.A. Butler that 'the Country wants greater change than is appreciated at Westminster'[5] and a letter to Central Office from a 'disaffected lifelong Conservative' averred that there was:

an "establishment" and that this establishment would rather lose the election than their power in the Party. We are looking for a 1963 leader. . . . We are sick of seeing old-looking men dressed in flat caps and bedraggled tweeds strolling with a 12 bore.

For God's sake, what is your campaign manager doing? These photographs of Macmillan's ghost with Home's face date about 1912.

The correspondent claimed that Edward Heath, or someone of similar appearance and background, was needed to lead the Party rather than 'these tired old men, with their 19th century appearance and their 18th century attitudes' but added that 'we don't believe he or his kind will ever be allowed to take the reins from the tired old men or the Etonians'.[6]

Debate over the Party's record in office was also conducted in its journals. Angus Maude, a former director of the Conservative Party College, argued that the main problem for the Party was how to appeal to both its traditional supporters and floating voters simultaneously. To Maude, there was an entirely new electoral perspective which the Party's policies did not meet.[7] The Tory journalist, T.E. Utley, took up this theme, arguing that the Government had been attempting to reconcile a series of conflicting demands for full employment, an expanding level of social services, economic growth, price stability and unrestrained trade unionism, and that this was a task for which the Conservative Party was ideologically unsuited.[8] One professed solution to this problem was provided by the Bow Group in its journal *Crossbow* which ran a series of articles in 1961 and 1962 advocating a mixture of economic modernization and efficiency. The main theme of this critique was that the government was responsible for making capitalism as efficient as possible and that on this issue the incumbent Conservative administration had failed.[9] To *Crossbow* the Conservative failure was both ideological – 'slogans irrelevant to the complex and often substantial problems of our age'[10] – and structural:

Have we not an ideal opening for a modern Conservative Party . . .? Is it not time to establish within the party some really effective policy committees who can set about building the bridges between problems and solutions – bridges that can in due course be incorporated in a dynamic Tory programme.[11]

For the Bow Group, therefore, economic modernization was the *sine qua non* upon which all other change was dependent and this in turn required a radical overhaul of party ideology and machinery. Even before the defeat of 1964, therefore, a vigorous debate was being conducted within the Party as to its record in government and future policies. Despite the criticisms and problems, the Conservatives lost the 1964 election by the narrowest of margins.[12] The defeat was enough however, in and of itself, to justify an overhaul of policy and organization.

A review of this type was a traditional Conservative Party response to electoral defeat, as Lord Blake, the Party's 'official historian' has commented: 'after every defeat . . . there was a constitutional reshuffle, change of committee nomenclatures and relationships and a general move for better representation of party sentiment'.[13] In the post-war period the defeat of 1945 compelled the party, in R.A. Butler's words, to 'rethink its philosophy and reform its ranks with a thoroughness unmatched for a century'.[14] Among other changes, the Conservative Research Department (CRD) was revived and expanded and the Conservative Political Centre (CPC) was established. By 1950 there had been a revolution in the Party's organization with the creation of a professional bureaucracy to service the political machine. At the 1950 general election the CRD had a staff of over fifty – it had been four during the 1945 election – and its role was widely expanded. At elections it was charged with the drafting of the manifesto, giving policy guidance, assisting with the Campaign Guide and Daily Notes and performing as a general supplier of information to the party at large. Between elections its role was to undertake longer-term research and to assist in the formulation of policy as well as preparing and advising on parliamentary briefs and acting as a general information clearing house.[15]

By the late 1950s, therefore, the CRD was established as the keystone in the Party's structure for policy formulation. As R.A. Butler explained, the Research Department

should be left to work up subjects on the research side. When these are ready for further public contact and/or advice, a small committee of enquiry should be set up under a member of the Front Bench to carry the work further, either with a view to publication or in order to have material ready for insertion in the party's final policy.[16]

The reports of such committees would then be submitted to the Policy Committee of the Leader's Consultative Committee – effectively a Cabinet or Shadow Cabinet Committee – and the Advisory Committee on Policy, the main forum for the consultation of extra-parliamentary opinion. Thus, a two-way exchange of information was established with the process controlled by the CRD. As Michael Fraser, one of the first appointments to the CRD in 1946 and its director between 1951 and 1964, recalled about the work of the subcommittees in 1961:

These committees, whose membership is normally drawn half from Conservative Members of Parliament and half from outside experts, are set up by Mr. Butler and serviced by the Research Department. They report to Mr. Butler and their reports are seen by the Advisory Committee on Policy, copies being sent to the Ministers concerned.[17]

By the 1960s a clearly defined and co-ordinated policy structure had evolved to which the CRD was central. There were four main elements to this. First, there was the Shadow Cabinet itself, formally called the Leader's Consultative Committee and having as its secretary the director of the CRD. This was the ultimate decision-making body of the party. Secondly, came the Steering Committee, sometimes known as the Chairman's Committee, chaired by Edward Heath between 1964 and 1970, and supported by the Official Group which was chaired by Sir Michael Fraser. This group comprised MPs and professionals from the CRD and Central Office and was responsible for assembling and drafting the manifesto. The third tier was the Policy Initiatives and Methods Committee, chaired by Fraser, where the CRD co-ordinated the work of the policy subcommittees and passed this to the Steering and Leader's Consultative Committees. Finally, there was the Advisory Committee on Policy, which took account of wider party opinion. Between 1964 and 1970 this was variously chaired by Sir Edward Boyle, Reginald Maudling and Heath, and had as its secretary, the director of the

CRD. In terms, therefore, of structure, personnel and operation, the CRD performed the central role in the formulation of policy and political strategy.[18]

The 1964 defeat was the occasion for a further organizational change which, although not as thorough-going as that which followed the 1945 defeat, had the effect of further enhancing the influence of the professional bureaucracy within the party. Central Office was reorganized with the CRD and CPC being integrated and new officials appointed. David Howell, a former editor of *Crossbow*, became Director of the CPC and Edward Du Cann was made Party Chairman in the expectation that his business experience and background would enable modern ideas about market research and publicity to be introduced. Sir Michael Fraser was made Deputy Chairman of the Party and secretary to the Shadow Cabinet, and Brendon Sewill, who had joined the CRD in the mid-1950s, became the new Director of the CRD.[19] Edward Heath became responsible for overall policy in October 1964 when he succeeded R.A. Butler as Chairman of the Advisory Committee on Policy and retained the position when he became Leader of the Party in July 1965. No new Chairman of the Research Department was appointed until 1970 and in effect the CRD 'came directly under the Leader of the Party from 1965 to 1970 with both Sewill and Fraser seeing Heath several times a week'.[20] With the accession of Heath to the leadership the policy review process began in earnest with a detailed examination of specific policy areas. Prior to the 1966 election there were 23 policy groups with a combined membership of 181 MPs and peers and 181 outside experts, while between 1966 and 1970 there were 29 groups with a combined membership of 191 MPs and peers and 190 outside experts.[21]

The post-1964 review concentrated on three main issues: first, the redefinition and differentiation of policy; secondly, the need to close, in Heath's phrase, 'the gap and conflict'[22] between different elements of the Party; and thirdly, the need to utilize modern electioneering methods and opinion poll techniques.[23] The whole exercise, however, was complicated by the prospect that a snap election could be called at any time, given the narrowness of Labour's majority.[24] In this sense the review exercise had to achieve the difficult task of providing a short-term manifesto which would at once modernize policy and organization, differentiate the party from Labour, unite the membership and provide a base for a longer-term review. Of the post-1964 policy groups the three most important were those concerned with industrial relations, economic policy and foreign affairs.

One of the first groups to meet was that on trade union law and practice. The Research Department had already decreed that 'a hard look at what is mainly 19th century law on trade unionism' would be an essential component in any policy review which sought to achieve industrial modernization.[25] Data was submitted by the party's Economic Intelligence Unit and by the CBI on labour costs, wages, inflation and company profits, but as a whole the group was dominated by lawyers and the chosen mode of dealing with the issue of industrial relations was, almost inevitably, legalistic.[26] It was taken as axiomatic that unofficial strikes, general industrial indiscipline and a balance of power in industry which was more favourable to organized labour than to employers were together responsible for inflation and were impediments to the modernization of the industrial structure. Underlying this interpretation was an analysis which viewed unions as economic monopolies, the curbing of whose power would enable the labour market to function properly. It also seemed to provide, through legislation, an alternative to incomes policy in controlling inflation. The group decided that the law should be amended in such a way as to inhibit breaches of collective agreements by unofficial strikes, redefine the rights of individual members with respect to their unions and extend the right of legal protection over existing contracts to employers. In other words, the group was seeking a fundamental reform of those trade union immunities which had been guaranteed by the 1906 Trades Disputes Act. The group was not without its tensions, however, with both Enoch Powell and Sir Keith Joseph urging stringency and Joseph Godber – the last minister of labour before the 1964 election – and Lord Blakenham, the former Party Chairman, urging caution. Godber and Blakenham argued that changing the law with respect to trade unions might have the effect of alienating the union movement from the Conservative Party, could involve a future Conservative government in conflict with organized labour, and was therefore not worth the electoral risk. Joseph and Powell took the contrary view that not to legislate would weaken support in the country and would fatally undermine any policy of industrial and economic modernization.[27] By May 1965 the group had recommended the establishment of an industrial relations court and the registration of trade unions. As Brendon Sewill noted when the programme was approved in September 1965, it was 'a very careful compromise between Sir Keith Joseph and Mr Godber'.[28]

The group focusing on future economic policy was chaired by Heath and included academic economists, bankers, businessmen and financial journalists as well as MPs. The range of topics – the role of sterling, defence expenditure, possible EEC entry and overseas expenditure, as well as fiscal, monetary and industrial policy – proved daunting however, and the group split into three sub-groups. Most of the work and the largest amount of controversy was generated by Subcommittee A, which was established to consider the reconstruction of the tax system. Once again, it was considered axiomatic that tax rates should be reduced, both to reward individual enterprise and to begin the process of supply-side reforms. The problem was to balance the tax yield against public-expenditure levels, which it would be politically impossible to reduce. General tax cuts were therefore ruled out but what was proposed was a substantial reduction in the upper income tax brackets to be offset by the introduction of a wealth tax. The rationale for this proposal was that 'if we are really to reduce the top rate of surtax and abolish the discrimination against investment income, a wealth tax is in practical political terms the only way we have any hope of doing it'. The suggestion was that this proposal would shift tax benefits from 'owners to earners' and thereby demonstrate a commitment to modernizing industry by rewarding work rather than wealth.[29] When the subcommittee's report was submitted to the main policy group, a sizeable minority was horrified by the proposal. Despite the fact that Heath favoured the recommendation, it was argued that the end result of such a policy would split the entire Party. The proposal was submitted to the Shadow Cabinet in 1966 but no agreement on it could be reached. The economic policy group went into temporary abeyance and the Party entered the 1966 general election with a traditional post-war demand management macro-economic package.

The foreign affairs group concentrated its attention on Europe. This was unsurprising given the extent of Heath's own passionate commitment on this subject. It was not, however, an issue without its problems. Sewill wrote to Heath that Europe was 'exciting, interesting and novel, but unfortunately with not much sign of being immediately practicable', adding that 'whilst efficiency and competition were obviously right and essential' they were like modernization, 'too technical and cold to be really inspiring'. Sewill suggested that the two themes could be combined and posed the question: 'should our aim be to increase our national efficiency so that we can enter Europe from strength and not from weakness, so that we can hope to lead Europe when we are in?'[30] The foreign affairs group report reaffirmed Conservative commitment to Europe and the policy of attempting to gain entry to the Common Market. To this end, much space was devoted to Britain and Europe and there was a commitment not only to joining the Community but also to economic and political integration.[31] The consensus was, however, more apparent than real; many were unhappy at the stress being placed on Europe in preference to the Commonwealth. Paul Williams of the Monday Club encapsulated this feeling by criticizing the fact that there was no Commonwealth affairs committee, a situation he felt 'typical of the worst of the current attitudes of the Tory Party'. When Heath attempted to mollify him, he responded that 'if, as you say, "the general lines of Commonwealth policy were firmly established and widely accepted in the Party", it would be very pleasant to know exactly what these lines are'.[32] Indeed, it was considered wise to keep foreign issues out of the wider arena of the Party altogether and once the foreign affairs group had reported, in August 1965, it was wound down and all foreign policy work was done via the Shadow Minister and Parliamentary Committee, with specific work coming from the Research Department directly to the Shadow Cabinet.[33] This, however, failed to alter the fact that on a range of issues – Europe, the Commonwealth, immigration and race relations (on which a broadly integrationist stance was taken in 1965) – there would be substantial difficulties between 1966 and 1970.

In early August 1965, and consequent on Heath's elevation to the leadership, it was decided to produce two draft documents, one to serve as an election manifesto, the other to serve as an 'approach document' for the Party Conference and for wider public consumption. The interim reports of all policy groups were collected and an attempt made to fit them to broad themes. What was required, the Research Department argued, was a 'weighty essay on the shape of future Tory policy, rather than a hold-all for everybody's pet scheme'.[34] Continuous redrafting went on throughout September and the policy document was published in October under the title *Putting Britain Right Ahead*.[35] Sewill warned Heath that the Party could now become the victim of its own success in the policy process. The

Party had to maintain its momentum until the anticipated election and, if it lost, for the full term of a Parliament thereafter. Policies could become outdated and, once a new policy had been adopted and expounded, it would be very difficult to retract.[36] James Douglas, who, as Senior Research Department Officer, had co-ordinated the work of the policy groups, wrote to all policy group secretaries arguing that whilst the interim reports had appealed to 'pacemakers' such as young executives, this was far too narrow a base on which to win an election and that the appeal needed to be expanded to a wider target audience.[37] Indeed, Douglas, Sewill and to a lesser extent Fraser, saw the issues of efficiency and enterprise as themes to be stressed and not as ends, although David Howell, the Director of the Conservative Political Centre, wanted to build on them to achieve concrete policies. Howell argued that management techniques needed to be 'vigorously applied', that merit should be encouraged to 'reverse the collectivist spiral' and that the 'National and European destiny are one'.[38] Douglas and Sewill, however, felt that 'the themes of management, competition and tax incentives . . . appeal to comparatively few voters. Many . . . would regard them with suspicion'. They argued that competition would be 'a disastrous word for us to use to present our policies to the general public' and stated that the main themes should be 'the building of a new prosperity and restraining the rise in the cost of living'.[39] These arguments over the ultimate ends of the policy process were intense enough for Heath to instigate a series of working lunches to attempt to resolve them.[40] Little was achieved, however, and the debate was all but paralysed between October 1965 and the election of March 1966. Indeed, the eventual manifesto, *Action Not Words*, appeared as a statement by the Leader with a list of specific promises attached. Despite what had been achieved, all of the opinion polls showed that some two-thirds of the electorate expected a Labour victory, that few voters blamed Labour for the nation's economic problems and that there was little public understanding of Conservative policies.[41] In the end, the Party sustained its second heaviest defeat in 50 years and faced the prospect of a full Parliament with Labour dictating events.

The post mortem which was conducted on the 1966 election made more use of public and private opinion polls than the Party had hitherto, and more attention was paid to them. The Party had first used survey research in 1958 and had employed an advertising agency, C.P.V. (Coleman, Prentiss and Varley), in 1959.[42] National Opinion Polls worked for the Conservatives in 1959 and 1962 and the same organization carried out a nationwide survey in 1963.[43] In 1965 Opinion Research Centre, headed by Humphrey Taylor, who had worked on previous NOP surveys for the Conservatives, was commissioned to conduct private polling. The aim of this work was to mount systematic, consistent and continuous tests of public opinion as to voting intentions, perception of policies, by-elections, the impact of political broadcasts and other specific issues.[44] Continuous panel operations were begun in 1965 with 4,500 electors being interviewed approximately every seven months in order to identify and analyze changes in voting intentions.[45] The key poll was a specially commissioned survey conducted for the Party by Gallup in the wake of the defeat. This (Table 10.1) compared responses to one question over the last five elections.

The trend revealed was unmistakable and potentially terminal for the Party. Many in the electorate were more prepared to identify with Labour even if they actually voted Conservative. As if this were not shock enough, further surveys provided more pause for thought. One finding was that some 30 per cent of the electorate had changed their voting intention in some way between 1964 and 1966 and that the majority of this group was drawn from the C2s, the skilled working class, the under-35s and women. What the surveys failed to detect was the meritocratic management voter upon whom many Tories had placed much stress; they highlighted instead the importance and volatility of the non-manual working class and women.[46]

This chimed in with a debate in the Party on these issues but it was a debate which tended to throw up rather contradictory strategies. On the one hand, there was a view that modernization had not been pursued vigorously enough and that this had alienated the meritocratic voter, though it was also argued that little had been done to alleviate pressure on the more traditional and, by extension, Conservative voting, middle class.[47] At least one commentator was prepared to suggest that the Tories had lost the 1964 election because they had lost control of the centre-ground of politics.[48] The centre, however, proved to be very difficult to define and identify. In various guises it appeared as comprising the technocrats, the new bourgeoisie or the salariat, with the common strand of identification being that, whatever it was termed, the key group had emerged from the working class but had few links left with it and that in some way it was at one and the same time the guarantor of electoral success and economic modernization.[49] But as an editorial in *Crossbow* reasoned:

Who are our future supporters going to be? And what kind of society are we going to offer them? . . . At the moment, we are in danger of becoming a rootless party and a boring party. A political party is a collection of interest groups, and if it loses the support of some of the old interest groups it can only survive by winning over new ones. It is therefore a false sense of political daring which allows us to face the alienation of some of our traditional supporters with complete equanimity . . . We should remember that the number of people attracted by strident calls for technology, dogmatic claims for more economic liberalism and even heartfelt appeals to the spirit of individualism is severely limited.[50]

In other words, the appeal of economic modernization had to be sufficiently all-encompassing to retain each of the elements of centrist support otherwise the Party would simply trade new supporters for old. Modernization, if pushed too far, could ultimately spell the end of the revamped One Nation strategy which had been followed since 1946. The inescapable conclusion stemming from both survey material and internal debate was that however the Tories explained their loss of support, they would have to change if the trend was to be reversed.

In 1967, Brendon Sewill explained the rationale behind the Conservative approach before 1966:

The Labour Party won the 1964 election by promising results; faster and steadier

Table 10.1 *Political support 1951–66*

'Leaving aside the question of which party you support, which party is best for people like yourself?' (%)

	1951	1955	1959	1964	1966
Conservative	40	42	38	36	34
Labour	43	44.5	41	40	45
Liberal	8	8	7	8	5
Others, and don't knows	9	7.5	14	16	16
Labour lead	3	2.5	4	4	11

Source: CCO 180/21/3/1–58 'Gallup Polls'

growth, more houses, lower interest rates, better social services etc. etc. This produced a natural reaction against talking about broad objectives. This was reinforced in the Conservative Party by the feeling that we had lost the confidence of the public because we had run out of ideas. Thus our natural reaction in recent years has been to seek 'Action not words', policies not aspirations, and to talk about means not ends.[51]

The conclusion was that of the 1965 policies, the issues of Europe, industrial relations, tax reforms and commitment to social services were viewed as positive whilst the questions of incomes policy and economic management were viewed as negative.[52] Sewill noted in his report on the 1966 election that:

If the Labour Government now moves to the left, our task of winning the next election should not be too difficult. Our most difficult problem will be if they attempt to continue in control of the centre. It is then likely that they will adopt a number of our policies – for example, Europe, trade union reform, housing, and some of our social policies – half heartedly and belatedly. We need to work out a method for dealing with this.[53]

In other words, it was likely that the forthcoming Parliament would witness a battle between the two main parties for the centre ground of politics. In this context, and in a comment on a paper proposing increased use of market research by the party, Sewill noted that:

much of the present boredom with politics comes because people cannot distinguish any question of principle between the two main parties . . . What we need is a Leader who can plot a course for the Party, and stir the masses, and awake the feelings of which people are as yet unaware.[54]

Aware that Wilson looked as if he would bid for the centre-ground and eschew any move to the left, James Douglas commented that he was 'frankly in a rather disheartened mood at the moment'.[55]

The policy exercise was now continued, the aim being, in Fraser's phrase, to put 'the clothing . . . on the bigger proposals between 1966 and 1970'.[56] In a speech at Carshalton in 1967, Heath committed the Party to the centre-ground and by extension attempted to pre-empt both Labour and any potential tensions within the Tories. His aim, in other words, was to differentiate the Party from Labour and at the same time reaffirm the concept of progressive Conservatism inherent in the centre-left of the Tory ranks since the policy review of the 1940s. Heath pledged himself to reverse 'doctrinaire adherence to collectivism', repair 'failure of confidence in free enterprise' and overcome the idea that the state could solve all problems, whilst at the same time reserving the right of government to intervene 'where industry needed help to speed necessary changes' or realise 'widespread changes of attitude'. Heath re-committed the party to full employment and promised that a Conservative government would deal with hardship as and when it occurred.[57]

The policy groups continued their work and once again the main focus and controversy centred on three areas: industrial relations, economic policy and foreign affairs. The reconvened trades union policy group had Sir Keith Joseph in the chair. Both Joseph and Nicholas Ridley sought to change what had been the emphasis of the group's work between 1964 and 1965. They wished to place the full onus for invoking the law onto management and reduce the role of government to the absolute minimum. These proposals did not command majority support however, and the industrialists in the group were particularly dismayed, arguing that they would result in disputes with both local and national unions. The CBI representatives in the group argued that since the current system encouraged strikes, inefficiency and low productivity, it was the responsibility of the government to redeem the situation.[58] This conflict was resolved when Robert Carr replaced Joseph in the chair. Carr's view was that specific policy pledges had already been made and that going over old ground would simply be counter-productive.[59] Under Carr the basic framework of rules by which the legislation would work were clarified and adopted in April 1967. The positive response to trade union reform in the 1966 manifesto inculcated within the Party the view that this was an issue on which they had a clear lead over Labour. Conscious also of Labour moves on the issue – the Royal Commission on Industrial Relations was due to report in 1968 and subsequent legislation was expected – the Party decided to make its own policies public as quickly as possible.

Fair Deal At Work was published in April 1968. The Donovan Commission reported in May 1968 and was quickly followed by the Labour Party's White Paper *In Place of Strife*. The Conservative proposals were different from Labour's. The document set out the legal immunities and privileges enjoyed by trade unions and argued that it was the duty of government to intervene and restrain 'irresponsible elements' from abusing them. The proposals gave the unions corporate legal status which entitled them to sue and be sued for breaches of contract, and defined trade disputes in such a way as to exclude sympathetic strikes, inter-union disputes and strikes to enforce the closed shop.[60] The policy group met to consider whether any response was necessary to either Donovan or *In Place of Strife* but decided that no substantial change was required to their own proposals. The few trade union leaders to whom the Party expounded its views replied that whilst they would oppose the proposals they would be obliged to accept them once they became law.[61] Within the Shadow Cabinet, however, there was a distinct lack of unanimity on this question and Heath himself was fearful of industrial trouble and the prospect that the issue might detract from negotiations over Europe. Heath eventually was persuaded by Carr and Sir Geoffrey Howe and the Party Conferences of 1968 and 1969 endorsed the document as policy.

The economic policy group reconvened in 1966, again under the chairmanship of Heath, and attempted to put some flesh on the bones of a policy which was recognized as a clear weakness of the 1964–6 exercise. Once again, however, this group ran quickly into difficulties. With the failure of the proposal for a wealth tax it had to fall back on savings in public funds, a reduced PSBR and price stability to bridge what would clearly be a revenue gap. Even on these issues the group was paralysed. At one meeting in April 1967 it was supposed to hear 'a weighty paper' by Brian Reading on economic policy but was instead treated, at the instigation of Iain Macleod, to an off-the-cuff briefing on the Budget so that the paper was never heard.[62] Tensions within the group were also apparent, with both Joseph from within and Powell from without pushing a less interventionist stance and stressing an anti-inflationary line – a position supported at least as far as incomes policy was concerned by Iain Macleod – and the Party's last chancellor, Reginald Maudling unwilling to abandon the policies which had been followed in the early 1960s and strongly advocating an incomes policy.[63]

Once again, these debates and tensions seriously delayed the process. Heath attacked the Labour Government for devaluing in 1967 but neither he nor Macleod could provide an alternative policy for sterling and Enoch Powell's proposal for a sterling float was ruled out because of IMF commitments. Eventually Heath was persuaded to disown a wages policy thereby placing the onus on management to either cut labour costs or suffer reduced profits. Given his commitment to 'no losers' made at Carshalton this would be a difficult circle to square. The group once again resorted to a highly detailed discussion of tax reforms, to such an extent that Sir Keith Joseph could ask in July 1968, if the group was ever going to begin to discuss economic policy.[64] Nothing of any substance, however, was done; no clear set of supply-side reforms was available, there was no coherent criteria covering government incentives and intervention, and even where the policy group had come up with radical proposals, such as those on denationalization, they were likely to meet severe criticism. Thus, Brendon Sewill could applaud the basis of Nicholas Ridley's proposals on denationalization but also argue that:

The paper is at the moment written starting from the assumption that denationalisation is right in principle. While all Conservatives naturally agree with this I feel that the next Conservative Government is going to be faced with so many urgent problems in the economic sphere that there will be a natural desire not to upset more apple carts than strictly necessary.[65]

In fact, on this issue, there were few details of either cost or feasibility and little detail of which public services could be sold to the public. The proposals were deemed politically unacceptable and made no impact in the manifesto. This was symptomatic of the hiatus at the centre of the economic policy group, as Brendon Sewill later recalled:

the central question, which was very apparent right through the 1960s, of what you did about incomes policies, none of which worked, was not tackled. The question of monetary policy was never mentioned. Enoch made some speeches but he was very much a lone voice to my memory and therefore we went into the 1970 election unprepared on what was going to be the crucial issue.[66]

In the summer of 1969 the economic policy group was disbanded so the conundrums about the economy were unresolved.

Despite the potential for splits in the Party over Europe and the Commonwealth (particularly in relation to Rhodesia) trouble erupted on neither of these questions but on the issue of immigration. The genesis of this question was the campaign begun by the former Commonwealth Relations Secretary, Duncan Sandys, to halt the inflow of Kenyan Asians whose entry was not controlled by the Commonwealth Immigrants Act. Labour announced that it would legislate to restrict entry but a number of Conservatives voted against the Bill's second reading. Heath now feared that the Party would be split into factions over the forthcoming Race Relations Bill. He hoped to placate the right by committing himself to 'drastic' immigration controls, and the left by opposing the Bill's methods and intentions and allowing them to vote with Labour.[67] In this he was pre-empted by Enoch Powell. Powell had proved one of the most stringent philosophical critics of the policy process. It was Powell who had posed the (then) unanswerable questions: on the role of monetary policy in macro-economic management; on Britain's dependence on American nuclear pro-curement and the costs of defence; on EEC entry and the inherent problems of European, and by extension, national statism.[68] On any of these issues Powell could have caused major difficulties within the Party but in the event he chose none of them and instead opted for immigration. The Conservative line on this in 1965 had been integrationist. Powell chose to expound the issues in dramatic language which obscured rather than revealed his main theme of urban squalor:

Those whom the gods wish to destroy, they first make mad. We must be mad, literally mad, as a nation to be permitting the annual inflow of some 50,000 dependants, who are for the most part the material of the future growth of the immigrant-descended population. It is like watching a nation busily engaged in heaping up its own funeral pyre. . . . As I look ahead, I am filled with foreboding. Like the Roman, I seem to see "the River Tiber foaming with much blood". That tragic and intractable phenomenon which we watch with horror on the other side of the Atlantic but which there is interwoven with the history and existence of the States itself, is coming upon us here by our own volition and our own neglect.[69]

The speech caused maximum impact, being delivered three days before the debate on the Race Relations Bill. The following day Powell was dismissed. Acrimony broke out within the Party; Quintin Hogg, the Shadow Home Secretary, declared that he would have resigned had Powell not been dismissed, the 1922 Committee attempted to have Sir Edward Boyle removed from his Shadow Ministry because he had voted for the Race

Relations Bill, Conservative peers in the Lords voted against and defeated the Mandatory Sanctions Order against Rhodesia and 45 back-bench MPs voted – and in so doing ignored a three-line whip – against the third reading of the Race Relations Bill.[70] Whilst there was never any danger to Heath's leadership on this issue and it was already questionable as to how much of the immigrant vote the Conservatives could hope to gain, the major problem was that the public perception of the Party would be that it was divided and unsuitable for government.[71] The only way in which Heath could heal the divisions was to stress the extent to which the Conservatives were already committed to severe restrictions on immigration.[72] The issue, however, continued to rumble on until it was overtaken by the Labour Government's own difficulties over *In Place of Strife* and incomes policy in 1969.

A further problem came from the Research Department which, although worried about the tensions in the policy process, was far more worried about the lack of clear evidence that the Party was effectively getting its general approach over to the electorate.[73] It was true that the Tories had gained a lead over Labour in 1967 which was held throughout 1968 and 1969[74] but what was worrying observers was the new volatility which such polls were revealing. Between 1945 and 1965 the gap between the highest and lowest party lead recorded by Gallup's monthly surveys had rarely exceeded 10 per cent. From 1965 onwards, however, the gap between these figures was much larger as Table 10.2 illustrates.

Table 10.2   *Variations in Conservative lead (%), 1965–70 (Gallup)*

	1965	1966	1967	1968	1969	1970
Highest lead	9	2.5	16	24°	21	9
Lowest lead	−6.5	−15.5	−11	5.5	3.5	−7
Range	15.5	18	27	18.5	17.5	16

Source: D. Butler and M. Pinto-Duschinsky *The British General Election of 1970* (1971) p. 173

The Gallup figures served to reinforce anxieties with respect to the floating voter and the elusive centre-ground; as David Howell noted, 'that over eleven million people should have cast themselves afloat in the electoral sea is a staggering commentary on the public mood with dangerous implications'.[75] The Party's private polls indicated that cross-switching was of a greater volume and frequency than hitherto and even when the Conservatives had a comfortable lead the numbers of people describing themselves as 'Labour' in the surveys remained ominously high.[76] Heath's own popularity continued to lag behind Wilson's to a considerable extent; in May 1968 with the Tories ahead in voting intention by 28 per cent, only 31 per cent were satisfied with Heath as Leader of the Opposition.[77]

It was the private polls which proved most worrying. These tended to show that where the sample electorate approved of a particular policy – as was consistently the case with industrial relations for example – the policy tended to remain little understood and was not dominant amongst issues about which voters cared most.[78] The problem for the Research Department was to establish dominant themes from the policy work in order to establish differentiation and in particular to attempt to move the Party towards a policy which the surveys continued to show the electorate was most concerned about – prices.[79]

Thus, the Party found itself with a range of policies in most areas which, at least as far as the electorate was concerned, remained unclear; and no policy in the one area where the electorate certainly desired one. As if this situation were not bad enough, it was, as Sir Edward Boyle told Margaret Thatcher,

extraordinary and rather disturbing . . . [that] a lot of Policy Groups are coming up with proposals, all perfectly sound in their own context, which would have the incidental effect of raising prices of something or other, and this is a tendency we must I am sure guard against.[80]

In other words the policies taken in aggregate could actually prove to be inflationary. The officials sought to remedy this situation by publishing a document which would outline Conservative philosophy and therefore be above the on-going debate about individual policies. As Sewill wrote, 'the Party wants to see some sort of purpose running through . . . [the new policies] . . . more than mere expediency . . . to demonstrate the practical application of traditional Conservative principles to the new problems of today'.[81] But even on this issue, splits emerged, Douglas-Home being favourable and Macleod openly hostile. Sir Keith Joseph noted that 'we don't need such a paper' and the issue was dropped.

By 1968, however, and primarily at the behest of Fraser, a policy document was prepared. To Fraser the main priorities were:

(1) pick out some plums with political attraction;
(2) do enough detailed work and no more than will ensure that what we propose in the package is intellectually respectable and can be done.[82]

Fraser argued that the earlier policy exercise had served to illustrate the existing depth of disagreement and that it was essential that Shadow Ministers take policy preparation more seriously. More had to be done to pull the work of the policy groups together; and as Fraser, Douglas and Sewill all argued, it remained essential that the Party differentiate itself and its policies from Labour.[83] To Douglas, the issues which ought to be emphasized were taxation, social policies, industrial relations and Europe. However, this attempt proved little more successful than that of 1967. The document had to be redrafted six times before it finally appeared under the title *Make Life Better*, but as Sewill commented:

I had thought that the idea at this stage in the Parliament was to show where the car was going more than what we were going to do inside the engine. But this was apparently not at all the idea of our leaders. They firmly gave instructions that we were to be much more specific, and have all expressed themselves much more pleased with the sixth draft than with any of the previous ones. . .[84]

To Sewill, the sixth draft was the one which had removed the connecting thought, the main reason for publishing in the first place. Despite his doubts, however, the document obtained a relatively positive response.[85]

By 1969, therefore, with a general election possible at any time, substantial problems remained for the Party to overcome. What had conspicuously failed to emerge from the policy process so far was an answer to the question of how the Conservatives would achieve their vision of modernization. Beset by Wilson's attempt to hold the centre-ground, Heath could only resort to attacking the worst examples of statism while at the same time restraining any tendency in the Conservatives to move further towards a free-market philosophy. This situation raised a whole range of largely rhetorical questions. What role, if any, would there be in a Conservative government for bodies like the Industrial Reorganisation Corporation, the National Economic Development Council and the National Board for Prices and Incomes? What was to be the Conservatives' attitude to defence in the wake of Labour's White Paper and the 1968 cuts – especially to the argument that defence commitments intruded in a negative manner on domestic economic policy? Could large-scale restructuring of industry be carried through without causing high unemployment – especially given Heath's commitments at Carshalton – and by what mechanism were skill shortages to be overcome? On what basis would a Conservative government intervene to support industry and what implications did this have for competition policy? Did membership of the EEC offer the protection of a super-cartel within which restructuring could be achieved at a reasonable pace or did it offer the harsh reality of a more open and competitive market which would cause restructuring along the lines of that which had taken place in the 1920s? To these fundamental questions the Conservatives had as yet no answers.[86]

Conservative difficulties may have been profound enough but problems were also mounting for Labour – from the devaluation crisis of 1967, through the subsequent balance of payments crises and consequent economic squeeze and incomes policy to the controversy over *In Place of Strife* in 1968 and 1969. The voters' disenchantment with Labour between 1967 and 1969 was registered in various ways. In September 1967 the Conservatives made by-election gains in Cambridge and Walthamstow West and in November, Labour lost Hamilton to the SNP, Leicester South West to the Conservatives and came third behind the Liberals in West Derbyshire. In March 1968, the Conservatives gained Meriden, Acton and Dudley and in the summer, Oldham West and Nelson and Colne. The lowest recorded swing to the Conservatives was 8.6 per cent at Cambridge and the highest, 21.1 per cent at Dudley. Even in seats which Labour was holding in by-elections, such as Manchester Gorton and Sheffield Brightside, the swing against it was 9.4 per cent and 17.1 per cent, respectively. If the swings at Meriden, Acton and Dudley were to be repeated nationwide, the Government faced annihilation at a general election. Nor was there any comfort whatsoever from the municipal elections of May 1968. Labour held only 450 seats – losing 639 in the process – compared to its previous post-war low point of 846 and a post-war average of 1,200. Also in May 1968 Labour trailed the Conservatives in the national polls by 28 per cent, which was far worse than the Conservative low point of 16.5 per cent in 1963.[87] The trend of by-election losses and substantial swings against Labour in seats held continued in 1969. The Conservatives gained Walthamstow East in March with a swing of almost 16 per cent, Birmingham Ladywood was lost to the Liberals in June and in the winter the Conservatives gained Swindon and Wellingborough on swings of 12.9 per cent and 9.7 per cent respectively. In that same winter Labour held seats at Islington North, Newcastle-under-Lyme and Paddington North, but only in Islington was the swing against them under 10 per cent.[88] For the Conservatives therefore the evidence was ambiguous. The Research Department continued to worry, on the basis of private polls, that the Conservative message was not getting across to the public, and indeed, that the message itself was obscure. On the other hand, the Party at large could draw enormous comfort from by-election and local election victories and from the trend of the published opinion polls. The Research Department continued to insist that the Party concentrate its attention on the deeper meaning of such polls, however, especially with respect to the new trend towards voter volatility and continuing voter identification with Labour.[89] What was required, the Research Department argued, was more clarity on substantive policy questions and a manifesto which would reflect such clarity.

A manifesto had been in draft since 1968, had been redrafted for the Party Conference of 1969, but had not yet been published. Redrafting began again in October 1969. Reaction to the manifesto within the Research Department, however, was at best muted, as one commentator noted:

it is not the sort of manifesto with which we can win a General Election . . . Few people read manifestos; but those who do have not been accustomed to being told this sort of economic realism at election time for years. One may say therefore that we will have to win the next general election in spite of, rather than with the aid of, our manifesto.[90]

A way to overcome the problems of producing an acceptable manifesto was suggested by James Douglas:

at this stage we do not need to stimulate ideas and discussion . . . so much as to get agreement, decision and follow-through on the ideas that are already around. Brendon and I have a sinister notion which is to incarcerate the Shadow Cabinet for a week-end where they can really concentrate free from distraction on their policy and strategy for the next Election.[91]

From this idea emanated the Selsdon Park Conference of January 1970.

The aim of collecting the Shadow Cabinet at Selsdon Park was to finally collate the work which had been done since 1966 and produce a coherent manifesto with clear underlying themes and organizational principles. In this sense, there was little that was new or novel in the policy field but in public relations terms the Party wanted to demonstrate just how different its policies were and to convey the impression of a Shadow Cabinet fit and primed to govern. The result of the conference was one of rather mixed success. It certainly brought more of the Conservative ideas and plans to public notice in a few days than at any time over the previous five years of the policy review.[92] This was partly fortuitous, as Quintin Hogg was permitted to make a tough statement on law and order, which allowed a rather minor issue to dwarf larger ones and drew from Heath the despairing remark that 'it's all gone mad'.[93] In policy terms, the Conference failed to resolve the problem of the hiatus at the core of economic policy, control of prices. In broad outline the economic policy maintained a reasonably centralist line between the perceived necessity of reducing state intervention-ism and the uncertain ground of neo-liberal deregulation. There was wide agreement on EEC entry, greater competition in industry and finance and supply-side reforms, such as reduced personal and corporate taxes, higher productivity and a freer labour market. But the only paper on the agenda at Selsdon which was not discussed was one by Brendon Sewill seeking clear decisions on incomes policy. As Sewill was later to recall:

There was a curious blank spot because everybody thought that inflation was the great problem but no one was actually prepared to say that the Keynesian principle that full employment was of paramount aim should be abandoned. Everybody said the trade unions were too powerful but nobody was prepared to say the only way to reduce their power was to increase unemployment. Nobody was prepared to take that mental leap away from the total Keynesian tradition in which everyone had grown up during the 1940s, the 1950s and 1960s.[94]

In the event, no agreement could be reached on the issue and once again it was shelved. Depressed by the long-term inability of the policy groups and the Shadow Cabinet to evolve any anti-inflation policy, the Research Department invented one. As Sewill, once again, noted:

For many, many years we had realised that the public considered the cost of living 'the most important issue'. This was the main theme of our advertising campaign in the year before the election . . . the Research Department had, at the very last moment, to invent a policy for dealing with inflation; and this was spatchcocked into the manifesto after the seventh draft when it was in final proof stage. This did not, however, prevent us from developing the cost of living as our main election issue, although our credibility was always a bit shaky.[95]

In other words, the issue which the Conservatives would highlight during the 1970 election campaign was the same one on which six years of discussion and argument had failed to achieve even the smallest amount of policy.

The Conservatives had reason to be pleased with the outcome of the Selsdon Conference. In February 1970 they enjoyed an average 10.5 per cent lead in the opinion polls, and the county council elections in April brought them further comfort. Throughout England and Wales there was almost no change in the position from the 1967 results, which was calcu-lated as being equivalent to a 9–10 per cent swing to the Conservatives since the 1966 election and which translated to a 7 per cent Conservative lead in the opinion polls.[96] From April, however, the trend of the opinion polls began to run against the Conservatives. On 28 and 29 of April, both Harris and Marplan gave Labour slender leads, the first time since March 1967 that any national poll had given Labour an advantage. In May, Labour did well in municipal elections with a swing which was one of the largest ever recorded in local contests over a twelve month period. The swing was rarely below 10 per cent in the big cities and reached 27 per cent in Hull. Translated to a general election, the results would give Labour a majority of 50 seats. By 12 May Gallup showed a 7 per cent Labour lead prompting Wilson to announce the dissolution on 18 May with the election one month later.[97] Indeed the polls were now not only showing a Labour lead but a continuing trend away from the Conservatives.

There were, however, two rays of hope for the Conservatives. The first was the fluctuating nature of the polls. On 14 June NOP gave Labour a 12.4 per cent lead while on the same day Gallup recorded a lead of only 2.5 per cent allowing some Conservative Party managers to discount the polls as unreliable. The second positive aspect for the Conservatives was that their private investigations were showing returns at variance with the national polls. The Conservative electoral strategy was to concentrate on those issues where they had a clearly different public image from Labour and to highlight prices in particular. Economic factors began to swing the campaign in favour of the Conservatives. On 15 June, the trade figures for May were released showing a deficit of £31 million. The following day Conservative private polls revealed continuing changes in attitudes on economic issues. The answers to two questions were especially revealing to party strategists (see Tables 10.3 and 10.4).

Table 10.3 *Economic Perceptions*

'The Conservatives say that another economic crisis is coming, Labour say it is not, who do you believe?' (%)

	8 June	11 June	15 June	16 June
Conservative	44	48	50	49
Labour	35	32	28	25
Neither/Don't Know	21	20	22	26

Source: CCO 180/27/9/1–2 'Opinion research summaries'

Table 10.4 *Party ability to deal with economic crisis*

'If there is an economic crisis which would you want to handle it, a Labour or a Conservative government?'(%)

	8 June	11 June	16 June
A Labour Government	44	43	41
A Conservative Government	39	43	45
Same/Don't Know	17	14	14

Source: CCO 180/27/9/1–2 'Opinion research summaries'

This provided clear evidence that the central themes in the campaign were getting across. Despite this, the national polls continued to show a Labour lead – on polling day Gallup gave Labour a 7 per cent lead, Harris a 2 per cent lead, NOP a 4.1 per cent lead, with only ORC giving the Conservatives a 1 per cent lead – all of which was in contra-distinction to the Conservatives' private poll.[98] There could be no reconciliation between the private and public polls and the eventual result lent heavy justification to the former, as Robert Carr, the Opposition spokesman on Employment was to recall:

In 1966 I went to the count believing I'd lost and was absolutely astonished when I won by 500 thanks to a Communist candidate. The mood was so different in 1970. All our canvassing results were showing that I was heading for a major majority and it didn't tie up with the public opinion polls. I knew that either my constituency was being absolutely freakish, which seemed improbable, or the overall public opinion polls were giving a very phoney result.[99]

In fact, at the declaration the Conservatives won 330 seats, Labour 287, the Liberals 6 and the SNP 1 and Labour's near 100 seat majority of 1966 had been turned into a Conservative majority of 30. The Conservatives had made a net gain of 66 seats – a post-war record – on a national average swing of 4.8 per cent.[100]

The Conservatives had achieved a remarkable victory. What was the role of the policy review process and the new-found commitment to opinion polls in that victory? Most of the available evidence would tend to support the adage that governments lose elections because of their own frailties as opposed to their rivals' strengths. For all of the vast amount of work which had gone into the policy review in the five years prior to the election, Conservative analysis of the results showed that they had made little impact on the young or upon the skilled, non-manual working class which had been their main target group following the 1966 defeat. In fact, the Conservative gains were made across the board in the A, B, C2, D and E social groups, though the latter three categories had long been regarded as Labour's 'natural constituencies'.[101] In broad terms, the parties tended to draw their support from the various sections of the community in much the same proportions as before and there was little evidence of any special turnover among target voters or critical seats. The evidence of the Party's own polls seemed to indicate that many people felt that the economic climate was likely to worsen and that the Conservatives were better equipped than Labour to deal with such a situation. In this sense, the Conservative attention to prices and the general economic malaise had proved correct, although the irony of this situation was well summed up by Brendon Sewill:

I was unhappy as we went into the 1970 election with an advertising campaign about the shopping basket and how the party was going to bring the cost of living down, but without any clue as to how we were actually going to do it. In fact, most of our policies were designed to put it up![102]

In other words the Conservative Party had won the election on the one issue where they had no policy and had also failed to convert their target groups. Sewill's conclusion to his report on the election result is also of note:

In the historical perspective the surprising thing is not that the Conservatives won the election but that, after five and a half years of Labour Government which even impartial observers would recognise as dogged by failure and unpopularity, we so nearly lost. The root cause of Labour's near success must lie in the public's greater identification with Labour; that to most people, in Harold Wilson's words, Labour is 'your party', and to most people the Conservatives are an alien exterior party; that Labour has a soft heart but also a soft head, that the Conservatives have hard hearts but also hard heads; so that the public turn to the Conservatives in time of trouble, but do not think of us as their party.[103]

To the extent that Sewill's analysis was correct, Labour lost the 1970 General Election because of its own failures and not Tory successes.

Notes

1 I would like to thank Dr Sarah Street, the Conservative Party Archivist at the Bodleian Library, Oxford and Alistair Cooke OBE of the Conservative Political Centre, for access to, and help with, sources. Thanks are also due to Nick Tiratsoo and Steve Fielding for reading and commenting on earlier drafts. Especial thanks to Patricia Hardy. All errors are my own.

2 J. Ramsden *The Making of Conservative Party Policy* (1980) p. 222.

3 R. Blake *The Conservative Party from Peel to Thatcher* (1985) pp. 284–96; D.E. Butler and A. King *The British General Election of 1964* (1965) pp. 9–56, 77–96; D.E. Butler and D. Stokes *Political Change in Britain* (1970) pp. 283–91; K Middlemas *Power, Competition and the State, Vol. 2, Threats to the Post War Settlement: Britain 1961–74* (1990) pp. 57–92; A. Roth *Heath and the Heathmen* (1972) pp. 161–78; 'Witness Seminar: 1961–1964. Did the Conservatives Lose Direction?' *Contemporary Record* Vol. 2 No. 5 (Spring 1989) and Ramsden op. cit. 219–30.

4 Quoted in Ramsden op. cit. 223.

5 Quoted in Ramsden op. cit. 223–4.

6 Quoted in Ramsden op. cit. 224.

7 *Spectator* 15/3/1963.

8 *Spectator* 10/5/1963.

9 *Crossbow* No. 16 (1961) 6.

10 *Crossbow* No. 19 (1962) 6.

11 *Crossbow* No. 18 (1962) 6.

12 Butler and King op. cit. passim.

13 Blake op. cit. 259.

14 R. A. Butler *The Art of the Possible* (1971) p. 126.

15 Blake op. cit. 259–62; Ramsden op. cit. 103–44; Butler and King op. cit. 84–95; A. Gamble *The Conservative Nation* (1974) pp. 38–60; J.D. Hoffman *The Conservative Party in Opposition* (1964) pp. 137–66.

16 Quoted in Ramsden op. cit. 132.

17 Quoted in Ramsden op. cit. 181.

18 Ramsden op. cit. 18 6–7.

19 D.E. Butler and A. King *The British General Election of 1966* (1967) pp. 53–5.

20 Ramsden op. cit. 237.

21 Butler and King 1966 op. cit. 59–73; Ramsden op. cit. 236–9 and D. Butler and M. Pinto-Duschinsky *The British General Election of 1970* (1971) pp. 66–8, 94–6. It is difficult to arrive at an exact figure for the total number of policy groups and their membership. Some groups met regularly, some rarely at all and many members served on more than one group. Groups also varied radically in size and composition.

22 Quoted in Butler and Pinto-Duschinsky op. cit. 94.

23 Butler and Pinto-Duschinsky op. cit. 95.

24 Butler and King 1966 op. cit. 44–5; Butler and Pinto-Duschinsky op. cit. 94.

25 Quoted in Middlemas op. cit. 270.

26 Conservative Research Department (hereafter CRD) 3/17/19–21 'Policy Group on Trade Union Law and Practice' 1965–6. This legalistic approach to the issue of industrial relations stemmed from a pamphlet by the Inns of Court Conservative and Unionist Society, *A Giant's Strength*, which was published in 1958.

27 CRD 3/17/20 'Policy Group on Trade Union Law and Practice' minutes and papers 1965–66.

28 CRD 3/17/19 'Policy Group on Trade Union Law and Practice' correspondence 1965–66.

29 CRD 3/7/6/9 'Future Economic Policy Group' 1965 and CRD 3/7/6/10 'Sub-group A of the Future Economic Policy Group on Taxation' 1965.

30 CRD 3/10/18 'Policy Group on Foreign Affairs' minutes, correspondence and papers 1964–65.

31 Ibid.

32 Ibid.

33 Ibid.

34 CRD 3/9/26 '1965 1st draft manifesto/documents and correspondence' 1965.

35 CRD 3/9/27 '2nd draft manifesto'; CRD 3/9/29 '3rd draft'; CRD 3/9/30 and 31 '4th draft'; CRD 3/24/3 '3rd draft policy document 1965'; CRD 3/24/4–6 '4th to 6th draft' 1965.

36 CRD 3/9/27 '2nd draft policy document and CRD comments' 1965.

37 CRD 3/24/9 'Policy Group letter books' 1965.

38 Ibid.

39 Ibid.

40 CRD 3/33/1 'Minutes of tactical meetings in Leader's room in House of Commons' 1965.

41 CRD/CCO files, Public Opinion files, (hereafter CCO) 180/11/3/1–5 'General Election 1966'.

42 R. Rose *Influencing Voters* (1967) pp. 37–44.

43 Ibid. and Butler and King 1964 op. cit. 91–3.

44 Butler and King 1966 op. cit. 67.

45 R.M. Worcester *British Public Opinion* (1991) pp. 23–4, 30. According to Worcester the party spent approximately £30,000 per annum between 1966 and 1970 on private polling, see p. 40.

46 CCO 180/21/3/1–58 'Gallup Polls'.

47 *Crossbow* No 30 (1965) 29–32.

48 E. Griffiths *The New Competitors* (Conservative Political Centre, 1965) passim.

49 For work on this theme see *Spectator* 30/3/1962; J. Biffen 'The Conservative party today' in M. Wolf (ed.) *The Conservative Opportunity* (CPC, 1965); T. Raison *Conflict and Conservatism* (CPC, 1965); D. Howell *Efficiency and Beyond* (CPC, 1965); R. Lewis *A Bonfire of Restrictions* (CPC, 1965) and M.

Schreiber 'Who are our supporters to be?' *Crossbow* No. 41 (1967) 21.
50 *Crossbow* No. 41 (1967) 5.
51 CRD 3/30/1 'Brendon Sewill, file on policy points, 1964–1970'.
52 Ibid.
53 CRD 3/9/51 'General election, reports' 1966.
54 Ibid.
55 Ibid.
56 Quoted in 'Symposium: Conservative Party Policy Making, 1965–1970' *Contemporary Record* Vol. 3 No. 3 (Feb. 1990) 36.
57 *The Times* 10/7/1967.
58 CRD 3/17/1 'Industrial Relations Policy Group, minutes and papers' 1966–1967.
59 Quoted in 'Symposium' *Contemporary Record* op. cit. 37.
60 Conservative Party *Fair Deal At Work* (1968) passim.
61 Ramsden op. cit. 267 and Middlemas op. cit. 277.
62 Ramsden op. cit. 273.
63 CRD 3/7/6/1 'Economic Policy Group, papers' 1966–7.
64 CRD 3/7/6/3 'Economic Policy Group, papers' 1968.
65 CRD 3/17/11 'Nationalised Industries, correspondence' 1967–8.
66 Quoted in 'Symposium' *Contemporary Record* op. cit. 38.
67 Butler and Pinto-Duschinsky op. cit. 76–7.
68 Middlemas op. cit. 261–4, 274. For Powell's own writings see J.E. Powell *Freedom and Reality* (1969); *Powell and the 1970 Election* (1970); *Income Tax at 4/3 in the £* (1970) and *Still to Decide* (1972). For biographical studies and analysis of his politics see T.E. Utley *Enoch Powell – The Man and his Thinking* (1968); P. Foot *The Rise of Enoch Powell* (1969); A. Roth *Enoch Powell: Tory Tribune* (1972) and T. Nairn 'Portrait of Enoch Powell' *New Left Review* 61 (May–June, 1970) 3–27.
69 Quoted in Butler and Pinto-Duschinsky op. cit. 76–7.
70 Butler and Pinto-Duschinsky op. cit. 77–8 and Middlemas op. cit. 275–6.
71 For an analysis of how the issue of immigration was viewed by the voters in the 1970 General Election, see Butler and Pinto-Duschinsky op. cit. 406–8.
72 Butler and Pinto-Duschinsky op. cit. 79–80.
73 CCO 180/27/9/1-2 'Opinion Research Summaries' 1963–1976.
74 Butler and Pinto-Duschinsky op. cit. 173.
75 D. Howell 'Towards stability' in *Conservatism Today* (Conservative Political Centre pamphlet No. 350, 1966) p. 43.
76 CCO 180/27/9/1–2 'Opinion research summaries'.
77 Butler and Pinto-Duschinsky op. cit. 174.
78 CCO 180/27/9/1–2 'Opinion research summaries'.
79 Ibid.
80 Quoted in Ramsden op. cit. 269.
81 CRD 3/24/8 'Policy Group Correspondence Files'.
82 CRD 3/24/17 'Policy Initiatives and Methods'.
83 CRD 3/24/15 'Policy Differentiation'.
84 CRD 3/24/20 'Policy document drafts, 1968'.
85 Ibid.
86 Middlemas op. cit. 280–81.
87 Butler and Pinto-Duschinsky op. cit. 34–5, 43, 383–5.
88 Ibid.
89 CRD 180/27/9/1-2 'Opinion research summaries'.
90 CRD 3/9/69 '1970 General Election, manifesto preparation'.

91 CRD 3/9/91 'Policy reviews, September 1969–January 1970'.
92 Ramsden op. cit. 275 and Butler and Pinto-Duschinsky op. cit. 129–30.
93 Quoted in Middlemas op. cit. 283.
94 Quoted in 'Symposium' *Contemporary Record* op. cit. 38.
95 CRD 3/9/95 'CRD Report on General Election 1970'.
96 Butler and Pinto-Duschinsky op. cit. 131–2.
97 Ibid. 133–6.
98 Butler and Pinto-Duschinsky op. cit. 176–9.
99 Quoted in 'Symposium' *Contemporary Record* op. cit. 38.
100 Butler and Pinto-Duschinsky op. cit. 338.
101 CRD 3/9/95 'CRD Report on General Election 1970' and Butler and Pinto-Duschinsky op. cit. 342–3.
102 Quoted in 'Symposium' *Contemporary Record* op. cit. 38.
103 CRD 3/9/95 'CRD Report on General Election 1970'.

Index